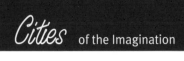

Cities of the Imagination

MOSCOW

A CULTURAL AND LITERARY HISTORY

CAROLINE BROOKE

W0010840

Signal

Signal Books
Oxford

First published in 2006 by
Signal Books Limited
36 Minster Road
Oxford OX4 1LY
www.signalbooks.co.uk

A catalogue record for this book is available from the British Library

ISBN 1-904955-22-3 Paper

Drawings by Nicki Averill
Cover Design: Baseline Arts
Cover Images: Alamy.com
Printed in Malaysia

CONTENTS

CHAPTER FOUR
RED MOSCOW—CITY OF SOVIETS AND SINCE (79)

CHAPTER FIVE
CITY OF WRITERS (113)

CHAPTER SIX
CITY OF THEATRES AND MUSIC (145)

CHAPTER SEVEN
CITY OF RICH AND POOR (183)

CHAPTER EIGHT
CITY OF UTOPIAS AND SLUMS (215)

CHAPTER NINE
CITY OF PALACES AND MONASTERIES (237)

Foreword: Moscow Sparrows

If you ever wondered where all London's sparrows went, then go to Moscow, a city which has its own Sparrow Hills and which, as the poet Mandelstam (who was unhappily exiled from St. Petersburg to Moscow) put it, either "huddles like a sparrow or expands like pie in the sky." Crowds of sparrows rush over the city, knowing as no stranger does where the best pickings are. Their only competitors are the hooded crows, as canny as their Scottish cousins in surviving a harsh winter. But the sparrows are cleverer. In Moscow Zoo, to feed the captive eagles, they leave a hole in the roof. Crows fly in to scavenge, only to be torn apart by hungry eagles: no sparrow will fall for such an obvious ploy. The sparrow's combination of bustling energy and deeply held suspicion sums up the Muscovite character.

For forty years I have been an itinerant visitor to Moscow, never staying longer than a season at a time, always glad to leave (mentally, and sometimes physically exhausted) but eager to return, once recuperated. I have endured a January of blizzards and -30°, when the day starts with a cigarette lighter applied to the lock of the car door and your lungs sting. Then the stranger in town, muffled up like an Eskimo, gives himself away by acting the clown at every metro exit, sliding and falling on the ice, which the authorities never clear from the pavements). January always left me black and blue, though I never broke a leg, and was equally gratified to find that the Macintosh notebook survived being periodically flung into the air and onto a curbstone. Summer is paradise by comparison, even if half the city is away seeing to the dacha or searching for mushrooms in the forests, and it can become unbreathably sticky in the city. The real excitement is to be found in between the main seasons. Spring arrives with a bang: from the sound of cracking ice to the explosion of leaves and lilac, often all over in a mere two weeks. Autumn, too, comes suddenly, with the first frost turning the city parks red and yellow, before a few weeks later ice starts to cover the pavements.

I have tried most conceivable ways of arriving in Moscow. Nothing is worse than Sheremetievo airport (built with the help of Ryanair), where the passengers disembark into an ill-lit, malodorous, subterranean anteroom to hell staffed by misanthropic border guards. True, passport control is today carried out by women who take minimal interest in their task, whereas in Soviet days your passport was scrutinized by a carefully selected psychopath from a Siberian orphanage. Better to take a western airline and land at Domodedovo, a fair imitation of Gatwick at a similar distance from the centre.

Arriving by road is more salutary: you really feel the thousand kilometres that separate you from the nearest frontier, and your greeting will be one of the traffic police (GAI, but pronounced gah-ee, not Gay) who man all the approaches to the city. They are as expensive as French motorway toll booth, but have the advantage of providing the motorist (especially the foreigner) with a compulsory ten-minute rest break while they digest your documents and your bribe. With time, one comes to understand them. Like the waiter in a prestigious French restaurant, they may well have had to pay to get their job and a large cut of their "tips" has to be passed to management. Unlike the Parisian waiters, the Moscow *gaieshniki* feel unloved and will often warm to drivers who speak to them as if they were human. They are also superstitious, so wearing a cassock or having at least a Bible on the front seat can guarantee you free passage.

Perhaps the best way to arrive in Moscow is by rail (there is a very decent train that runs overnight from Helsinki to Moscow). You arrive at a railway station which still has relics of former magnificence. More important, the border crossing is limited by the timetable to an hour or even less. Furthermore, you get a physical sense of Moscow's remoteness without the discomfort of driving along Russia's dangerous and tedious roads. And on trains, as any reader of Dostoevsky and Tolstoy knows, your life can be radically changed by your encounters: you are more likely to strike up a friendship with a Muscovite in a train compartment hundreds of kilometres away that anywhere in the city.

In a country where until recently most males served in a brutal army and where nothing anyone needed, from a pound of butter to a university degree, could be obtained without what might be called short cuts or good acquaintances, a talent for trickery evolved into virtuoso skill. In Moscow these skills are at their height. Moscow can be proud of its thieves and conmen, not to mention its hooligans. (Russians refuse to believe that Hooligan is an Irish surname: it sounds like an etymologically native Russian word.) Park your car for ten minutes in an unguarded place (which is why the guarded car park can cost more than the hotel room), and then drive off. You will have gone ten miles before you try to switch on a radio that is no longer there, so neat is the workmanship. Flash your money in a shop, and five minutes later as you stroll down Tverskaya you will see someone drop what looks like a bundle of dollar notes in front of you. Naively you will look around and call out to those ahead of you, assuming that someone has dropped the bundle. Next to you a shabby type will suggest in a whisper that you pick it up and share it. Indignantly you refuse and march on. A minute later you are stopped by an exquisitely dressed couple who say that they have reason to suspect you of picking up a bundle of dollars they have lost. You express sympathy and innocence, mention the shabby man, and ask them to call the police—half-heartedly because you rightly fear that the police will only complete the ruin of your day. The apparent victims say that they would be content if you show them your wallet. You do so, put it away, and they depart with an apology. You feel sorry for their loss until the next day you open your wallet to find it magically empty: a not too exorbitant charge for a lesson in how not to be a good Samaritan in Moscow.

These conman talents make Moscow theatres worth a visit: when the Soviet Union broke up, so did the theatres, and Moscow now teems with small theatres where you can sit and dine, like Banquo's ghost, with unbelievably versatile actors playing Chekhov's Three Sisters at their name-day party, or you can watch actors swinging on ropes over the stalls like Tarzan to an audience packed into the gallery. True, for every two unforgettable evenings there will be one dud, but this is an acceptable risk. Classical concerts, however, are not what they used to be: many of the best Russian conductors and instrumentalists, trained in the harshest musical schools of the world, now lead the orchestras of Britain, the USA and Germany. Russian cinema, protected rather than stunted by Soviet censorship, has now been swamped by Hollywood, even though the seats are now reupholstered and bug-free. The museums and art galleries are now better lit and a little less crowded than they used to be. True, if you are a foreigner you now pay six times more to go in; you can go with a Russian friend and keep your mouth shut to get a cheap ticket, but even so the eagle-eyed attendant will probably take one look at you and shriek: "Foreigner!"

The unimaginable wealth in which Moscow's richest five per cent wallow has its advantages. The new Russians have clogged up Moscow's roads with their SUVs, but some of their loot has gone into property, and there are whole areas, especially south of the river, which have been restored to pre-revolutionary grandeur. There, and in the north-west area of the centre, once again Moscow is a city worth exploring on foot: the art nouveau buildings humanize this enormous metropolis. What is more, now that some many Soviet street names have been replaced by their old pre-revolutionary names, you can even use an antiquarian Baedeker to explore.

Today, Moscow has fast food (some of it very good), and you don't have to walk interminably and then queue to get a decent coffee or beer. And unlike London, people live as well as work in the centre, so that it does not die at the weekend. Public transport has survived reasonably well: the metro has the same frequency and even more coverage than before, but the best value are those heavy-weight wooden-seated suburban trains known as *elektrichki*, which for very little outlay will trundle (rather than whisk) you to forests, villages, monasteries, not all of them vandalised by the "cottages" of the new rich. In the metro everyone fights for their personal space and few cubic feet of air; on the benches of the *elektrichka*, especially at the week-end, the Moscow crowd, off to see friends, restore the dacha or scour the forests, becomes warm and friendly.

The buses, stuck in endless traffic jam with no lanes of their own, are to be avoided in the centre; the trams and trolley-buses are now a dying breed. One good round trip was to be had on the trolley-buses that circled the Garden Ring road. Now they move so slowly that Mandelstam's lines "You and I will take the A and the B, To see who dies first" are proving clairvoyant.

In most cities I make a bee-line for the zoo and the botanical gardens. Moscow Zoo (which in 1893 Anton Chekhov called a "graveyard for animals" before delivering his own pet mongoose there) has been renovated, but thousands of tons of concrete have not made it much less distressing. I recommend only a short visit to the musk-ox and the warthog, which respond bravely to their dismal environment by prolific breeding—an example which Moscow's human beings, to the distress of their government, refuse to follow. As for the Botanical Gardens in which Moscow's only magnolia struggles to stay alive, let alone flower, forget it. Go instead to the great forest-parks of the outskirts, to Bitsevsky Park with its natural spring and chorus of green and red frogs which one could swear are rehearsing the new Russian anthem without words. You have a chilling mixture of pure resin-flavoured air with a grim history. Here was one of Lavrenti Beria's villas, still exuding an air of unspeakable sadism, and nearby is Butovo, one of the killing grounds where tens of thousands of Moscow's intellectual elite were slaughtered in 1937 and 1938. Moscow's outlying parks and its cemeteries give you a different, perhaps deeper insight into Russian history than does a tour of the Kremlin.

Much of my time in Moscow has been mis-spent in archives, with head stuck under a derelict microfilm reader and laptop surreptitiously charging from the archive's mains. Even more important than what is revealed by millions of documents and photographs, is the realization that in Moscow nothing is ever thrown away, however much destruction and confiscation went on. Moscow houses have no fireplaces and very few stoves. Letters are hidden, but kept, and everything that ever happened to anyone, no matter how much the perpetrators would wish it obliterated, is somewhere recorded. Perhaps that is Moscow's attraction (charm is the wrong word): it is a city built on buried knowledge. "Moscow doesn't believe in tears" is an old saying, but behind that ruthless motif lie centuries of weeping, which is why a stay in modern Moscow has the same deep effect on the visitor as a sojourn in ancient Babylon.

Donald Rayfield
March 2006

Preface

This book is organized in a form that is partly topographical and partly thematic, linked to Moscow's concentric circle layout. Chapters One and Two focus on the very heart of the city, the area around the Kremlin and Red Square, tracing the history of Moscow through these districts and the buildings that stand in and around them. Chapters Three to Seven move outwards and encompass the whole of the area within and just around the Garden Ring, each chapter concentrating on a particular theme: the Russian Revolution and its impact on the city; the experience of Soviet rule during the twentieth century; areas and buildings with literary, theatrical or musical connections; and the contrast between rich and poor in pre-revolutionary Moscow. Chapters Eight and Nine move beyond the Garden Ring to investigate the housing situation in twentieth-century Moscow and to explore some of the pre-revolutionary palaces and monasteries on the outskirts of the city.

Note on Transliteration
While I have generally adopted a modified version of the Library of Congress system for transliterating words from Russian, in the case of names I have usually tried to provide the spelling that will be most familiar to English readers (hence Tchaikovsky rather than Chaikovskii or Chaikovsky). I have also made some changes in an effort to help pronunciation, which has resulted in a number of anomalies. For example, the Russian letter "е" has been transliterated "ye" when it appears at the beginnings of words (Yeltsin, Yesenin) but not otherwise, except in cases where to do so will result in a more familiar spelling (Sheremetyevo). I have usually adopted "yo" as the transliteration for the Russian "ё" although I have used the more familiar spelling of Andrei Rublev rather than Rublyov.

Acknowledgements
I would like to thank friends in Moscow, in particular Larissa Mashkova who first introduced me to the city; Irina Khutsieva who took me on numerous walking tours around the backstreets of central Moscow; and Tatyana Bart who has helped to make recent trips to Russia vastly more enjoyable. Thanks are also due to numerous teachers, students and

colleagues who, over the years, have helped to stimulate my interest in Russian history and culture. Rosamund Bartlett made some very helpful comments on the manuscript and James Ferguson has been a most constructive editor. The Library of the School of Slavonic and East European Studies, University College London was an invaluable source of information and the Department of History at Queen Mary, University of London helped to fund one of my trips to Moscow when I was doing the research for this book. Particular thanks go to my parents who displayed their characteristic generosity in offering financial support during the six month "sabbatical" when I did most of the writing.

This book is for Adam, without whom it would never have been started, let alone finished.

Introduction

How many times in my sorrowful separation
In my wandering fate
Have I thought of you, O Moscow!
Moscow... how much there is in this sound
That flows together for the heart of the Russian!
How much echoes in it!

Pushkin, Eugene Onegin

Moscow is a city that is constantly reinventing itself.

It has acquired many different descriptive titles over the centuries: Holy Moscow, or the Third Rome, for its status as a major centre of the Orthodox Church; Moscow of the taverns, where people gathered to drink endless cups of tea and eat enormous meals of soups, pies and pancakes; later Calico Moscow for the dominance of the textiles trade. In the nineteenth and early twentieth centuries it was often described as a "big village" as peasant migrants moved into the city; and during the Soviet period the name of Moscow came to be synonymous with communist ideology as the centre of the Third International.

The changing seasons help to show some of the many different faces of the city. Spring comes late to Moscow after the interminable thaw, but brings with it a string of festivals: Orthodox Easter when devout Orthodox believers attend church at midnight and process through the church holding red candles before returning home to eat their specially prepared cake, the *kulich* with *paskha*, a sweetened curd cheese. Easter is swiftly followed by two major public holidays: May Day, which was a big event in Soviet times, and the grand public celebrations of Victory Day that marks the anniversary of the end of the Second World War on 9 May.

Summer is a time when many Muscovites, rather like Parisians, do their best to get out of the city. Children are sent off to summer camp, while the elderly tend to spend their summers staying at the dacha if they are fortunate enough to own one. One cannot blame them: Moscow can become extremely hot and unpleasant over the summer months and mosquitoes are a major nuisance. The composer Sergei Rachmaninov once asked, rhetorically, "what could be worse than Moscow in the summer?" and Chekhov expressed his views on the subject in vivid terms in a letter to a friend in June 1886: "You should be ashamed of staying in stuffy Moscow… Living in town in summer is worse than pederasty and viler than bestiality…"

The autumn, on the other hand, can be a lovely time. September is often a golden month of Indian summer, beautifully described by Tolstoy in *War and Peace*:

> *there had been the extraordinary autumn weather that always comes as a surprise, when the sun hangs low and gives more heat than in spring, when everything shines so brightly in the rare clear atmosphere that the eyes smart, when the lungs are strengthened and refreshed by inhaling the aromatic autumn air, when even the nights are warm, and when, in those dark warm nights, golden stars startle and delight us continually by falling from the sky…*

Chekhov came to dislike the Moscow winter and, particularly after the onset of the tuberculosis that would eventually kill him, he took to spending his winters in warmer parts of the Russian empire. He was able to recognize some of its charms, however, and offered a lyrical description of the early stages of winter in Moscow in his short story *The Lady with the Little Dog*:

> *Everything was already like winter: the stoves were heated and it was still dark in the morning… The frosts had set in. When the first snow falls and the first day you go out for a sleigh ride, you are glad to see the white ground, the white roofs, the air is so soft and wonderful to breathe and you remember the days of your youth*

The first snow fall can indeed be a magical time, yet as Walter Benjamin, the German Marxist intellectual who visited Moscow during December 1926 to January 1927 was to discover, the later months of winter can be something of a trial as the harsh temperatures make every action out of doors a struggle. "During my first few days I am above all struck by the difficulty of getting used to walking on the sheet ice of the streets," he wrote. "I have to watch my step so carefully that I cannot look around very much." He was greatly appreciative of a spell of warmer weather when the sun shone during January when he began to think more fondly of the city.

A City So Irregular

Benjamin was one visitor who noted in Moscow a curious intermingling of the urban and the rural in the city streets. "The Russian village plays hide-and-seek in them," he observed. His explorations of Moscow courtyards led him to find spaces where children played in and around the little sheds that were built to store wood and coal, and his trip to the suburbs of the city gave him a vivid sense of the village character of Moscow in the 1920s. An earlier visitor, the English clergyman William Coxe, who came to Moscow in the late 1770s, had similarly remarked on the great diversity of the city and the multiplicity of different types of building that he saw all jumbled in together:

> *I was all astonishment at the immensity and variety of Moscow, a city so irregular, so uncommon, so extraordinary and so contrasted, never before claimed my attention… Wretched hovels are blended with large palaces; cottages of one story stand next to the most stately mansion… In a word, some parts of this vast city have the appearance of a sequestered desert, other quarters, of a populous town; some of a contemptible village, others of a great capital.*

This variety remains very much in evidence today. Medieval churches stand alongside glitzy new shopping malls; eighteenth-century palaces are fronted by Soviet-era statues to heroes of the international revolutionary movement; the fabulous wealth of some flaunts itself in the face of the desperate poverty of others.

Instability and flux have been two of the most characteristic features of Muscovite development over the centuries: street names have changed, statues have been moved, buildings torn down and rebuilt, sometimes several times over. The net result of all of these changes is that an extraordinary range of different symbols are layered one upon another, turning the very fabric of the city into a palimpsest. Where once hammers and sickles were affixed to the pediments of eighteenth-century palaces, today plaques devoted to the exploits of communist luminaries adorn the façades of buildings housing mobile phone shops.

Muscovites themselves have often discerned a certain charm in this variety and the intermingling of old and new. "Moscow is a city of slow historical growth," wrote the anarchist Prince Pyotr Kropotkin in the late nineteenth century,

*and down to the present times its different parts have wonderfully well
retained the features which have been stamped upon them in the slow
course of history… Each quarter is a little world in itself; each has its
own physiognomy, and lives its own separate life.*

It is something of a cliché to say that the city stands at the crossroads
between Europe and Asia, but like many clichés it contains more than
a grain of truth. Moscow today may appear to be doing its best to
emulate the wild capitalism of Las Vegas, with its ever-increasing
network of casinos, slot-machine arcades and strip clubs, together with
runaway advertising hoardings, yet its historical development has
encompassed many eastern influences, ranging from the Mongol
occupation in medieval times through to the close links with
Byzantium and Moscow's status as one of the major centres of Eastern
Christianity.

Orthodox believers have long regarded Moscow as the centre of the
Orthodox Church, the city of the golden domes and the heir to
Byzantium. The city was said to have "forty times forty" churches, and
after the fall of Constantinople in 1453 and Moscow's assumption of
the title of the Third Rome, the legend spread that the city had been
founded on seven hills. In fact, unsurprisingly, the number of churches

in Moscow was considerably smaller than this and the number of hills is debatable. Orthodoxy permeated the streets of old Moscow where onion domes studded the skyline and the sound of the bell chimes filled the air. Although many of Moscow's monasteries and churches were pulled down in the Soviet period, many still remain and are being restored.

The city is often spoken of as if it were a woman, specifically a mother and as a centre of family life. Tolstoy famously described this phenomenon in War and Peace:

Every Russian looking at Moscow feels her to be a mother; every foreigner who sees her, even if ignorant of her significance as the mother city, must feel her feminine character...

After the Russian capital was moved from Moscow to St. Petersburg in the early eighteenth century, Moscow became a place where aristocrats who preferred to avoid the court would spend the long winter months, entertaining their friends with generous dinners, parties and balls. Pierre Bezukhov in *War and Peace* viewed Moscow as somewhere cosy and comforting, where he could escape from the bustle and hurry of life in the northern capital: "when he saw those old Moscow ladies, the Moscow balls, and the English Club, he felt himself at home in a quiet haven. In Moscow he felt at peace, at home, warm and dirty as in an old dressing gown."

Food was always very important to Muscovites, and convivial meals, whether in private homes or in the city's numerous taverns and restaurants, often feature prominently in literature depicting pre-revolutionary life. Muscovites were said to have large appetites and the portions on offer in the taverns were legendary. Sucking pig, sturgeon, cabbage soup, pancakes and all different sorts of pies were the stuff of these tavern meals, while aristocrats would vie with one another to offer up the richest and rarest delicacies: sturgeons of enormous size, stuffed meats, oysters, caviar, asparagus, strawberries and crystallized fruits. During Lent, craftsmen in the central Kitai gorod district would gather to hold pancake-eating competitions, washing down the piles of food with *kvas*, a refreshing drink made from fermented bread, which is often to be found on sale outside metro stations in the summer months.

Hospitality was very important to pre-revolutionary Muscovites, who were always inviting one another around for tea. The samovar, the Russian tea-urn, was the focal point of many households, where friends and neighbours gathered to discuss the affairs of the moment. Tea was the Muscovite drink (as well as vodka, of course); in St. Petersburg they were said to prefer coffee. This tradition of hospitality remains a feature of modern-day Moscow: guests in Muscovite homes are routinely stuffed with excellent food and drink until they can hardly move. The duty to offer lavish hospitality to guests does not extend beyond the home, however, and many visitors have noticed—both in previous centuries and in our own—the contrast between the Muscovite's public, often rather brusque and sometimes unfriendly, persona and their private warmth and generosity.

The contemporary detective novelist Boris Akunin, whose translated works include *The Winter Queen*, described Moscow as "an incredible city: it doesn't let you see its charms at the first glance, but penetrates into your soul little by little." Vast in size—its rapidly expanding population stood at around eleven million in 2004—there is a great deal here to discover. For those who are drawn to its history and culture and who have the time and the inclination to explore the city, there are considerable rewards in store. Moscow is an exciting and diverse city, a city with an extraordinary past and present, a city of excesses and of extremes, an exasperating and exuberant place to live and a fascinating place to visit. "To tell the truth," Walter Benjamin wrote in a postcard home, "one does not tire that easily of seeing this city."

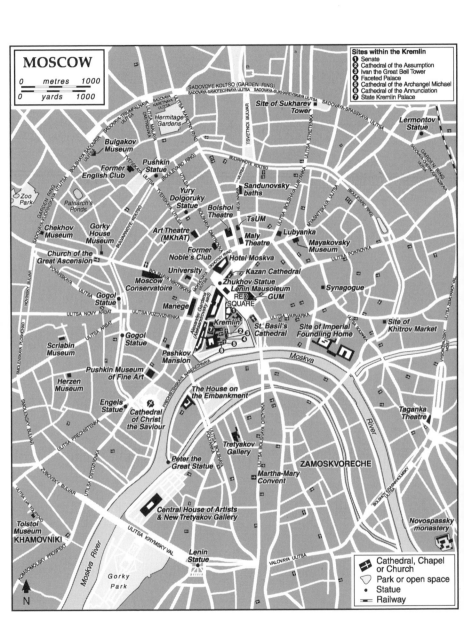

MOSCOW

0 metres 1000
0 yards 1000

Sites within the Kremlin
1 Senate
2 Cathedral of the Assumption
3 Ivan the Great Bell Tower
4 Faceted Palace
5 Cathedral of the Archangel Michael
6 Cathedral of the Annunciation
7 State Kremlin Palace

SADOVOYE KOLTSO (GARDEN RING)
SADOVAYA-SAMOTECHNAYA ULITSA   SADOVAYA-SUKHAREVSKAYA ULITSA

Site of Sukharev Tower

Lermontov Statue

Hermitage Gardens

Bulgakov Museum

Pushkin Statue

Former English Club

Zoo Park

Patriarch's Ponds

Sandunovsky baths

Yury Dolgoruky Statue

Bolshoi Theatre

TsUM

Chekhov Museum

Gorky House Museum

Art Theatre (MKhAT)

Maly Theatre

Lubyanka

Mayakovsky Museum

Church of the Great Ascension

Former Noble's Club

Hotel Moskva

Kazan Cathedral

University

Moscow Conservatoire

Zhukhov Statue
Lenin Mausoleum
RED SQUARE   GUM

Synagogue

Gogol Statue

Manege

Kremlin

St Basil's Cathedral

Site of Imperial Foundling Home

Site of Khitrov Market

Scriabin Museum

Gogol Statue

Pashkov Mansion

Moskva River

Herzen Museum

Pushkin Museum of Fine Art

Engels Statue

Cathedral of Christ the Saviour

The House on the Embankment

Taganka Theatre

ZAMOSKVORECHE

Tretyakov Gallery

Peter the Great Statue

Martha-Mary Convent

Central House of Artists & New Tretyakov Gallery

Novospassky monastery

Tolstoi Museum

KHAMOVNIKI

ULITSA KRYMSKY VAL

Lenin Statue

Gorky Park

N

Cathedral, Chapel or Church
Park or open space
• Statue
Railway

Chapter One
THE KREMLIN

The word *kremlin* simply means a fortress. Yet rather like the word *soviet*, with its seemingly innocuous meaning of a council, the Moscow Kremlin has outgrown its dictionary definition. Every ancient Russian city had its *kremlin*, but none has acquired the symbolic significance that Moscow's Kremlin commands. The Moscow Kremlin has acted over many centuries as a fortress, a religious centre and the focus of Russian political power and hence the very name has come, over time, to stand for much more than a purely geographical landmark.

It is difficult, even today, to approach the complex of cathedrals, palaces and gardens that lie within the Kremlin walls without a sense of awe. The poet Mikhail Lermontov famously rhapsodized on the majesty of the surroundings in 1833:

> *What can compare to the Kremlin which, having ringed itself with crenellated walls and adorned itself with the golden domes of the cathedrals, sits on a high hill like the crown of sovereignty on the brow of an awesome ruler...? No... neither the Kremlin nor its crenellated walls, nor its dark passages, nor the splendid palaces can be described. They must be seen, they must be seen. One must feel all that they say to the heart and the imagination.*

Foreign visitors have often been more circumspect. The English merchant Richard Chancellor described the Kremlin in the mid-sixteenth century as "a very faire castle, strong and furnished with artillerie", although his general impression of the city was rather more ambivalent. He commented of Moscow that "our men say that in bignesse it is as great as the Citie of London, with the suburbes thereof. There are many and great buildings in it, but for beautie and fairenes, nothing comparable to ours... [it is] very rude and standeth without all order."

Three centuries later the French aristocrat, the Marquis de Custine, who set out on his visit to Russia in 1839 in a mood of fond nostalgia for *ancien régime* Europe, was shocked by the repression that he found. The Kremlin for him seemed to epitomize the barbaric quality of Tsar Nicholas I's Russia. It was, he said

> *impossible to approach the fabric [of the Kremlin] without a shudder... the Kremlin is the work of a superhuman being, but that being is malevolent... It is a habitation which would suit some of the personages of the Apocalypse... the sombre cathedrals of the Kremlin, with their narrow vaults and thick walls, resemble caves; they are painted prisons, just as the palaces are gilded gaols.*

Perhaps the French ambassador during the First World War, Maurice Paleologue, best encapsulated the multifaceted character of the complex of buildings that make up the Kremlin, when he described it thus:

> *this curious conglomeration of palaces, towers, churches, monasteries, chapels, barracks, arsenals and bastions, this incoherent jumble of sacred and secular buildings, this complex of functions as fortress, sanctuary, seraglio, harem, necropolis and prison, this blend of advanced civilisation and archaic barbarism, this violent contrast of the crudest materialism and the most lofty spirituality—are they not the whole history of Russia, the whole epic of the Russian nation, the whole inward drama of the Russian soul?*

These last words could well apply to the Kremlin today. The mixture of symbolism contained within the Kremlin can be said to contain the whole epic of the Russian nation: indeed, it gives the distinct appearance of a state in the midst of an identity crisis. On the front of the Palace of Congresses the imperial double-headed eagle shares its space uneasily with carvings of Soviet hammers and sickles. This confusion was formalized into Russian law by President Putin in December 2000 when a new law on state symbols came up with an interesting compromise to settle the problem of Russia's symbolic heritage. It decreed that the old Soviet national anthem should be resuscitated, albeit with a set of new words (written by the original author); the Soviet army flag was readopted as the flag of the Russian army and the Romanov double-headed eagle crest and flag became state symbols. Defending this decision, Putin argued that Russia needed to come to terms with its past rather than whitewash uncomfortable memories. "If we agree," he said, "that the symbols of the preceding epochs, including the Soviet epoch, must not be used at all, we will have to admit then that our mothers' and fathers' lives were useless and meaningless, that their lives were in vain. Neither in my head nor in my heart can I agree with this."

The juxtaposition of contradictory symbols, visible in many places, is a curious and noteworthy feature of the city as it enters the twenty-first century. Moscow is in many ways a city of contrasts and of extremes, and not just in terms of its symbolic heritage. There is the obscene wealth of the New Russians, the designer-clothed *nouveaux riches* of the 1990s who flaunt their mobile phones as they sit with their friends in expensive cafés, coexisting side by side with the grinding poverty of the old women who stand outside metro stations in the dead of winter selling packets of cigarettes and bottles of vodka to supplement their meagre pensions. There is the scale of the place: the vast dimensions of many of the twentieth-century buildings that make passers-by appear like ants in comparison, contrasting sharply with the more intimate spaces of the city, the courtyard playgrounds with their rusting Soviet-era climbing frames that can be found if one ducks behind many apartment blocks, even in the central districts.

Founding Legends

The foundation of Moscow and its Kremlin is surrounded by improbable-sounding legends. According to one story, the city was founded by one of Noah's descendants, Mosokh, in Old Testament times, hence the name. Another version tells of how the boyar or nobleman Stephan Kuchka, while out hunting one day, was saved from a wild boar by a double-headed eagle. The eagle seized the boar and dropped its corpse on a nearby hill. According to the legend, Kuchka founded a village on this hill that would later become Moscow and the two-headed bird thus became the symbol of the Russian royal house. Poetic details aside, it is certainly the case that the Kremlin lies on a hill at the confluence of two rivers, the Moskva and the Neglinnaya, and that there is evidence of settlement here long before the Prince of Suzdal, Yury Dolgoruky, arrived in the mid-twelfth century.

The Rus themselves were originally Vikings or Varangians who moved south from Scandinavia to settle along the trade routes of Eastern Europe from around the eighth century onwards. They would become the overlords of the Slavic tribes that inhabited these regions and they founded the city of Kiev. Kiev became a major political centre until the twelfth century when Kievan Rus broke up and smaller principalities based around towns further to the north such as Novgorod, Suzdal and Vladimir began to play a more important role.

The official date of the foundation of Moscow, from which the increasingly lavish anniversary celebrations are calculated, is 1147 when the settlement made its first appearance in the Russian chronicles. Yury Dolgoruky, son of Vladimir Monomakh, Prince of Kiev, constructed the first wooden fortress on Borovitsky hill overlooking the two rivers in the mid-twelfth century, and it was from this fortress that the Moscow Kremlin was to develop. His name "Dolgoruky" or "long-armed" derived from his reputation as a ruthless and grasping empire-builder, and a statue of him was commissioned by another ruthless and grasping empire-builder, Josef Stalin, to mark the 800th anniversary of the city's foundation. Finally unveiled on Tverskaya Square in 1954, after the dictator's death and missing the deadline for the anniversary celebrations by several years, the statue remains in place today despite Khrushchev's best efforts to have it replaced by a more internationalist symbol less redolent of the power and might of the Russian state. Incidentally, if you walk past the statue to investigate the back of the square, you will find one of the few Lenin statues to remain in central Moscow. The building behind him is the former Central Party Archives.

Moscow remained a relatively small settlement for several centuries. Sacked by the Mongol horsemen who swept westwards in the later 1230s under Batye Khan, grandson of the more famous Genghiz, the population fell under the fabled "Mongol yoke" and were forced to pay tribute. Russia was ruled indirectly by the khans for the next two and a half centuries, and it was in their role as tax collecting collaborators that the princes of Moscow first came to extend their control over the surrounding towns and built up their power base in the area. The early fourteenth-century Prince Ivan I, grandson of Alexander Nevsky whose legendary feats against the Teutonic Knights are portrayed in the film by Sergei Eisenstein, acquired the nickname

"Kalita" or "moneybags" on account of his role as agent of the Mongols. It was under Ivan's rule that the centre of the Russian Orthodox Church was moved to Moscow from Vladimir in 1326 and he was to enlarge the area within the Kremlin walls.

In the later fourteenth century Moscow played an important role in helping to overthrow the Golden Horde, the name eventually taken by Batye Khan's branch of the Mongol empire. The first great Russian military victory against their eastern rulers was led by the Muscovite Grand Prince Dmitry at the field of Kulikovo on the banks of the Don river in September 1380. He was given the title "of the Don" (*Donskoi*) in recognition of this feat and Dmitry Donskoi returned to Moscow in triumph, only to see the newly-built white limestone walls of the Kremlin torn down by the Mongols in an act of revenge two years later. Muscovy would remain under Mongol control for another century, yet with hindsight the Battle of Kulikovo can be seen as having marked the beginning of the end of the Golden Horde.

The Kremlin Churches
Maurice Baring, the British diplomat and journalist who spent time in Russia in 1905-6, accurately described the Kremlin as "a citadel of cathedrals". Although erected initially as a military fortress, the Kremlin from its earliest times also served as a religious centre. The Russians had adopted the Eastern variant of Christianity in 988. The story goes that Grand Prince Vladimir of Kiev sent out emissaries to investigate the merits of the different religions practised by neighbouring states. Catholicism was rejected on aesthetic grounds; Islam because of the requirement to give up alcohol—"drink is the joy of Rus and we cannot do without it," as the Grand Prince himself put it—but the Orthodox religious rite was reported to be so beautiful that

> *we knew not whether we were in heaven or on earth. For on earth there is no such splendour or beauty and we are at a loss to describe it. We only know that God dwells there among men, and their service is fairer than the ceremonies of other nations. For we cannot forget that beauty.*

So Orthodoxy it was, a politically astute choice in any case given Russia's proximity to the centre of Eastern Christianity in Byzantium.

It is worth trying to attend a Russian service at some point during a visit to Moscow, as the rituals and music of the Orthodox Church are very beautiful and provide a bewitching introduction to aspects of Russian culture. Services can last for several hours but most worshippers will only attend for a certain portion of that time; there are no seats, so the congregation stands or wanders around while the service is in progress. Worshippers do not take part in the liturgy, nor do they join in the singing: they are there to observe. Icons serve as a focus for prayer and a wall of icons—the iconostasis—can be found separating the main body of the church from the priest's inner sanctuary. Religious Russians will often have a collection of icons at home and stalls selling miniature reproductions can be found today in many metro stations. The iconostasis is usually constructed according to a standard pattern. The lowest row of icons depict the local saints, including the patron saint of the particular church, the second row shows Christ with the Virgin, John the Baptist and the Disciples, the third row depicts the feast-days of the church, there may be a fourth row of Old Testament prophets, and finally the top row celebrates Church patriarchs.

The earliest religious buildings in the Kremlin were made of wood. The Church of the Saviour in the Woods (*Spas na boru*) dated back to the early thirteenth century although it was rebuilt in stone several times before its final demolition in the 1930s. It was during the fourteenth century that the first stone churches in the Kremlin were erected. The two main religious houses of the Kremlin dated from the fourteenth century and survived until the Stalin era. These were the Monastery of Miracles (*Chudov*), dating from the 1350s, and the Convent of the Ascension (*Voznesensky*) which was founded a few decades later. The Chudov Monastery is said to have been built on land that had been occupied by the Mongols which was given to the Metropolitan Alexei by the Khan in gratitude for curing his mother of her blindness. The Convent, situated next to the Saviour (*Spasskaya*) Tower, was established by Dmitry Donskoi's widow Yevdokiya. It became the place where women of the royal household, including the wives and mothers of Tsars, were buried. An English visitor, Captain Colville Frankland, who travelled in Russia in 1830-31, was scathing in his assessment of the appearance and moral virtues of the Kremlin nuns, writing of the convent at this time:

here I saw all the nuns, and d—d ugly they were. They looked like travestied men. Nothing can be more unbecoming than their high black cap, shaped like the helmet of the infantry of the feudal times; and their long, slovenly, black and dirty gown, or rather coat… the morals of the cloister are said to be dreadfully depraved; I hear of things so grossly licentious, that I can with difficulty attach credit to them. I must here observe, that the nuns in Russia are not confined to the convent, excepting at night, so that they have abundance of opportunity for depravity. The young Russ seigneurs of my acquaintance assure me that the convents are complete bagnios and that the favours of any particular nun may be had for asking…

Six great walled monasteries were constructed around the southern and eastern flanks of the city as part of a ring of protection against Mongol raids: the Novodevichy, Donskoi, Danilov, Simonov, Novospassky and Andronikov monasteries. These will be explored in Chapter Nine.

It was during the later fifteenth century under Ivan the Great (Ivan III, 1462-1505) that Mongol control was ended and Muscovy came to dominate the surrounding Russian lands including the politically important towns of Tver and Novgorod. Ivan shrewdly chose to marry the niece of the Byzantine Emperor, Sophia or Zoe Paleologue in 1472, a connection that would provide the foundation for Moscow's claim to be the "Third Rome" after the fall of Constantinople to the Ottomans in 1453. Ivan the Great made it his business to identify Moscow as the heir to Byzantium and the centre of the Orthodox Christian world, and it was most probably at this time—romantic legends about Stephan Kuchka notwithstanding—that the Byzantine double-headed eagle was adopted as an emblem by the rulers of the city. It was from this point on that the idea developed of Moscow as having a sacred mission to lead the Christian world: "for two Romes have fallen, the third stands and there will be no fourth."

Sophia Paleologue is said to have been monstrously ugly, to have weighed twenty-five stone (three hundred and fifty pounds) and to have broken her bed on the first night she spent in Moscow, but she nonetheless brought with her a number of positive assets. It was she who was responsible for inviting a team of Italian architects—Antonio Fryazin, Alevisio Novi, Marco Ruffo, Pietro Solario and Aristotle

Fioravanti—to Moscow in order to carry out a massive programme of building works in the Kremlin. The later fifteenth century witnessed the rebuilding of the Kremlin walls and the construction of a series of towers to help defend them. Two of the main Kremlin cathedrals were designed by Italian architects: the Cathedral of the Assumption (*Uspensky*) and the Cathedral of the Archangel Michael; so too were the Ivan the Great Bell Tower and the Faceted (*Granovitaya*) Palace. Italian influences are particularly in evidence on the exterior of the Cathedral of the Archangel with its Venetian scallop shell motifs.

The walls of the Kremlin are interspersed by nineteen towers, many of which date from the 1490s and all of which are different in design. Perhaps the best known and certainly the most photographed of the Kremlin towers is the Saviour Tower (*Spasskaya bashnya*) on Red Square, first built in 1491 and with its tent roof and famous clock installed by the Scottish clock-maker Christopher Galloway in 1625. Fronted by an icon of the Saviour, this was the main entrance to the Kremlin used by the Tsars and is still the entrance favoured by officialdom today. In the nineteenth century a mechanism of chimes was installed which allowed the clock to play tunes: religious and tsarist, later secular and revolutionary. It now chimes the quarter hour and plays the Russian national anthem. Other towers along the Kremlin wall have been used in the past as prisons, storehouses and in one case—the Vodozvodnaya tower—as a water pumping station.

Kremlin Cathedrals

Cathedral Square—"the incomparable circle of five cathedrals, ancient, holy friend", as the poet Marina Tsvetaeva described it—was laid out in the fourteenth century and was the focal point of pre-revolutionary political life in Moscow. Crowds gathered here to witness important church services, imperial proclamations and the like. In *War and Peace*, the young Petya Rostov makes his way to the square on the occasion of the Tsar's visit to Moscow, where "the crowd outside spread out and hawkers appeared selling *kvas*, gingerbread and poppy seed sweets." Tourists can visit the three cathedrals on the square either by purchasing separate tickets or by joining an all-inclusive guided tour.

The most important of the Kremlin cathedrals is undoubtedly the five-domed Cathedral of the Assumption or Dormition (*Uspensky sabor*), which celebrates the feast of the Virgin Mary's assumption into heaven. This was the place where Tsars were crowned, patriarchs and metropolitans were buried, and important state services were held; coronations continued to be held here even after the capital of Russia was moved from Moscow to St Petersburg in the early eighteenth century. Described by one nineteenth-century visitor as "a very curious and interesting church, of I know not what style of architecture, but partaking of the Norman, Saxon, Byzantine and Lombard," it combines traditional Russian features with western European architectural techniques. Its Italian architect, Aristotle Fioravanti, travelled around the ancient cities of Novgorod, Suzdal and Vladimir in 1476-7 to study traditional Russian church design. While taking the Cathedral of the Assumption in Vladimir as a model, he nevertheless gave a sense of light and space to the interior of the Moscow cathedral that was unusual for Russian churches of the period.

Pride of place among the cathedral's icons goes to the fabled Virgin of Vladimir, said to have been painted by St. Luke and brought from Byzantium to Kiev in the twelfth century and thence to Vladimir from where it was brought to Moscow in 1395. The original icon now hangs in the Tretyakov Gallery while a later copy is held in the cathedral. Icon-painting tended to follow fairly strict conventions: portrayals of the Virgin and Child that follow the earliest Byzantine models show a rather austere Virgin with the Child on her left arm; he holds a scroll in his left hand and raises his right hand in a blessing and there is little sense of any connection between the two figures. Later images—the Virgin of Vladimir is a good example—show a more tender and touching image of mother-love, with the Child reaching up to embrace his mother, her head inclined towards him.

The smaller Cathedral of the Annunciation (*Blagoveshchensky*) is ahead and to your right as you exit from the Cathedral of the Assumption and stand facing the square again. With its nine gold domes, it served as the private chapel of the royal family. The existing building dates from the 1480s and was constructed by Russian masons from Pskov, but the cathedral was to be substantially rebuilt following a fire in 1547. Ivan the Terrible ordered the addition of four new domed chapels, gilding them with gold looted in the sacking of Novgorod, and in 1572 a new porch was added in the south-east corner for use by the Tsar himself. Having incurred the displeasure of the ecclesiastical authorities because of his rapid turnover of wives (the Church

disapproved of anyone marrying more than three times: Ivan got through seven wives) he was condemned to enter the church through a separate doorway and observe services through a grille. This power of Church over state would later be curtailed, first with the Church reforms of the seventeenth century and finally by Peter the Great, who abolished the Patriarchate in 1721, bringing the Church wholly under state control.

The nineteenth-century traveller, Captain Colville Frankland, was unimpressed by the interior of the cathedral, remarking that it was "ornamented with curious frescoes, among which are the heads of heathen philosophers… this church contains a great variety of musty and disgusting relics set in silver frames, which the deluded and absurd people were kissing with great veneration." Present-day visitors may beg to differ in their assessment of the iconostasis, a survivor of the 1547 fire, which contains icons painted by the great master Theophanes the Greek together with his student Andrei Rublev. A German visitor, Field Marshal Helmuth von Moltke, visiting Moscow in 1866 for the coronation of Alexander II, was more impressed by what he saw: the cathedral was, he said "narrower, more peculiar and more gorgeous than all the others. It is a perfect little jewel-box. The cross and cupola are of pure gold, and the pavement is inlaid with jasper, agate and cornelian from Siberia." The provenance of the jasper flooring is the subject of some dispute: some say it was donated by the Shah of Persia to Tsar Alexei Mikhailovich in the seventeenth century.

Another, much smaller, religious building dating from the time of Ivan the Great is the unassuming white single-domed Church of the Deposition of the Robe (*Rizhpolozheny*) that lies in the shadow of the Cathedral of the Assumption. It takes its name from the miracle-working robe of the Virgin Mary deposited in Constantinople in the fifth century AD; an earlier church on this site was built to mark the liberation of Moscow from the Tatars on the day of the Feast of the Deposition of the Robe. The church was used by Church elders as a private place of prayer and as a concealed route from the Tsar's palace to the cathedral, used in particular by the women of the royal household.

Between the Cathedrals of the Assumption and the Annunciation stands the Faceted Palace, the oldest surviving secular building in Moscow. Built in the late fifteenth century by the Italian architects Marco Ruffo and Pietro Solario, its name derives from its white stone exterior and patterned façade. The palace has two storeys and the upper floor with its grand vaulted hall was used by the Tsars on grand occasions such as state banquets and the reception of foreign ambassadors. Augustin von Meyerberg, an ambassador sent from the Austrian Emperor Leopold to the Muscovite court, described his frosty reception by Tsar Alexei Mikhailovich in this hall in 1661 as follows:

The hall was large enough, but in the centre was a large column which supported the vault and diminished its beauty very much... Many boyars, courtiers and councillors... were seated on the right side of the Tsar, in all his state, and some of them on the left, everyone with his head uncovered. Not one deigned to honour us by a bow, neither on our entrance or departure. It was difficult to see the Tsar, seated on a silver-gilt throne, placed not in the centre but in the left corner of the hall between two windows. This throne was raised three steps above the steps of the councillors; but it was so narrow, and the obscurity of the room so diminished its splendour that it did not look magnificent at all... And on a bench at the Tsar's right there was a basin, ewer and towel, with which to wash and dry his right hand after we had profaned it with our lips when he presented it to us to kiss, since the Muscovites look upon us, and all who acknowledge the Roman Church as the Mother Church, as Pagans.

The grand entrance to the palace from Cathedral Square is up the Red Staircase, a structure that was demolished in the Soviet period but rebuilt in the 1990s. Visitors expecting the staircase to live up to its name may be disappointed: like Red Square, the name originally meant "beautiful" rather than "red". It was from this vantage-point that the young Peter the Great is said to have witnessed the first atrocities committed in the revolt of the *streltsy* or musketeers against members of his mother's family in 1682. Here too, Napoleon is supposed to have stood and watched on that fateful day in 1812 as the fires that would eventually consume the entire city began to blaze. One would have thought he might have been able to find a better vantage point from which to view the city.

The Cathedral of the Archangel Michael was the third of the Kremlin cathedrals to be rebuilt in stone by Italian architects under Ivan III, not long before his death in 1505. Notable for its Italianate exterior topped by one gold and four silver domes, the cathedral became the final resting place for Moscow's rulers. In Marina Tsvetaeva's 1916 poem dedicated to fellow poet Alexander Blok she wrote of how:

At home in Moscow—where the domes are burning
At home in Moscow—in the sound of bells,
Where I live the tombs—in their rows are standing
And in them Tsaritsas—are asleep and Tsars.

The tombs do indeed stand in their rows: forty-six in total, contained within metal and glass cases: here you can see the graves of Dmitry Donskoi, Ivan the Great, Ivan the Terrible and his sons, and Mikhail Romanov, among many others. From Peter the Great's time onwards the tradition changed and the Tsars of Russia were customarily laid to rest in the Cathedral of St. Peter and St. Paul in the new capital of St. Petersburg. The dark, frescoed interior of the Archangel Cathedral, with its high ceilings and gold chandeliers, provides a dramatic contrast with the white exterior of the building.

Towering high above the other Kremlin buildings, the Bell Tower of Ivan the Great was constructed in the early sixteenth century to replace an earlier church and bell tower on the same site. Further storeys were added to the tower over the decades that passed until it reached the height of 265 feet during the reign of Boris Godunov at the beginning of the seventeenth century. Godunov had sponsored the extension of the tower in part as a job-creation scheme during a time of economic crisis. The tallest structure in Russia, it dominated the Moscow skyline and could be used by guards as a look-out post to watch for invading armies. Napoleon's attempt to have the bell tower blown up as he retreated from Moscow in 1812 caused serious damage to the building, but happily failed to destroy it. Although the bell tower is not open to tourists today, visitors in the past were able to go up the tower to enjoy what Lewis Carroll in 1867 described as "a beautiful view of Moscow, lying around us on all sides, its spires and golden domes all flashing in the sun."

The Development of the City
The city of Moscow, as a brief glance at a map will indicate, is laid out according to the principle of concentric circles. In earlier times these circular settlements were enclosed by ramparts and later by stone walls: the Kremlin wall at the centre with the *Kitai gorod* district (the name literally means China Town in modern Russian, although it almost certainly had a different meaning originally), the home of merchants and those boyars who were not favoured with residences within the Kremlin, huddled next to it. Moving outwards from the city centre next comes the White City (*Belyi gorod*) and then the land enclosed within the Earthern Rampart (*Zemlyanoi val*). The Kitai gorod wall was constructed as a defensive barrier in the 1530s, replacing an earlier soil rampart, and the area developed as a trading quarter with merchants' houses and warehouses still standing today. The wall itself, with its swallow-tail battlements, gates and towers, was described by the Bolsheviks as a "relic of savage and medieval times" and was torn down in the early 1930s to lessen traffic congestion in central Moscow. Only a small fragment now remains in the shadow of the Metropol Hotel on Okhotny Ryad, although this has to be distinguished from the rebuilt section surrounding the archway entrance to the designer shopping arcade on Tretyakovsky proezd.

In the 1570s a white stone wall with twenty seven towers was constructed around the old Belyi gorod, following the line that more than three centuries later became the Boulevard Ring. Many of the traffic intersections along the Boulevard Ring today bear the names of the old gateways into Moscow: Prechistenskie vorota, Arbatskie vorota,

Nikitskie vorota, Petrovskie vorota and so on, the word *vorota* meaning "gates". Later in the same century an earthern rampart and moat were built around the Earthern town, which was subsequently enclosed by the Garden Ring.

Ivan IV or Ivan the Terrible, as he became known, ascended the throne at the age of three in 1533 and was the first ruler of Russia officially to adopt the title "Tsar", the word derived from the Latin "Caesar". The year of his coronation, 1547, coincided with a serious fire in Moscow in which much of the centre of the city was destroyed and Ivan's maternal uncle Yury Glinsky was lynched by angry crowds who blamed his family for starting the blaze. The rumour had spread among the crowd that Ivan's grandmother, Anna Glinskaya, was a witch who had made a magic potion out of human hearts which she had used to set the city ablaze. According to Ivan's own account of his uncle's murder, written twenty years later, the

> *mass of insensate people... pulled him inhumanly into the Cathedral of the Assumption, and killed this innocent man in the church. Opposite the metropolitan's palace they stained the floor of the church with his blood, dragged his body through the front door and exposed him on the market-place as a criminal.*

As a psychological explanation for the Tsar's later psychopathic tendencies this gruesome experience may be argued to have left its mark on the young Ivan.

In the 1550s Ivan's troops, together with their Cossack allies, conquered the cities of Kazan on the Volga and Astrakhan on the Caspian Sea, marking the final defeat of the khans and consolidating Moscow's political and economic influence in the region. It was in the later stages of his rule that Ivan's "terrible" reputation was forged with the creation of the *oprichnina*, his own private fiefdom in which his new private army, the *oprichniki*, were set loose to root out traitors and heretics. Described by later writers as the original secret police, the *oprichniki* rode around the land on black horses, dressed in long black robes and identifiable by their symbol of a dog's head and a broomstick. "They bite like dogs," it was said, "and then they sweep everything superfluous out of the land." Prince Andrei Kurbsky, who fled from their attentions in 1564, described them as "children of darkness...

hundreds and thousands of times worse than hangmen". In Novgorod in 1570 somewhere in the region of three thousand people were tortured and killed by the *oprichniki* in a week-long orgy of violence after the fall of the city.

The image of Ivan the Terrible is probably most familiar to modern-day westerners through the film made by Sergei Eisenstein in the 1940s. Originally planned in three parts, Eisenstein died in 1948 before he was able to finish it. The first part of the film, released in 1944, shows Ivan as hero, leading his troops to victory against Kazan. The second part, a much darker portrayal of the Tsar's inner torments and paranoia, was promptly banned by Stalin with Eisenstein subjected to a torrent of official criticism for "portraying the progressive army of *oprichniki* as a band of degenerates, similar to the American Ku Klux Klan and Ivan the Terrible, a man of strong will and character, as weak and spineless, something like Hamlet." Stalin had famously remarked in conversation with the director that Ivan's problem was that he had not been decisive enough in destroying the boyar clans who had plotted against him.

Another famous depiction of Ivan the Terrible is the painting by Ilya Repin (1885) which hangs in the Tretyakov Gallery. It shows the Tsar seated on the floor, one arm around the waist and the other clutching the head of the son, another Ivan, whom he has just killed, as blood flows down the young man's head and his father stares off into the distance in horror at what he has just done. Ivan struck and killed his son in 1581 in a fit of rage, three years before his own death, with the result that the crown passed to his feeble-minded son Fyodor.

The Seventeenth Century
It was after the death of Ivan the Terrible's son Fyodor that Russia fell into the period of political instability and turmoil known as the Time of Troubles (1598-1612). Fyodor died without leaving an heir, his nine-year-old half-brother Dmitry having died in mysterious circumstances in Uglich in 1591, and his brother-in-law, Boris Godunov, was elected to succeed him. Rumours persisted about how Dmitry had met his untimely end, with the finger of accusation increasingly coming to be pointed at Godunov himself. In the nineteenth century re-workings of this story, both in verse by Pushkin and later in opera by Musorgsky,

Godunov is portrayed as being tortured by a guilty conscience after the murder of Dmitry.

A series of pretenders emerged, each claiming to be the dead Dmitry. The first of these "False Dmitrys" was a defrocked monk called Grigory Otrepev from the Chudov monastery in the Kremlin who gathered support for his cause in Poland, returned to Moscow and was accepted as the new Tsar after Godunov's death in 1605 and crowned in the Cathedral of the Assumption. Yet his Polish connections—in particular his marriage to a Polish Roman Catholic, Marina Mniszek—did not go down too well with Muscovites and the first False Dmitry was eventually torn to pieces by an angry mob in May 1606.

Describing these events in lurid terms, the nineteenth century French writer Prosper Mérimée wrote of how

> the mob threw themselves upon him with horrible cries of triumph, and beating him, dragged him to a room of the palace which had already been sacked… his clothes were ripped off him and a baker's kaftan put on him…soon a disfigured, slashed corpse with the stomach slit open and the arms chopped by sabres was dragged out onto the steps.

His naked body was left on display in Red Square for three days as the beneficiary of the coup, the noble boyar Vasily Shuisky, sought to scotch rumours that he had escaped assassination. Rumours spread that the False Dmitry had been in league with the Devil and his body was later cast into a ditch and eventually burned. His ashes are then said to have been fired from a cannon in the direction of Poland, whence he had come.

Shuisky, having been proclaimed the new Tsar, set about trying to convince people that the genuine Dmitry was really dead: his body was exhumed in Uglich and reports were spread abroad that miracles had been performed at his graveside, paving the way for his eventual canonization. His remains, which were said to have been perfectly preserved, were brought to Moscow and re-interred in the Cathedral of the Archangel, and a special shrine was constructed here in honour of the new St. Dmitry. Shuisky's attempts to secure his own position were ultimately unsuccessful, however, and after a series of revolts against his rule, including one headed by a second False Dmitry, he was deposed by the mob in 1610. In a deeply unpopular move, the boyar ruling council then offered the crown to the Prince of Poland. Widespread resentment against Polish rule was rallied by the Patriarch of Moscow, Germogen, who declared that no one should accept rule by a Catholic. The Polish occupation was eventually ended in October 1612 when a people's militia led by Kuzma Minin and Prince Dmitry Pozharsky advanced on Moscow from Nizhny Novgorod and expelled the invaders, an event commemorated by the statue of the two resistance leaders on Red Square that was erected two hundred years later. A boyar assembly was convened which selected Mikhail Romanov to be the new Tsar, and the Romanov family would rule Russia for the next three hundred years.

The Terem Palace adjoins the Faceted Palace and was built in the 1630s for the first Romanov Tsar, Mikhail Fyodorovich. Squashed between other buildings, it is difficult to see the red and white façade of the building which rises in stepped layers up to the attic or *teremok* from which the palace takes its name. The lower floors contained storerooms and workshops, the upper floors comprised state rooms and the Tsar's private apartments. A series of private chapels offered the women of the royal household a place to pray: three of the Terem Palace churches share a common roof, identifiable by its eleven small gold domes topped by ornate crosses.

The Romanov era was not without its periods of instability and conflict. Violent scenes were witnessed in the Kremlin in 1648 when the people of Moscow, angered at increasing food prices, taxation and unemployment as well as by corrupt officialdom, took to the streets to demand change. A Dutch witness of the events described how the people "were not able to hold out any longer: yea they desired rather with their wives and children to undergoe a present death, then to suffer any longer in such transcendent oppression."

The troubles began when the Tsar, Alexei Mikhailovich, was returning home from a pilgrimage and a crowd gathered to meet him. Seizing the bridle of the Tsar's horse, the people complained about their situation and demanded redress. Reports vary as to what happened next, whether the Tsar refused to receive their petition or whether he promised to do what he could to help, but then his boyars attacked the crowd, beating them with knouts. Either way, the result was a great riot and the storming of the Kremlin. The mob broke into the house of

Alexei's leading statesman, his brother-in-law Boris Morozov, looted valuables, drank his vodka, killed one of his servants and set the house on fire. Another leading boyar, Nazar Chistoi, who was alleged to have inspired the increase in the salt tax that had so enraged the people, was betrayed by a servant and beaten to death, with his body then flung into a cess pit.

When his musketeers, the *streltsy*, refused to clear the crowds from the Kremlin, Tsar Alexei realised that he would have to make some concessions. He offered up one of his officials, Levonty Pleshcheev, a man notorious for his exploitative and unjust nature, for public execution. No sooner was Pleshcheev brought out than he was lynched by the mob. Olearius, the Duke of Holstein's ambassador to Muscovy, described the scene:

> *His head was beaten to such a pulp that his brains splattered over his face. His clothing was torn off and the naked body dragged through the dirt around the market place, while they cried: "Thus will all such scoundrels and thieves be treated."*

Fires broke out in the White City, spreading across the Neglinnaya river to threaten the Kremlin. The crowds hurried to plunder the burning buildings with the result that "not a person wanted to escape or could, since all were as drunk as could be from the vodka they had pillaged from the cellars... Many who completely lost consciousness were suffocated by the smoke and fumes, and burned up." It was said that the fires only died down when a monk thought to cast Pleshcheev's body into the flames and burn it to ashes. Eventually the Tsar was able to calm the disturbances by promising that he would exile Boris Morozov from Moscow and replace his most unpopular advisers with just and pious men. He also created a new office that could receive popular petitions for consideration; never again would they be presented directly to the Tsar.

Positioned against the western wall of the Kremlin and facing the Palace of Congresses, the Poteshnyi Palace offers a good example of mid-seventeenth century architecture from the reign of Tsar Alexei Mikhailovich. Built in 1652 as the private mansion of the Tsar's father-in-law, it was taken over by the crown after his death and a stone passageway was constructed to link it to the Terem Palace. The name *poteshnyi* means "amusements" and the palace takes its name from the theatre that was located here during Tsar Alexei's reign. The palace was used as housing for Soviet leaders after the revolution and Stalin had his private apartment here until 1932 when his wife Nadezhda Alliluyeva committed suicide by shooting herself in her bedroom.

The Cathedral of the Twelve Apostles is the first religious building that will be seen by a visitor entering the Kremlin through the tourist entrance via the Trinity Gates. Together with the Patriarch's Palace, the Cathedral is inseparably bound up with the name of the seventeenth-century Patriarch Nikon who was instrumental in precipitating the great schism in the Russian Church of 1666-7. Nikon, the son of a peasant who rose to be elected Patriarch in 1652, built his own palatial apartments beside those of the Tsar as a manifestation of the might and power of the Church in Russia. The message was understood by visitors, one of whom—Archbishop Paul of Aleppo who visited the palace shortly after it was completed in 1655—remarked that "these buildings are an object of wonder to everyone; for scarcely in the royal palaces is there anything to equal them."

Nikon had strong views about religious architecture, insisting that Russian churches should have unadorned exteriors and that "in observance of the rules of the Holy Apostles and the Fathers the Lord's church should have five cupolas and not resemble a tent." The tent roof design visible in earlier Moscow churches such as the Church of the Ascension at Kolomenskoe and the Church of the Nativity of Our Lady in Putinki on Malaya Dmitrovka ulitsa was henceforth abandoned and the Cathedral of the Twelve Apostles was built according to Nikon's preferred design with its five silver domes and plain exterior walls.

Nikon was not simply concerned with the aesthetics of church architecture. His views on church roofs formed part and parcel of a much wider concern for the purity and authenticity of Russian Orthodox practices. It was his fear that errors and mistranslations had crept into rituals over the centuries since Russia's adoption of Christianity that led him to introduce a package of reformist measures designed to purge the Church and thereby strengthen it. Most controversially, these included the ruling that believers should follow the Greek practice of crossing themselves with three fingers rather than with the traditional two. Far from strengthening the Church, Nikon's reforms had the opposite effect: many believers were simply not prepared to accept that the rituals that their fathers and their fathers' fathers had strictly adhered to could now be denounced as false. The adoption of Nikon's reforms brought a major schism in the Church. The large minority who refused to go along with the new measures split off from the Church and formed their own communities of "Old Believers", insisting to the last that they were the truly Orthodox and that "if we are schismatics, then the holy fathers, Tsars and patriarchs were also schismatics." They believed that "to make the sign of the cross with three fingers is a Latin tradition and the mark of the Antichrist." The Russian term for the Old Believers, *Raskolniki* (literally meaning "schismatics") may be familiar to readers as the name given to the antihero of Dostoevsky's *Crime and Punishment*, Raskolnikov, a man who cuts himself off from societal norms.

Peter the Great: Moscow Abandoned

Moscow's star began to wane with the dawn of the eighteenth century and the reign of Peter the Great. The turbulent events surrounding Peter the Great's rise to power saw three separate revolts by the Muscovite *streltsy* or musketeers. The first came almost immediately after his ascension to the throne following the death of his half-brother Fyodor in 1682; rebels who preferred the claims of his older, feeble-minded half-brother Ivan, stormed the Kremlin and killed members of Peter's mother's family, the Naryshkins, including his uncle Ivan who was tortured and killed in the tower of St. Constantine and St. Helena. One story has it that the ten-year-old Peter and his mother came out onto the Red Staircase and witnessed the beginnings of this bloodbath as the first victim, Artamon Matveev, counsellor to Tsar Alexei, was killed and flung down the steps onto the spears of the *streltsy* waiting below.

In the seven years that followed, Peter and Ivan ruled as joint Tsars under an unofficial regency dominated by their elder sister Sophia. A special double throne was built for them which contained a secret compartment for Sophia herself to sit in: this throne can be seen today in the Kremlin Armoury Palace. In 1689, on hearing rumours that a new *streltsy* coup was in the offing, Peter fled to the Trinity Monastery and organized his resistance: the rebels once again were defeated and Sophia, who was blamed for instigating the attempted coup, was sent to a nunnery. Finally in 1698, following Ivan's death, a further attempt was made to overthrow Peter, taking advantage of his temporary absence in western Europe. Again the revolt was put down, this time with particular brutality. These events were to provide the material for Modest Musorgsky's opera *Khovanshchina*, "The Khovansky Affair", named after the leader of the *streltsy* in 1682: a fictional plot based on the events of the three rebellions and weaving in the story of the Old Believers who supported the mutiny against the Tsar. The opera ends with the mass self-immolation of the Old Believers in despair at the direction being taken by the new Russia but putting their faith in God's salvation.

If the *streltsy* were fearful that Peter represented a threat to their traditional way of life, they were quite right to feel that way. Peter's efforts to Europeanize his country would be far-reaching, encompassing changes in noble dress and even a tax on beards. Boyars were fined 100 rubles a year if they wished to remain hirsute; a French biography of Peter dating from 1730 recounted how in Moscow for this reason

> the Tsar was regarded as a tyrant and a pagan; and there were many old Russians who, after having their beards shaved off, saved them preciously, in order to have them placed in their coffins, fearing that they would not be allowed to enter heaven without their beards.

Peter's dislike of Moscow and what he saw as its backwardness and obscurantism may well have been crystallized by these events, and these feelings were only strengthened by his experience of travel in western Europe. After some attempts to modernize Moscow (building a new College of Mathematical and Navigational Science and introducing paving stones and street lighting to the city), he eventually abandoned it altogether. In 1703 Peter founded his new city of St. Petersburg on the Gulf of Finland, and in 1712 he moved his court north to the new "Window on the West". The impact on Moscow was crushing: its population dropped precipitously and it lost its dominant influence in Russian political life for the next two hundred years, barring a short period under the youthful Tsar Peter II (1727-30) when the capital was briefly returned to Moscow.

Writing in 1787, Prince Mikhail Shcherbatov sought to put into words the city's own feelings about what followed in his *Petition of the City of Moscow on being relegated to Oblivion*:

Alas! He left me whether out of necessity, to build a fleet, to institute commerce, and to direct in person the war then taking place, or out of disdain for my ancient customs, he transferred his capital to the newly built city bearing his name... My best citizens left my walls to found their homes in a strange land and crowds of peasants were sent to cultivate a marshy and infertile soil; my buildings, which no order was given to restore, fell to ruins, and it was forbidden to erect new ones.

Comparisons soon began to be drawn between the old capital and the new and a certain rivalry developed between the two cities that has continued in one form or another to this day. Moscow was always depicted as the more truly Russian city with its onion domes and narrow, winding streets, St. Petersburg as a foreign creation laid out on a westernized grid of broad avenues. Writing of this phenomenon in 1834, Pushkin recalled how:

At one time there really was a rivalry between Moscow and Petersburg. Then in Moscow there were rich nobles who did not work, grandees who had given up the court, and independent, carefree individuals, passionately devoted to harmless slander and inexpensive hospitality, then Moscow was the gathering place for all Russia's aristocracy, which streamed to it in winter from every province... Five thousand people filled the hall of the Noble Assembly twice a week. There the young met; marriages were made. Moscow was as famous for its brides as Vyazma for its honey-cakes; Moscow dinners became a proverb. The innocent eccentricities of the Muscovites were a sign of their independence. They lived their own lives, amusing themselves as they liked, caring little for the opinion of others... From afar haughty Petersburg mocked, but did not interfere with old mother Moscow's escapades.

The independence of Muscovites was also commented on by the English traveller, Captain Colville Frankland, who remarked that:

There is a liberty of speech and thought, and action, in Moscow, which does not exist in Petersburgh; this makes it an agreeable place to an Englishman... almost all the men of liberal opinions, and those whose politics do not suit those of the day, retire hither, where they may find fault with the Court, the Government, &c. as much as they please, without much fear of interruption. I have no doubt that a great deal more may be learnt in this city of the real state of Russia in one month than one could gather with the utmost industry in six, in Petersburgh.

And an American visitor in 1871 contrasted the two, arguing that:

The one, fully aware that progress cannot be improvised, seeks to overcome obstacles gradually: the other expects at once to realize Utopia... In a word, at St Petersburg men reason, at Moscow they dream: in the former intelligence and moderation dominate, in the latter, visionary dreams and precipitation... Moscow is ready to sacrifice everything, even Russia, for its visions of the great Slavic Empire of the future.

With the court now ensconced in St Petersburg, the Kremlin fell into disuse. A series of fires in the early eighteenth century cleared away many of the close-packed boyars' homes that had been clustered within the Kremlin wall, and others were demolished to make way for the building of the Arsenal in the north-west corner of the fortress. The Arsenal stands to the left of the tourist entrance to the Kremlin and cannons captured from Napoleon's *Grande Armée* line the outside of the building.

A particularly ferocious fire destroyed many of the smaller Kremlin buildings in 1737 and was responsible for inflicting fatal damage on the Tsarina Anna's great bell that stands today in front of the Ivan the Great bell tower. The crack occurred when water was poured over the bell while it was still hot from the fire. An earlier bell had crashed to earth in a previous fire of 1701; no attempt was made to replicate Anna's "Tsar Bell" and it stands today as a curio for tourists to wonder at, alongside the "Tsar Cannon" that was cast in 1586 and

never used. The philosopher Pyotr Chaadaev remarked sardonically on how

> *in Moscow… every foreigner is taken to look at the great cannon and the great bell—the cannon which cannot be fired and the bell which fell down before it was rung. It is an amazing town in which the objects of interest are distinguished by their absurdity; or perhaps that great bell without a tongue is a hieroglyph symbolic of this huge, dumb land, inhabited by a race calling themselves Slavs as though wondering at the possession of human speech.*

Catherine the Great, who began life as the German Princess Sophia of Anhalt-Zerbst, came to Russia after her marriage into the Romanov family at the age of fifteen. Having ousted her husband, the unfortunate Peter III, in 1762, she became the sole ruler of Russia until her death in 1796. Catherine was not particularly fond of Moscow: she spent as little time here as possible and felt that its unplanned and disorderly layout was symptomatic of its general backwardness. "Moscow is a world of its own, not just a city," she remarked to Voltaire. Her reign witnessed a number of radical projects to redevelop Moscow, most of which were only partially realized. In the late 1760s she commissioned the court architect Vasily Bazhenov to devise a plan to modernize the Kremlin: his proposals encompassed the construction of a massive new four-storey palace along the south side of the Kremlin overlooking the river that would, had it ever been built, have enclosed many of the existing buildings within its walls. Part of the Kremlin wall was demolished in preparation for the building work to begin, but it was soon called off as Catherine lost interest in the project and it ran out of money. An English visitor, E. D. Clarke, who saw the plans and Bazhenov's wooden model of the palace in 1810, described it as "one of the most curious things in Moscow… had the work been completed, no edifice could ever have compared with it."

The wall was soon rebuilt, and a later Kremlin project saw the building of the Senate, a neoclassical construction designed by Bazhenov's star pupil Matvei Kazakov. Kazakov, who was also responsible for building a large number of noble mansions in Moscow at this time, designed the Senate in the shape of a triangle with three inner courtyards and a large circular hall. With the Russian flag flying from its large green dome above the great hall, the Senate now serves as the President's official residence. Further developments that took place in the city during Catherine's reign included the paving of some streets, the laying of water pipes and the tearing down of the old Belyi gorod wall and its replacement with the ring of attractive tree-lined boulevards that have lasted down to this day.

Napoleon: Invasion and Conflagration

Many of Kazakov's fine new mansions would not survive for long. The burning of Moscow in 1812 left three quarters of the city in ruins, although miraculously the Kremlin withstood the worst of the blaze. After suffering defeat at the hands of the French at the Battle of Borodino at the end of August, the Russian army abandoned Moscow to Napoleon's troops and many of the inhabitants fled. One Russian officer recorded in his diary the appearance of the city on 1 September as the army retreated:

> *While we were walking through the city, it seemed that I had come upon another world. Everything around me was ghostly. I wanted to believe that everything I saw—the despair, fear and confusion of the inhabitants—was only a dream and that mere apparitions surrounded me…The ancient towers of Moscow, the tombs of my ancestors, the sacred shrine where our sovereign was crowned—all called to me, all demanded revenge.*

Their belongings loaded into carts, Moscow's wealthier citizens took to the roads and fled the city, leaving behind them an empty shell for the French to occupy. Fyodor Glinka, a Russian officer who wrote an account of the war, reported that by 2 September when the French entered the city, he could barely recognize the capital, "which I have so often seen in its shining magnificence, amidst celebrations and feasting… They've taken from Moscow the throng, the bustle of people, the frenzied passions, the clatter of carriages, the wealth of ornament— and Moscow, orphaned, empty, differs not in the least from a simple provincial town."

The first of the fires started almost immediately. Blamed by the French on the local inhabitants, it was claimed that the Governor-General of the city, Count Rostopchin, had ordered that the city be set alight so that the invaders be deprived of its riches. "To burn down their own cities!" cried Napoleon, "A demon has got into them! What ferocious determination! What a people!" Having originally broken out in the Kitai gorod district to the east of the Kremlin, by the afternoon of 3 September the fire had spread far and wide and, in the account left by the French General de Caulaincourt:

> it had already reached the houses around the Kremlin. The wind, which had veered slightly to the west, fanned the flames to a terrifying extent and carried enormous sparks to a distance, where they fell like a fiery deluge hundreds of yards away, setting fire to more houses and preventing the most intrepid from remaining in the neighbourhood. The air was so hot and the pinewood sparks were so numerous, that the beams supporting the iron plates which formed the roof of the arsenal all caught fire. The roof of the Kremlin kitchen was only saved by the men placed there with brooms and buckets to gather up the glowing fragments and moisten the beams. Only by superhuman efforts was the fire in the Arsenal extinguished.

Eventually the French were forced to evacuate the Kremlin and Napoleon headed north to take refuge in the Petrovsky Palace on the St. Petersburg road. The novelist Stendhal, who was with the French army at the time, described how as they left the city centre, their way was "lit by the finest blaze in the world which was in the form of a huge pyramid resembling the prayer of the faithful whose base is on earth and whose spire reaches to heaven. The moon, I think, appeared above the holocaust. It was a magnificent sight." By the time the fires had burned themselves out, Moscow lay in ruins. In Tolstoy's memorable description in his great historical novel *War and Peace*, Pierre Bezukhov gazes on the devastated city from its western edge at Maiden's Field:

> No flames were seen, but columns of smoke rose on all sides, and all Moscow as far as Pierre could see was one vast charred ruin. On all sides there were waste spaces with only stoves and chimney stacks still standing, and here and there the blackened walls of the brick houses. Pierre gazed at the ruins and did not recognize districts he had known well. Here and there he could see churches that had not

*been burnt. The Kremlin, which was not destroyed, gleamed white
in the distance with its towers and the belfry of Ivan the Great…it
was plain that the Russian nest was ruined and destroyed.*

A Russian soldier, surveying the scene with Pierre comments: "How is
one to help feeling sad? Moscow—she's the mother of cities. How can
one see all this and not feel sad?"

For the French army, the fires brought defeat at the very moment
of their victory. Winter was fast approaching: the snows fell unusually
early that year, and it was impossible for the French to live out the
winter in the devastated city. Just over a month after his army had first
entered the city, Napoleon gave the order to retreat. By the end, as
Tolstoy would later put it, "the aim of each man when he left Moscow
was no longer, as it had been, to conquer, but merely to keep what he
had acquired," and looting became endemic among the French soldiers.
Directions were given for mines to be laid and for the Kremlin to be
destroyed: parts of the wall and towers were badly damaged in the
explosions that ensued, although the worst of the planned destruction
failed to materialize, thanks once again, in part, to the weather.

The French occupation had come as a terrible shock to most
Russians. The writer Ivan Turgenev was devastated by the news: "What
misfortune can be compared with the taking and burning of Moscow?"
he confided in his diary, "What a deep impression this has made in my
heart! It seems to me that I've lost everything in the world and that all
that is left is to die. Bitter tears flow from my eyes, embodying the truth
of my feelings, for I myself cannot believe what I see and yet,
unfortunately, see so clearly. Moscow! Russia! I am lost in frenzy and
grief!" As the French retreated and the Russians re-entered the city, the
extent of the devastation became clear. In the words of one observer,
"here lie only the ashes of homes… everywhere the traces of
desolation… Around me is the gloom and stillness of graves… Was it
long ago that swarms of people seethed and clamour never ceased within
Moscow's walls?" Another Muscovite wrote to her husband that "you
would not believe what has become of Moscow, it is unrecognizable, and
one can not look upon these ruins without weeping."

Reconstruction and Revolution
Napoleon's claim that "Moscow, one of the most beautiful and wealthy

cities of the world exists no more" was something of an overstatement. The city was rapidly rebuilt with new public spaces laid out in the immediate surroundings of the Kremlin. Theatre Square, home to both the Bolshoi and Maly theatres, dates from this time and the Neglinnaya river that had formed a moat around the Kremlin was channelled into an underground pipe. This left space for the creation of the Alexander Gardens (*Aleksandrovsky sad*), named in honour of the reigning Tsar, Alexander I, to the west of the Kremlin wall. A sense of what the Kremlin looked like before the moat was removed can be found in the Tretyakov Gallery: two paintings from the early nineteenth century by F. Y. Alekseev show the river running alongside the Kremlin wall with bridges leading up to the main tower gates.

It was during the reign of Alexander's brother, Nicholas I—the gendarme of Europe, as he became known—that the south-western corner of the Kremlin was redeveloped with the construction first of the Great Kremlin Palace and then of the Armoury. Many older buildings were demolished to make room for these new palaces designed by the architect Konstantin Ton. The Great Kremlin Palace, with its yellow and white columned façade standing high on Borovitsky hill and gazing down to the river below, became the main residence of the imperial family in Moscow. Its opulent halls are not normally open to the general public and are used for grand occasions of state; in the Soviet period they were used as the venue for Party congresses. One early visitor, the Earl of Mayo, who viewed the building in 1845 as it was still under construction, was unimpressed by the grandeur that he saw around him. "It is an enormous pile without the smallest pretensions to architectural beauty and looks more like a Manchester cotton factory than the Imperial residence of the sacred Kremlin," he wrote. "How the Russian committee of taste could have induced themselves to set up an eye-sore of such gigantic proportions on so holy a spot, can only be conceived by those who have mused upon the edifices of Trafalgar Square."

The Armoury Palace (*Oruzhenaya Palata*), together with the State Diamond Fund, is usually the last stop on a tour group itinerary. Now a museum, the Armoury offers visitors the chance to view the most precious treasures of the Russian state: the Crown of Monomakh, allegedly passed down from the Byzantine Emperor to Prince Vladimir of Kiev, the Diamond Throne of Tsar Alexei, coronation robes, state carriages and Fabergé eggs. There is an extensive collection of western European silverware from the sixteenth and seventeenth century that was offered to the Russian state by foreign ambassadors: the English items are of particular interest as much Tudor silver was melted down by Cromwell during the English Civil War.

Palaces and churches aside, there are very few public monuments or statues in the Kremlin. Those that once stood within its walls have mostly been removed after their subjects fell into political disfavour. From 1898-1918 the Kremlin was home to a statue of Tsar Alexander II, the great Tsar-Liberator, responsible for the Emancipation Proclamation of 1861 that freed the Russian serfs from their lives of servile bondage. Alexander had been assassinated by a terrorist bomb in St. Petersburg in 1881 and the monument was erected by his grandson, the ill-fated Nicholas II. A massive edifice topped by a tent-like canopy and not wholly dissimilar to the Albert Memorial in London, it stood in the Kremlin gardens, visible from the opposite bank of the river. After the revolution, Lenin ordered that the memorial be removed and replaced by a statue of Tolstoy. This never materialized and in the 1970s a statue of Lenin was erected on the spot, one that would suffer the same fate as its predecessor when it too was taken down in 1995.

Another tsarist-era monument that once stood in the Kremlin was the cross dedicated to the memory of Grand Duke Sergei Alexandrovich, brother-in-law of Nicholas II and Governor-General of Moscow, who was blown up by terrorists in 1905. The cross stood on the site of his assassination just inside the Nikolskie gate of the Kremlin. Boris Pasternak recalled hearing about the attack in a poem entitled "Childhood":

For the third day snow had fallen.
It's still falling in the evening.
During the night
The weather cleared.
In the morning
—a thundering peal from the Kremlin:
The patron of the Arts School...
Sergei Alexandrovich...
Killed...
In these early days of February

I fell in love with the storm.

The cross, with its associations both with the Orthodox Church and with the Romanov family, was an obvious target for Bolshevik iconoclasts and Lenin himself helped to pull it down just in time for the May Day celebrations in 1918. A replica has since been erected in the Novospassky Monastery in the southeast of the city after the reburial of the Grand Duke's remains in the family vault there in 1995. The Grand Duke's widow Elizaveta Fyodorovna, sister of the Tsarina and granddaughter of Queen Victoria, dedicated her life to the Church after his death and founded the Martha and Mary Convent south of the river on ulitsa Bolshaya Ordynka. The church here was built by the architect Shchusev, later famous for building the Lenin Mausoleum. Elizaveta herself suffered a similarly tragic fate to her husband after the Revolution when she was killed by being thrown down a mineshaft in the Ural Mountains by Bolshevik agents. She has since been canonized and a recent statue of her can be seen in the convent courtyard.

Popular discontent in the city during the first decade of the new century was fuelled by serious overcrowding in the workers' districts and this tension would rise in the years leading up to the Great War, before spilling over into revolution in 1917. House-to-house fighting took place in Moscow in the aftermath of the Bolshevik coup in the capital Petrograd (as St. Petersburg was patriotically renamed during the war) on 25 October. After changing hands twice, the citadel was captured by Lenin's supporters on 3 November and a grand ceremony was held on Red Square to mark the funerals of the early martyrs of the Revolution. Several buildings in the Kremlin sustained serious shrapnel damage in the prolonged assault. The American journalist John Reed, who visited Moscow shortly after the Bolshevik take-over, went to inspect the damage to the Kremlin and reported in *Ten Days that Shook the World* that one of the cupolas of the Cathedral of the Assumption had been damaged, a shell had hit the corner of the Ivan the Great bell tower, and the Chudov monastery had been hit about thirty times and sustained damage to the exterior of the building.

The Soviet Kremlin

It was in March 1918 that the new Soviet government made the decision to move the capital back to Moscow. With the loss of Poland

and the Baltic States, St. Petersburg had become very close to the country's western border and was hence vulnerable to attack. Originally approved as a temporary measure, some Bolsheviks were anxious about the idea that they might be seen to be endorsing conservative Slavophiles' long-held hopes of a return to the ancient capital. Once the transfer had taken place, however, the question of moving the capital back again was never even considered.

The Revolution turned earlier social norms on their head as across the country workers and peasants moved into the homes of the former ruling classes: the Kremlin was no exception in this regard. The government took it over and turned its cathedrals into museums and its palaces into office space and apartment blocks. The Senate became the home of the Soviet Government and many of the most important Soviet leaders lived in the same building: above the shop, as it were. Lenin and his wife Nadezhda Krupskaya had a modest set of rooms in the Senate, and this apartment was preserved as a museum long after his death. Stalin, too, took over a flat here after his wife's suicide, although he spent the bulk of his time either in his dacha outside Moscow or on holiday in the south.

The Soviet period brought major upheaval to the fabric of the Kremlin. Several buildings were torn down to make room for new construction projects: the Church of the Saviour in the Woods, the Chudov monastery and the Voznesensky convent were all demolished to provide space for a new Military School built in the classical style (this later became the home of the Presidium of the Supreme Soviet and now provides government office space). The double-headed eagles were removed from the tops of the Kremlin towers and replaced by red stars although this change was not made until 1935: in photographs from the 1920s and early 30s the Imperial crest still punctuates the skyline at the very heart of Soviet power. A cinema was installed in the Great Kremlin Palace for Stalin's interminable movie evenings with his unfortunate colleagues, evenings that were invariably followed by drunken carousing until dawn.

Before the Revolution the Kremlin had been open to the public; ordinary people would have to wait until after Stalin's death before access was permitted by the Soviet authorities. The move to reopen it was made by Khrushchev in 1955, since then public access has been mostly straightforward. The government is still liable to close the

Kremlin at short notice if security concerns are deemed to make this necessary: fears about possible Chechen terrorist attacks have brought heightened security measures in recent years and tourist access has sometimes been restricted as a result.

The Palace of Congresses, now renamed the State Kremlin Palace, was the most dramatic new architectural addition to the Kremlin during the Soviet period. An ugly 1960s building made of concrete and glass, its saving grace is that the foundations were laid low down, making it far less obtrusive than it would otherwise be. Stalin's successor, Nikita Khrushchev, ordered the building of the new palace and a competition was held to produce the final design. The hall of the palace contains seating for six thousand and was purpose-built to house Party congresses. It is now used as a stage for opera and ballet performances, tickets for which are usually easy to obtain from the many ticket kiosks found in metro stations and on main streets in the city centre.

During the 1990s President Yeltsin ordered the refurbishment of the Kremlin palaces at vast expense. Public scandal erupted around the restoration project as the Swiss firm hired to undertake the work, Mabatex, was alleged to have bribed Russian officials in order to secure the lucrative contracts. Swiss investigators put out an arrest warrant for Pavel Borodin, who at that time worked as the manager of the Kremlin estate. In 2000 he was removed from that position by President Putin and transferred to another role.

Let us leave the Kremlin now, with a final backward glance over the complex of yellow and white classical buildings, sparkling golden domes and dark fir trees. Lewis Carroll had his final visit to the fortress by night back in 1867. In his words:

> *On our way home [we] passed through the Kremlin and so got our last impression of that most beautiful range of buildings, in perhaps the most beautiful aspect of which it is capable—a flood of cold, clear moonlight, bringing out the pure white of the walls and towers, and the glittering points of light on the gilded domes, in a way that sunlight could never do.*

Chapter Two
RED SQUARE

Red Square, the beautiful square in the original meaning of the name, has a long history as a commercial, religious and political space. A trading centre from the end of the fifteenth century, it was famous for its Easter fairs when stalls selling all manner of weird and wonderful goods—tortoises, goldfish, toy monkeys, musical instruments, icons, carpets, sweets and balloons—sprang up across the square attracting huge crowds of visitors. The fairs continued into the early twentieth century, and Alexander Pasternak, brother of the more famous Boris, left a description of one such occasion: "On this day Red Square was unrecognizable. Naturally vast, it became tight and circumscribed; generally quiet, it whistled, roared and squealed; normally respectable, it was overtaken by Bacchic revelry."

The square also served as a place of executions: the body of the first False Dmitry was put out on display here in 1606; later that century the rebel Cossack leader Stenka Razin, subject of many popular ballads, who had organized a peasant uprising against Tsar Alexei Mikhailovich, was beheaded and quartered on Red Square. A poem about the event by the Soviet writer Yevgeny Yevtushenko has Razin musing to himself on his fate:

> *I have sinned in this*
> > *that in a world of evil*
> *I was a good idiot.*

> *I sinned in this,*
> > *that I thought of doing battle*
> *For a good Tsar.*
> > *There are no good Tsars, fool…*
> *Stenka,*
> > *you are perishing for nothing!"*
> *Bells boomed over Moscow.*

They are leading Stenka
  to the place of execution…

Here it was, too, that Peter the Great ordered the execution of the mutinous *streltsy* in 1698, an event immortalized in the huge oil painting *On the Morning of the Execution of the Streltsy* (1881) by Vasily Surikov, which hangs in Moscow's Tretyakov Gallery. The painting depicts a mass of women and children crowded around the Lobnoe Mesto in front of St. Basil's Cathedral, weeping over their doomed menfolk while Peter himself looks on from beside the Kremlin wall.

After the transfer of the capital to St. Petersburg, Red Square was deprived of its central symbolic role in Russian state affairs for two hundred years, only regaining its political significance following the 1917 Revolution. The first shots of the Bolshevik Revolution in Moscow were fired here and during the Soviet period the square came to be used as a staging ground for parades of physical fitness or of military might. The great Victory Parade of June 1945 celebrating the defeat of the Nazis was held on Red Square; Stalin watched from atop the Mausoleum as Marshal Zhukov, the great Soviet war hero, inspected the troops from his white horse and the captured red and black German standards with their swastika emblems were flung to the ground at Stalin's feet. Stalin had hoped to lead the parade himself but backed out of this plan after he was thrown from his horse during a secret riding practice session.

The square has also been used as site for unofficial demonstrations of one kind or another over recent years. The nineteen-year-old West German pilot Mathias Rust landed his light aircraft here in May 1987, sparking a diplomatic incident and the arrest of many security officials who had failed to anticipate his escapade. Rust himself was sentenced to four years' hard labour and still claims to this day that his actions helped to bring about the ending of the Cold War. A group of more than two thousand Crimean Tartars, deported from their homeland during the Second World War, staged a demonstration in the square in August 1987, demanding that they be permitted to return to Crimea. More recently, I can remember witnessing a demonstration in 1996 by naked western anti-fur protestors whose antics sparked utter bemusement among fur-coated Russian observers. Today, the square is basically a tourist attraction although it is also used on occasion for concerts. Paul McCartney gave a guest appearance in Red Square in 2003 to a great crowd of adoring fans. (The Beatles were, and still are, hugely popular in Russia where during the Soviet period they were officially stigmatized as "propaganda of an alien ideology".) Muscovites who could not get tickets stood as close to the square as they could in order to hear the music even if they could not watch the show.

Not everything in the square is as it has always been. A sense of how the square looked at the turn of the nineteenth century can be gleaned from the picture of Red Square in 1801 by Fyodor Alekseev which hangs in the Tretyakov Gallery. It shows the moat that used to run down the western side of the square, with bridges joining it to the Kremlin gates, as well as the trading stalls that once ran along its length. These were removed after the 1812 fire. Tram tracks once ran across the square, but were removed in the early 1930s. The statue of Minin and Pozharsky, the liberators of the city from the Poles in 1612, stood in the centre of the square for a hundred years before being moved to its current position in front of St. Basil's. Other structures such as the Voskresenskie gates, the Iverskaya chapel and the Kazan cathedral were torn down after the Revolution and only rebuilt in the 1990s after the end of Communism.

The main entrance to Red Square from the north is through the Resurrection (*Voskresenskie*) Gates, also known as the Iverskie Gates, one of the seven sets of gates in the Kitai gorod wall. This twin-arched structure with its green tent roofs is a modern replica of the gates that were erected in the sixteenth century during the reign of Ivan the Terrible's imbecile son Fyodor to replace an earlier entrance erected at the time the wall itself was built in the 1530s. In 1669 the Chapel of the Iberian Virgin (*Iverskaya*) was built in front of the gates, between the arches. This shrine held a copy of a Greek icon of the Virgin from Mount Athos that had been given to Tsar Alexei in 1648. A nineteenth-century German visitor described how

> *...her hand and the foot of the child are covered with dirt from the abundant kissing; it sits like a crust in little raised points, so that long since it has not been hand and foot that have been kissed, but the concrete breath of pious lips. The doors of the chapel stand open the whole day, and all are admitted who are in sorrow... Here come the peasants early in the morning before going to market... hither*

come the healthy and the sick, the wealthy and those who would become so, the arriving and the departing traveller, the fortunate and the unfortunate, the noble and the beggar...

Everyone took their hats off as they passed through the gates. It was customary for Tsars to pray at the shrine before they entered the Kremlin. In *War and Peace*, Pierre Bezukhov, driving through Moscow on his return from St. Petersburg, noticed "the Iberian shrine with innumerable tapers burning before the golden settings of the icons," and the twentieth-century poet Marina Tsvetaeva wrote of the Iverskaya's "small door where people pour in their crowds," leading into "the chapel of stars, the refuge from evil where the floor is polished by kisses." A 1916 painting by Aristakh Lentulov depicting crowds of people approaching the chapel hangs in the New Tretyakov Gallery. Like so many other places of worship in Moscow, the shrine attracted the attention of militant atheists after the Revolution. Arthur Ransome, who was visiting Moscow in 1919, described how close by the chapel someone had erected a stone tablet with the inscription "Religion is the opium of the People"; he witnessed how an illiterate peasant crossed himself before the chapel and then crossed himself no less solemnly in front of the stone inscription as well. A notably iconoclastic poem written in 1927 by Sergei Tretyakov runs as follows:

All for combat!
Force is best.
A bullet to the brain
Of Basil the Blest.
Smash all the icons
And the signs they have made.
Explode the Iverskaya
With a hand grenade!

The gates and the chapel were destroyed in 1931 in order to open up the entrance to Red Square for tanks and political parades, despite popular protests against the move. In a famous phrase, the Moscow Party chief "Iron Lazar" Kaganovich, faced with pleas from architects that the destruction of old monuments such as the gates would spoil the area's aesthetic character, announced that "my aesthetic requires the accommodation of multiple columns of demonstrators crowding into Red Square simultaneously." The gates and the chapel were rebuilt in 1995 as part of Mayor Yury Luzhkov's programme for restoring Moscow's architectural ties with the imperial past.

St. Basil's

The crazy, colourful onion domes of St. Basil's at the southern end of Red Square date from the time of Ivan the Terrible. After his victory over the Mongol khans at Kazan on 1 October 1552, Ivan ordered the construction of a new cathedral to mark the event and to celebrate Moscow's victory over the infidels. Originally known as the Cathedral of the Intercession of the Virgin by the Moat and dedicated to the feast day on which the battle for Kazan had taken place, it soon became popularly known as St. Basil's, after the "holy fool" Basil (Vasily) the Blessed, who was buried in an earlier church on this site. The eight little chapels that surround the central church of the Intercession of Our Lady are each said to mark a Muscovite victory and an extra chapel was built over the grave of St. Basil in 1588.

The story goes that the two architects, Barma and Postnik, who were commissioned to build the cathedral, were subsequently blinded on the orders of the Tsar so that they might never build anything so beautiful again. The cathedral was clearly intended to have an impact on viewers with its extravagant exterior that contrasts so dramatically with the narrow little chapels within, decorated with floral motifs on the walls. It certainly did produce an impact. The nineteenth-century poet Mikhail Lermontov described the onion domes of St. Basil's as having been "scattered all over the building without symmetry or order like the offshoots of an old tree climbing over its bared roots." In the Baedeker guidebook to Moscow of 1914 the cathedral was summed up as "quaint and fantastic in the extreme". The Marquis de Custine, never a man to use one word where ten would do, described the view of St. Basil's from a distance as follows:

it appears as an immense cluster of little turrets forming a bush, or rather giving the idea of some kind of tropical fruit all bristled over with excrescences, or a crystallization of a thousand rays: the scales of a golden fish, the enamelled skin of a serpent, the changeful hues of the lizard, the glossy rose and azure of the pigeon's neck, would all, as regards colour, serve as comparisons: above, rise minarets of a brownish red. The effect of the whole dazzles the eye, and fascinates the imagination. Surely, the land in which such a building is called a house of prayer is not Europe: it must be India, Persia or China!—and the men who go to worship God in this box of confectionary work, can they be Christians?

Lewis Carroll, who was shown around St. Basil's "by undoubtedly the most atrocious guide I have yet met with," said of the cathedral that it was "as quaint (almost grotesque) within as it is without". Another foreigner, this time Walter Benjamin, who visited Moscow in 1926, remarked on how "the lower portion of St. Basil's Cathedral could well be the ground floor of a boyar's mansion. But the crosses atop the domes often resemble gigantic earrings attached to the sky... the warm, cosy colours of its façade shine onto the snow." He was unimpressed by the interior, which he described as "poorly maintained... cold and empty", and he disliked the floral patterns painted on the interior walls. Like Carroll, Benjamin was extremely rude about the tour guides who showed him around Moscow's landmark buildings (the tradition of tedious and/or uninformative guided tours is one that was proudly perpetuated in the Soviet period by the state tour company Intourist).

Intourist alumni can still be found in abundance and are happy (for a fee) to inform the incautious visitor at great length and in interminable detail about the height, breadth and width of the walls and time taken to build any number of significant buildings.

The cathedral was looted by the Poles during the Time of Troubles, and intermittent fires in the seventeenth and eighteenth centuries destroyed parts of the building. In 1812 Napoleon ordered that St. Basil's, which had already been plundered by the French, should be destroyed, but fortunately the orders were never carried through. St. Basil's was damaged by the fighting in Moscow in the days following the October Revolution, and the first Commissar for Enlightenment Anatoly Lunacharsky is said to have offered his resignation on hearing the news, saying "I cannot bear it any longer… I am powerless to stop this barbarism."

St. Basil's came under threat on a number of occasions during the Soviet period as well. Closed to worshippers in 1929 and handed over to the Historical Museum, the cathedral was removed from the register of protected buildings in 1933, and Kaganovich, the Party First Secretary in Moscow, is said to have advocated its demolition. The great Soviet conservationist Pyotr Baranovsky threatened to commit suicide if St. Basil's was destroyed, and the story has it that he chained himself to the main door of the cathedral and said that the demolition gang would have to blow him up as well. He repeated his criticisms of the "idiotic and criminal" scheme to destroy the cathedral in a telegram to Stalin and was arrested and sent to the labour camps of the Soviet Gulag for his pains. In 1935, at a meeting to consider the General Plan for the reconstruction of the city, one city planner reportedly jogged Stalin's elbow when the leader picked up the model of St. Basil's to see how the square would look without it.

The cathedral has nonetheless survived to this day, although recent signs of cracks in the brickwork and evidence that St. Basil's is steadily sinking have prompted the government to undertake structural work to underpin its foundations. These had been damaged in part by the use of the Red Square for military parades in the Soviet period, when columns of tanks and missile launchers trundled across the square and, more recently, by rock concerts. Recent plans for a new hotel complex with a massive underground car-park on Red Square are unlikely to help matters and may undermine the foundations still further.

The statue standing in front of St. Basil's is of Kuzma Minin and Dmitry Pozharsky, the butcher from Nizhny Novgorod and the Muscovite prince who were responsible for ending the twenty-three month Polish-Lithuanian military occupation of Moscow and driving the Poles out of Russia in 1612. The statue was commissioned in advance to mark the two hundredth anniversary of the event; little did the commissioners know, however, that the anniversary year would itself be marked by a second patriotic war and a further occupation of the city, this time by the French. It was finally erected in 1818; the inscription on the base reads: "To Citizen Minin and Prince Pozharsky from a Grateful RUSSIA 1818." It was the city's first statue in honour of specific historical figures and was designed by Ivan Martos who had studied in Rome. The standing figure of Minin is dressed in a traditional Russian smock, reminiscent of a Greek tunic and thereby in keeping with the classical design. The statue was cast in St. Petersburg, where Martos worked at the Academy of Fine Arts. The carvings around the plinth show the people of Nizhny Novgorod collecting money to finance the resistance movement.

The Lobnoe Mesto in front of St. Basil's is a stone structure that was used both for executions and for public pronouncements. Some see the name as deriving from Golgotha, the Place of the Skull (the word *lob* in Russians meaning forehead), while others argue that the origins of the name derive from the Latin word for a high or raised place. The present structure was designed by Matvei Kazakov in the 1780s. It was on this spot that Stenka Razin and later the *streltsy* were executed. More recently, in August 1968, a group of seven Soviet dissidents chose the Lobnoe Mesto as the site for their protest against the Soviet decision to crush the Prague Spring. Knowing that such protests were illegal, they gathered together quietly and then pulled out towels and pieces of cloth from under their clothing and raised them above their heads so that onlookers could see the slogans daubed on them: "Hands off Czechoslovakia!" The group was quickly bundled away by the KGB and put on trial.

The Lenin Mausoleum

A central feature of the western side of the square is the red and black stone Lenin Mausoleum in front of the Kremlin wall. Lenin died in January 1924 in the estate south of Moscow known today as Gorki

Leninskie, and his corpse was returned to Moscow by train (the funeral train can still be seen near Paveletskaya station south of the river). His body then lay in state in the Columned Hall of the former Nobles' Club, while half a million people queued in sub-zero temperatures in order to get the opportunity to file past and pay their respects to the leader of the Revolution. Alexander Pasternak described his night spent waiting in line:

> *Crowds began to collect in long queues stretching across Okhotny Ryad and here, as on Red Square, pyres burned to warm the soldiers and cavalrymen controlling the crowds, which were in any case quiet and orderly... Stoically, the crowds froze, stamping numbed feet and beating their arms. Like everyone else that night, I was dressed for the Arctic. I only reached the Hall at dawn.*

After the funeral on 27 January the body was placed in a temporary crypt to give others the chance to visit it, and a debate began between his former comrades as to whether or not it should be preserved. His widow, Nadezhda Krupskaya, opposed the idea, as did Trotsky, who felt that the plan was simply an attempt to pander to the religious sensibilities of the peasantry, replacing the relics of the saints with those of Lenin. In the end the embalmers had their way as the body was clearly beginning to rot in its temporary mausoleum by the Kremlin wall. Brown and green patches were appearing on the skin, the ears, nose and fingers were deteriorating, and the eyes were sinking into their sockets. A refrigerator was imported and work began on embalming the corpse and designing a more permanent structure in which it could be housed. Lenin's heart and brain had already been removed during the autopsy, and a special Institute for the Study of Lenin's Brain was set up to try and find the source of his genius.

Interest in methods of embalming had been sparked at this time by the discovery of Tutankhamen's tomb in the Valley of the Kings, and there were some Soviet scientists and politicians who cherished the hope that there would come a time when dead bodies could be brought back to life. The mausoleum itself was designed by Aleksei Shchusev, initially in wood but later in red and black stone on a pyramidal design somewhat reminiscent of Aztec tombs in Mexico. The mausoleum with its holy relic became a place of pilgrimage for the remainder of the

Soviet period, in a curious imitation of the religious practices that the atheistic Bolsheviks so vehemently rejected. Visitors queued up to descend into the darkened crypt and view the body, lying in its dark suit and looking for all the world like a waxwork. The changing of the guard outside the mausoleum became a popular sight with visitors, and ceremonial events were held here, with wreath laying on important holidays. A stand was constructed on top of the mausoleum from which the Communist Party leadership could watch parades; a room behind the stand was equipped with a bar for anyone who felt the need for a quick shot of vodka. Western "Kremlinologists" in the Cold War period developed the habit of analyzing who was standing where during these line-ups as a way of gaining some insight into shifting alliances and power struggles in the Politburo.

In July 1941, shortly after the German invasion of Russia, orders were given for Lenin's body to be evacuated. A small team of scientists responsible for maintaining the body were sent with the specially constructed traveling coffin on a special train to Tyumen in western Siberia, where it stayed until March 1945 when, with the Red Army marching on Berlin, it was felt safe to bring Lenin back to Moscow. Three biochemists were sent to Berlin shortly after the ending of hostilities to requisition chemicals and equipment for use in the mausoleum. In the post-war period, the scientists from the mausoleum laboratory branched out into preserving the corpses of other communist leaders: Klement Gottwald, Ho Chi Minh and Kim Il Sung were all embalmed by Russian scientists.

Debates were rekindled after the fall of Communism as to what should be done with Lenin's body. The goose-stepping ceremonial guards were assigned to other duties and visiting hours were sharply reduced; some people talked of pulling the mausoleum down altogether. In 1998 when the last Tsar, Nicholas II, was reburied in St. Petersburg, further calls were made for Lenin's interment and the liberal politician Boris Nemtsov confessed that he had "a mystical kind of feeling that as long as we don't bury Lenin, Russia is under an evil spell." Others argued that Lenin himself had expressed the desire to be buried next to his mother and his sisters in St. Petersburg and that his wishes should be respected. In 1999 Yeltsin's chief of staff gave a press interview in which he said that Lenin would "definitely" be removed, but refused to be specific as to when this might take place. Moves to rebury the body have always met with stringent resistance from the still-powerful Communist lobby; demonstrations have been held at the mausoleum demanding that Lenin be left alone, and the Communist politician Gennady Seleznev pointed out that "there is a mass of people for whom the name of Lenin is a religion." At the time of writing, Lenin's body remains *in situ* at the symbolic heart of the Russian state.

The Kremlin wall adjoining Red Square had been a burial ground for Soviet heroes and officials since 1917 when the bodies of the 238 "Martyrs of the October Revolution" who died in the fighting for Moscow were buried in two mass graves by the Nikolskie gate to the Kremlin. Others who are buried here include all of the General Secretaries of the Communist Party with the exception of Nikita Khrushchev (who lies in Novodevichy cemetery); the astronaut Yury Gagarin; the writer Maxim Gorky; Lenin's wife Nadezhda Krupskaya and his mistress Inessa Armand; Marshal Zhukov, the hero of the Second World War; and most of Stalin's henchmen. When Stalin died in 1953 his body was originally placed beside Lenin's in the mausoleum, but after the denunciation of his crimes by Khrushchev he was removed in 1961 and re-interred a few yards away in the Kremlin wall. A handful of westerners are buried here too: John Reed; "Big Bill" Haywood and Charles E. Ruthenberg, two American communists (half of Ruthenberg's ashes are buried here, the other half in Chicago); and Arthur MacManus, one of the founders of the British Communist Party.

The red brick towers of the Historical Museum occupy the northeastern end of the square on the site where Moscow University had its first home in 1755: a plaque on one corner of the building commemorates this date. The museum itself is from the early 1880s and was built to house exhibits collected for the 1872 Polytechnical Exhibition organized by Moscow University. Pavilions had been erected in and around the Kremlin for the occasion and after the exhibition closed, sites were designated in the city centre for permanent collections to be housed. The Polytechnical Museum on Novaya ploshchad also dates from this era. The architect of the Historical Museum was a man of English descent; Vladimir Shervud, or Sherwood, sought to emulate the Russian style popular at that time, with an attempt to replicate in brick the older traditions of wooden architecture. The design with its red brick and tall towers was intended to fit in with the nearby Kremlin and Kitai gorod walls.

The Kazan Cathedral

The Kazan Cathedral is yet another religious building that was originally built to commemorate a military success, this time the victory over the Poles of 1612. Prince Pozharsky founded the church in gratitude for what he believed had been the aid given to him in battle by the icon of the Blessed Virgin of Kazan, which he had carried with him. The cathedral itself has had a chequered history. Built in wood in 1632, it burned down and was replaced by a stone structure in 1636 notable for its multiple rows of decorative arched gables on the exterior. These gables, very common in early Russian church architecture, are known are *kokoshniki*—a word that also means a traditional peasant woman's headdress, which the gables are thought to resemble. The Archpriest Avvakum, leader of the Old Believers at the time of the great church schism in 1666-7, was arrested here for his opposition to Nikon's church reforms; in the late eighteenth century the cathedral became a meeting place for the mutinous *streltsy*. In 1812 General Kutuzov came to pray here before riding off to do battle with the French at Borodino.

Parts of the cathedral had been rebuilt over the years, so much so that by the early twentieth century little of the original building remained. In the mid-1920s, Pyotr Baranovsky was given permission to undertake restoration work in order to return the building to its original state. Walter Benjamin, described its interior in 1929:

> *first you enter into a spacious anteroom with a few scattered pictures of saints… It is gloomy; its half-light lends itself to conspiracies. In rooms like this, one can hatch the shadiest deals, even pogroms, should the occasion arise. Adjoining this room is the actual place of worship. It has a few small stairs in the background that lead up to the narrow, low platform on which one advances past the pictures of saints. Altar upon altar follows in close succession… The lateral walls are taken up by very large pictures of saints. Those portions of the walls that are not hidden by pictures are covered in luminous gold. A crystal chandelier hangs from the cloying, painted ceiling.*

As the moderate 1920s gave way to the militant "cultural revolution" of the late 1920s-early 1930s the Kazan Cathedral came under attack. Closed down in 1930, it became a workers' cafeteria, and proposals were put forward to turn the building into a cinema. Baranovsky was arrested in 1933 and sent to a labour camp in Siberia; the cathedral was demolished in 1936 shortly after his release. Stalin's government gave an indication of exactly what it thought of religious buildings when it turned the space into a public urinal. Reconstructed in the post-communist era by Oleg Zhurin, a young associate of Baranovsky, the new replica cathedral was consecrated in 1993.

GUM and the Hotel Rossiya

When the rows of trading stalls were cleared away from Red Square in the aftermath of the 1812 fire, commerce on the square did not cease but simply moved into a more permanent home. The present-day GUM shopping complex was completed in 1893 by Alexander Pomerantsev on the site of an earlier trading centre built by Osip Bove. Known as the Upper Trading Rows, the complex was built in the Russian style of that era, its ornate exterior copied from medieval church architecture combined with the very latest in technical innovations in lighting, heating and ventilation. Skylights in the ceiling helped provide illumination, and reinforced concrete was used in the construction of the internal walkways. Inside, the Trading Rows, then as now, offered a mass of small shops along three parallel passages. An American visitor in the 1890s described the merchants who worked here:

> ...with their ample beards spreading over their bosoms, clad in long, dark-coloured coats or caftans, tall boots and cap with visor, they sit gravely in their shops playing draughts or drinking tea while their clerks walk up and down in front praying passers by with obsequious bows... to enter and buy... The abacus and glass of tea are indispensable accessories of Russian commerce.

During the Soviet period, the Upper Trading Rows became known as GUM, standing for the State General Store, and were converted into an exclusive department store for the use of the Soviet elite and privileged foreigners. The American writer Martha Gellhorn, who paid it a visit in 1972, said it was "a hybrid born of Macy's basement and an oriental bazaar, and you'd have to be Russian not to see it as a big black joke... I.... spent one boiling hour on a single purchase." Since the demise of communism, GUM has been largely taken over by a series of expensive boutiques and designer clothes stores. Early in 2004 a luxury goods company bought a fifty per cent stake in the building and announced plans to open a huge supermarket with the aim of eventually turning GUM into a Russian version of London's Harrods.

Another site of imminent changes bordering Red Square is the Hotel Rossiya, a twelve-storey grey concrete monstrosity that, at the time of writing, looks out over the river, offering spectacular views of the Kremlin. The hotel was completed in the 1960s, and with nearly 3,000 rooms it boasted of being the largest hotel in Europe and included a concert hall and cinema as added attractions. Mainly known as a haven for bedbugs, cockroaches and prostitutes, as well as for the serious fire that killed more than forty people in 1977, it attracted the ire of Mayor Luzhkov, who ordered its demolition in the summer of 2004. Plans have been announced to fill the site with a new hotel and shopping complex. One professor from the Moscow Architectural Institute was bold enough to complain, saying "I'm concerned about the idea of demolition according to taste—that is, if you don't like it, raze it. History does not have taste: it leaves its marks." Nonetheless, the Hotel Rossiya is earmarked for demolition. While its architecture is unlikely to be widely missed, the destruction of one of the few remaining affordable hotels in the city centre is more regrettable.

Ulitsa Varvarka and the Plague Riots, 1771

Ulitsa Varvarka, in Soviet times called ulitsa Razina after Stenka Razin, the executed seventeenth-century peasant rebel, leads out of Red Square from behind St. Basil's, past a series of small churches and down to Kitai gorod metro station. The intersection where the road comes out to join Staraya ploshchad (Old Square) and the metro was once the site of the Varvarskie gates in the Kitai gorod wall. This was where the great plague riot of 1771 is said to have begun. The plague that struck Moscow during that year may have killed as many as twenty per cent of the city's population, and reports in the British press in October of that year revealed that "The Accounts we receive from Moscow are very melancholy... Great Numbers die daily of a malignant Fever which prevails there." At its height, somewhere between four and five hundred people were dying of plague each day. Even the governor of Moscow abandoned the city.

Charles de Mertens was a doctor from Brussels who came to Moscow in 1767 to work at the Imperial Foundling Home. He left a substantial *Account of the Plague which Raged at Moscow, 1771*, detailing some of the events that he witnessed. He remarked on how easily the infection spread throughout the city: "The common people live crowded together in small wooden houses... it is easy to conceive how favourable these low and crowded habitations must have been to the harbouring and spreading of contagion." The textiles trade that dominated the business world in Moscow at this time did nothing to help matters: rats and fleas could hide in the bales of wool and silk brought into the city from the south, and the warehouses were usually located near to rivers, giving easy access to the rats. The rivers of Moscow were generally in a disgusting state: one description of the Neglinnaya at around this time told of how:

> both it and the ponds along it not only are of no use to the city, but are a real menace to human health from the consumption of that water, for during a greater part of the year there is an unbearable stench from it, so that inhabitants living close to it are in danger from the corruption of the air.

The first signs of the plague hit the city in the later part of 1770 but the number of cases soon abated as the winter set in. With the coming of warmer weather, the epidemic flared up again the following year. Attempts by the authorities to curb the spread of the disease by quarantining the infected and restricting traditional practices such as having relatives wash and kiss the bodies of the deceased caused outrage among ordinary townspeople, who in any case felt deep suspicions about the number of foreign doctors who were employed to try to stem spread of contagion.

The plague riots began in September when a great crowd gathered at the Varvarskie gates to seek protection from infection from the supposedly miracle-working icon of the Virgin Mary that hung there. The authorities were understandably concerned at this development as crowds provided an excellent opportunity for the disease to spread. Stories differ as to exactly what happened: one account has it that the icon had been taken down to pass around the crowd and Archbishop Amvrosy stepped in to remove the image from above the gates; another contemporary version states that a group of imposters were trying to collect money from the crowd for permission to worship there or in order to pay for a silver casing for the icon. Whatever the exact facts, it is clear that the Archbishop was involved in trying to disperse the crowd for their own safety when they suddenly turned the full force of their anger and fear against him. A foreign newspaper report described what happened next:

> *The blinded Multitude... immediately gathered themselves together, and plundered the Archbishop's House; but not finding him there, they went to the Convent, where this worthy Archbishop was killed by them in the most cruel and barbarous Manner. As soon as the Government of Moscow heard that the People were in an Uproar, they sent Troops against them; by whose Hands many of these Wretches fell victims to their own Credulity and blind Bigotry.*

The Convent mentioned in this report was the Donskoi Monastery in the south of the city: Amvrosy tried to seek sanctuary there but was dragged out from behind the iconostasis and beaten to death by the mob. In the words of a witness, "they pierced the eyes, cut up the face, pulled out the beard, stabbed the chest, broke the bones" of the unfortunate cleric.

De Mertens relates what happened next: the mob broke into the hospitals and began conducting religious ceremonies at the bed-sides of the sick as well as digging up the dead bodies of victims for reburial. They argued that as it was pre-ordained who would die, then attempts by doctors to interfere were an insult to God and:

> *in their paroxysm of phrensy, the populace attempted to wreak their vengeance upon those who had laboured for their preservation. After they had sacrificed one victim to their blind rage, they fought for the physicians and surgeons. Some of the lowest rabble broke into my house, and destroyed every thing they could lay hold to.*

It was only with great efforts that de Mertens was able to keep the Foundling Home under a strict quarantine, and the plague never reached it. The authorities were able to quell the disturbances by sending in the army, but the riots helped to spread the contagion still further and the death rate rose in the aftermath of these events. Houses were burnt down or disinfected and serfs who volunteered to work in the hospitals were promised their freedom. As autumn turned into winter, the epidemic slowed. It is said that Catherine the Great herself ordered that the bell in the Alarm Tower of the Kremlin should be silenced after the ringleaders of the mob had used it to summon crowds together during the plague riots.

Zhukov's Statue

In front of the Historical Museum stands a recent equestrian statue of the hero of the Great Patriotic War (as the Second World War is commonly known in Russia), Marshal Georgy Zhukov. Zhukov was responsible for masterminding the defence of Moscow in autumn 1941 when the Germans advanced on the city; visitors arriving at Sheremetyevo airport who are interested to see how far the Germans penetrated should look out for the anti-tank defences left as a memorial by the side of the road at Khimki as they drive into the city centre. Transferred from Leningrad where the nine hundred day siege was already underway, Zhukov was telephoned by Stalin. He recalled the conversation in his memoirs:

> Stalin phoned me and asked: "Are you sure we'll be able to hold Moscow? It hurts me to ask you this. Answer me truthfully, as a Communist."
> "We'll definitely hold Moscow. But we'll need at least two more armies and another two hundred tanks."
> "It's good that you are so confident…"

Zhukov set to work organizing the necessary defences and in the end he did indeed succeed in holding Moscow and driving the Germans back from the city. Stalin's faith in Zhukov's skills as a military strategist meant that he eventually stopped interfering in military decisions and allowed his generals to direct the Russian defence effort at Stalingrad and beyond.

Since 1991 Zhukov has been appropriated by the post-Soviet authorities as a suitable war hero; his treatment by Stalin after the war when he was demoted and sent to work in the Ukrainian backwater of Odessa probably aided his reputation in the long term. The fact that he was one of the few people who was able to disagree openly with the dictator and get away with it similarly has done his image in post-Soviet Russia nothing but good. In 1994 an Order of Zhukov was introduced in the Russian army, putting the Soviet general alongside his pre-revolutionary forbears who also have medals named after them: Generals Suvorov and Kutuzov, who fought Napoleon's army in the earlier Patriotic War of 1812. It is said that Yeltsin originally planned to position the statue on Red Square but was dissuaded from the idea.

The sculptor, Vyacheslav Klykov, is also known as the man who has long campaigned to have a statue of the last Tsar of Russia put up in central Moscow. This campaign has thus far proved unsuccessful and the two statues that he has erected to Nicholas II in provincial towns have both fallen victim to political vandalism. Another example of Klykov's work in central Moscow is the statue of St. Cyril and St. Methodius, founders of the Cyrillic alphabet, which is to be seen on Slavyanskaya ploshchad near Kitai gorod metro station.

The Alexander Gardens

To the west of the Kremlin wall lie the Alexander Gardens (*Aleksandrovsky sad*), laid out in the 1820s in the time of Alexander I. They were planted over the site of the Neglinnaya river after it had been confined to an underground pipe. Here, in the shadow of the Kremlin wall, is the Tomb of the Unknown Soldier, lying directly on your left as you enter from Manezhnaya ploshchad. It was erected more than twenty years after the victory in the Great Patriotic War at a time when the Brezhnev regime was seeking to reinforce its legitimacy by invoking past Soviet triumphs. A ceremonial guard was stationed at the memorial during the 1990s, perhaps to give the soldiers who had been decommissioned from the task of honouring Lenin's tomb something to do. Sentry-boxes on each side of the flame itself are manned by guards in long black leather boots with helmets tilting forward over their eyes. The inscription on the tomb reads "Thy name is unknown. Thy victory is immortal," and a series of further red slabs to the left of the tomb commemorate the twelve "hero cities" of the Second World War, cities where major battles or sieges took place (Moscow, Leningrad, Odessa, Kiev, Minsk, Stalingrad, Sevastopol, Novorossiysk,

Kerch, Tula, Smolensk and Murmansk). Each slab bears the city's name and a five-pointed star.

The eternal flame itself was carried to Moscow from Leningrad, from the memorial erected on the Field of Mars in 1957 to those killed in the October Revolution. In a speech given to mark the unveiling of the new memorial, the first secretary of the Moscow Party proclaimed that:

This fire... transfers across an entire half-century the undimmed flame of October, illuminating the stages of the great path taken by the Soviet people under the leadership of the Leninist party... It is as if the soldiers of the revolution and the soldiers of the Great Patriotic War have closed ranks into one immortal rank, illuminated by the Eternal flame of glory, lit by the living in honour of the fallen, who will always live.

By tradition, newly married couples come here to lay flowers on their wedding day in an act of symbolic deference to their grandparents' generation, twenty-seven million of whom lost their lives in the defence of their motherland in 1941-5.

The gardens themselves are a pleasant place to walk: a peaceful spot with trees, benches, municipal bedding plants and refreshment stands selling hotdogs, ice-cream and beer. Half way down the garden stands the Obelisk to Revolutionary Thinkers, a monument with the names of such international revolutionary luminaries as Marx, Engels, Liebknecht, Luxemburg , Campanella, More, Proudhon and Fourier, as well as a handful of Russians: Chernyshevsky, Lavrov, Bakunin and others. Originally, the obelisk was erected in honour of the Romanov family: it was put up in 1913 to mark their tricentennial year as rulers of Russia. After the Revolution, Lenin himself proposed that rather than demolishing the monument altogether, the regime should simply erase the original inscription and replace it with more politically-correct sentiments. An inscription at the base of the monument exhorts the workers of the world to unite.

Manezh Square

The current Mayor of Moscow, Yury Luzhkov, is a larger than life figure whose popularity among Muscovites is demonstrated by the huge majorities he has won in the mayoral elections. Having become mayor in 1992 after the resignation of the incumbent he went on to win nearly ninety per cent of the popular vote in 1996 and just under seventy five per cent in 2003. Luzhkov is a master of the photo-opportunity, he makes frequent walk-abouts wearing his trademark cap, and he likes to present himself as a man of action, someone who gets things done. On the 850th anniversary of the founding of the city, in August 1997, he even issued orders for the clouds to be dispersed in order that rain should not spoil his planned celebrations (the attempt was only partially successful).

Luzhkov formed his own political movement—*Otechestvo* or Fatherland—to run in the 1999 Duma elections, trading on his distinctive brand of populist Russian nationalism. He was talked of as a plausible presidential candidate for 2000, but in the event, after Yeltsin's anointment of Vladimir Putin, Luzhkov chose to stay out of the race and offered his endorsement to the front-runner. It is Luzhkov who has been responsible for many of the changes in Moscow over the last decade: the rebuilding projects, new statues, changing of street names and the often controversial decisions to tear down old buildings. Although he has claimed that all he is seeking to achieve is "a slow return to the natural order of things", his changes, taken as a whole, have transformed the appearance of the city in ways that have not always found favour with the general public.

Luzhkov has been much criticized for his patronage of the Georgian sculptor Zurab Tsereteli, whose works adorn many public spaces in the city. Tsereteli is responsible for the design of the Manezh development, the statue of Peter the Great that stands near the new Tretyakov Gallery on the southern embankment of the Moskva river, the war memorial in the Victory Park off Kutuzovsky Prospekt and many other statues throughout the city, including one of Luzhkov himself which can be seen in the courtyard of the house on Petrovka where Tsereteli's own Museum of Modern Art is housed. One of the more notorious Tsereteli monuments is the horrible statue of Peter the Great steering a sailing ship situated just across the river from the Cathedral of Christ the Saviour. It was erected to commemorate the 300th anniversary of the founding of the Russian fleet in 1996, although the decision to site it in Moscow, a city that Peter disliked so much that he built himself a new capital several hundred miles away, was seen by many as curious. Rumours abound that the statue had originally been commissioned by a US patron to serve as a monument to Christopher Columbus but that when it was rejected, Tsereteli used his "court connections" to have the recycled statue erected in Moscow instead.

The area that is now Manezhnaya ploshchad was for a long time filled with small houses and shops which were cleared in the general redesign of the city centre in the 1930s. Left as a vast empty space for many years, it was only in the 1990s that the area was transformed with the creation of an underground shopping complex that is said to be the largest in Europe. The original design proposed an even more extensive development, going deeper underground, but the plans were changed to avoid complications with the metro system. The excavation work necessitated by this project unearthed some interesting archaeological discoveries: part of the white sixteenth-century stone bridge that used to lead over the Neglinnaya river into Red Square was uncovered in the work. A small museum of archaeology was set up on the square near to the shopping complex to provide a home for these finds.

Tsereteli was responsible for the decorative features on the arcade; white balustrades surround the artificial canal and Disney-style animal statues depicting stories from Russian folk tales sit in pools, attracting crowds of children and their parents on hot summer days. A complex of fountains finishes off the whole ensemble. On top of the shopping centre itself, a series of benches and street lamps surround the glass domes which provide light to the complex below. One of these is decorated with a map of the world with Moscow at its centre; on top of the map stands a mounted statue of St George, the patron saint of Moscow, killing the dragon. (St George doubles as the patron of the Russian army, and the Cross of St George is the highest military medal a Russian soldier can be awarded.)

The shopping complex itself, with its shiny marble colonnades and opulent designer shops selling fur coats, handbags and cosmetics, has not been particularly popular with Muscovites. Some have criticized its rather brash and tasteless design, others have taken an ideological stance against the encroachment of capitalist values into the heart of the former Soviet capital. In August 1999 a group calling itself Revolutionary Writers claimed responsibility for planting a bomb in the amusement arcade on the bottom floor of the Manezh shopping centre that injured around forty people. A note found at the scene belligerently declared: "Philistines, we don't like your way of life... A hamburger half eaten by a dead consumer is a revolutionary hamburger!"

The Manège

Shortly after the close of polling in March 2004 on the day that Vladimir Putin won his second term in office, a massive fire broke out in the Manège, an early nineteenth-century hall in the classical style that stands opposite the Alexander Gardens. The two events did not appear to be connected, and the fire, which caused the deaths of two firemen, was blamed on an electrical fault. The hall had originally been erected in the reign of Alexander I not long after the ending of the Napoleonic war: the Tsar had asked for a riding school to be erected that would be big enough to allow elaborate cavalry exercises to take place under one roof. The building was officially opened in 1817 but the exterior was finally completed only in 1825. It was used primarily by the military but it also served civilian purposes: the French composer Hector Berlioz gave a concert here during his visit in 1868. In his memoirs he described how:

> as they could not find a hall large enough for the first concert they had the idea of giving it in the Manège Hall, a hall as large as the central hall in our Palais de l'Industrie at the Champs-Elysées. I thought the idea crazy, but it was incredibly successful.

After the Revolution, the Manège became a car park for the Soviet government and after Stalin's death it was converted into an exhibition space and became known as the Central Exhibition Hall. It was here that Nikita Khrushchev made his notorious attack on abstract painting during an exhibition held in the hall in December 1962. Having described the modern works as "dog shit", he became embroiled in an argument with the artist Ernst Neizvestny who informed the premier that he knew nothing about art and that his comments were ridiculous. Ironically, Neizvestny would later be asked by the Khrushchev family to design his tombstone in Novodevichy cemetery: in the striking design, Khrushchev's head appears between two interlocking pieces of black granite and white marble. In Neizvestny's assessment of Khrushchev:

He began to lead out country out of the darkness and he exposed Stalin's crimes. The dawn broke for all of us, heralding the imminent rise of the sun. The light began to dispel the darkness. This is reflected in the tombstone... It is no accident that the head is on a white pedestal, or that the background remains dark...

Controversial plans to redevelop the Manège building, replacing its historic wooden roof beams and adding underground car parking and a restaurant, had already been drawn up when the building was gutted by fire in 2004. The Ministry of Culture had previously tried to block moves to excavate the foundations of the Manège in order to create parking space, arguing that it would ruin the site, but after the fire it seems inevitable that the car park lobby will have its way. The roof, which had been in need of restoration for years, is likely to be rebuilt using modern materials. The excavation of the site in summer 2004 uncovered a number of archaeological finds including tools, weapons, coins and the remains of a pre-Mongol era cemetery.

Walking back from the Alexander Gardens towards ploshchad Revoliutsii (Revolution Square), after the Historical Museum one passes another red brick building, this time of the old City Duma and former Lenin Museum. Constructed in the 1890s by the architect Dmitry Chichagov, it was used by the municipal Duma or parliament as Moscow's town hall. (The word *duma*, incidentally, is derived from the Russian verb "to think", contrasting with the English word parliament deriving from the French for "to say".) Demonstrations took place outside this building during the February Revolution of 1917 as members of the Duma took over responsibility for running city affairs. In 1936 the building was given over to the Central Lenin Museum, housing reconstructions of rooms where Lenin lived or worked, photographs, documents and curious gifts donated by foreign admirers including portraits of the great leader painstakingly constructed from sunflower seeds. This museum was closed down in the 1990s and Yeltsin offered to return it to the Moscow City Duma. They declined the offer and the building is now earmarked to become an annex of the Historical Museum.

Hotel Moscow

The Manezh shopping mall is only one of many redevelopments in and around this area. On a vast site bordering Manezhnaya ploshchad and in front of the entrance to Red Square, taking up an entire block, the Hotel Moskva is, at the time of writing, in the process of being demolished and rebuilt. The original hotel was built during the 1930s by a group of architects including the prolific Shchusev. The site had been cleared as part of the reshaping of the city centre with the demolition of part of the Grand Moscow Hotel and other smaller buildings in the area: if the 1935 Master Plan for the redevelopment of the city had been fully realized, the hotel would have stood facing the Palace of Soviets with its enormous Lenin statue (planned to take shape on the site of the Cathedral of Christ the Saviour).

The first design for the hotel was for a purely constructivist building with clean lines and geometric shapes; the final asymmetrical grey hulk is attributed to Stalin's personal interference with the architects' plans. One story has it that, on being presented with two alternative designs for the building, Stalin ticked both of them and the architects, too scared to ask him what he meant by this, sought to incorporate both designs into the finished building; it may be that Stalin did not understand that he was being asked to choose between them and merely ticked to indicate that he had looked at them both. An alternative story explains that Stalin added his own squiggles to the designs which were then interpreted to mean that he wanted the blocks on either side of the entrance to be different, with arched windows on one side but not the other. One Russian visitor who saw the finished construction said that it evoked a "fairy tale palace"; anything less like a fairy tale palace would be quite hard to imagine: it has always put me more in mind of a multi-storey car park. Current plans envisage the rebuilding of the hotel to the original design, but this time with underground parking facilities; no doubt the cost of a room will soar when the redevelopment is complete. During the demolition workers came across a stash of explosives dating from the period of the Second World War when key landmarks in Moscow were mined as a precautionary measure in case the Germans should take the city.

Mayor Luzhkov's approach to redeveloping the centre of Moscow has been much in evidence in this chapter, and has been highly controversial among residents and conservationists. Alexei Komech, director of the Art Research Institute, has been a vocal critic of

Luzhkov's programmes, in particular his fondness for tearing down buildings only to replace them with replicas. In his view,

> *Moscow is being deliberately destroyed. In the 1920s and 1930s this was happening for ideological reasons: there was no place for old building in the new Soviet utopia. Today it is happening for purely commercial reasons. The Bolsheviks hated old Moscow. The current Moscow government does not hate it, it simply does not recognize it... Luzhkov simply does not see the difference between a copy and the original.*

Luzhkov has countered this view by arguing that "sometimes recreation is the most effective way of preserving the past. We have some idiots for whom the preservation of old bricks is an end in itself. Where possible, old stones should be preserved, but I say bricks are simply molecules from which you can create any image." There is an extraordinary lack, on his part, of any real concept of authenticity: one might perhaps draw parallels with the Russian fondness for plastic over real flowers in graveside offerings. Some critics suspect that part of the reason for destroying and rebuilding old buildings is so that ownership can be quietly transferred from the state to a private company.

More than three hundred supposedly protected buildings are said to have been destroyed since Luzhkov came into office in 1992; many more have been demolished leaving only the façade intact. As one architect put it: "Just as Stalin and Brezhnev destroyed Moscow in their day, Luzhkov is doing the same now. If he could, he'd put underground parking under St. Basil's Cathedral." To give Komech the last word: "The tragedy of Moscow is not that separate listed buildings have been knocked down, but that the cityscape has been altered. We shall soon have a metropolis with some monuments, but the historic city will be gone forever."

Chapter Three
CITY OF UPHEAVAL

From the terrace at the front of Moscow University up in the Sparrow Hills a spectacular panoramic view spreads out before you. Anton Chekhov was one of many who enjoyed the view from here; he declared that in order to understand Russia one would have to come and see Moscow from this spot. During the Soviet period, this south-western district of the city was renamed the Lenin Hills but it has now returned to its original name. Most of the faculties of Moscow University moved up here after the Second World War; the nearest metro station is Universitet on the red line. Two earlier visitors were the young radicals Alexander Herzen and his childhood friend Nikolai (Nick) Ogarev who, fired up by the tragic example of the Decembrist rebels who had made an unsuccessful stand against the autocracy in 1825, came here to swear their famous oath that they would dedicate their lives to the struggle against social injustice. In his autobiography, *My Past and Thoughts*, Herzen described the scene:

> *Flushed and breathless, we stood there mopping our faces. The sun was setting, the cupolas glittered, beneath the hill the city extended farther than the eye could reach; a fresh breeze blew on our faces, we stood leaning against each other and suddenly embracing, vowed in sight of all Moscow to sacrifice our lives to the struggle we had chosen.*

Radical Circles

Moscow became a centre of radical thought in the 1830s and 1840s during the reactionary reign of Tsar Nicholas I. Intellectual activity focused around the discussion circles which met, usually on a weekly basis, in the private home of one of their members. These circles provided a space in which young radicals could meet together, form friendships and express their feelings about the autocracy in relative freedom. Two of the most important of the Moscow discussion circles were the group organized by Herzen and Ogarev and a rival set-up which met at the house of Nikolai Stankevich. Herzen was one of the most famous Moscow radicals of this era, and often regarded as one of the fathers of Russian socialism. Born in Moscow in the inauspicious year of 1812 as the illegitimate son of a wealthy aristocrat, he was given the name Herzen, meaning "heart" in German, as a sly reference to the circumstances of his conception. The house where he was born stands on 25 Tverskoi Boulevard and is now a literary institute; in the early Soviet period the writers Osip Mandelstam and Boris Pasternak had apartments in the building. A statue of Herzen stands in the courtyard.

Herzen and Ogarev studied together at Moscow University, at that time based in its old buildings in the city centre, and Herzen had his first brush with authority when he was involved in leading a riot against the unpopular Professor Malov, who was chased from his lecture theatre by angry students throwing their galoshes at him. The writer Mikhail Lermontov is said to have been involved in the same incident. Their time at university spanned the period 1830-31 when the institution had to be closed for a year because of the cholera epidemic. During their student years the two friends formed a circle of likeminded fellow students who met together to discuss the writings of European thinkers such as Saint-Simon and Schelling along with other recent progressive ideas.   Soviet-era statues of the pair of them, Herzen standing with his arms folded and a rather irritated expression on his face, now stand outside the classical Moscow University building on ulitsa Mokhovaya opposite the Kremlin. Their main meeting place was just around the corner on 23 Bolshaya Nikitskaya, which was Ogarev's home. Herzen reminisced of these meetings about how:

> *in his bright cheerful room with its red and gold wallpaper, amid the perpetual smell of tobacco and punch and other—I was going to say eatables and drinkables, but now I remember that there was seldom anything to eat but cheese—we often spent the time from dark till dawn in heated argument and sometimes in noisy merriment.*

In 1834 Herzen was arrested for writing politically subversive remarks in private letters discovered by the police. Held for a month in the police station on ulitsa Prechistenka, he was then transferred to the military prison at Krutitskoe podvore near the Simonov monastery and finally exiled to the provincial town of Vyatka. He did not return to Moscow until 1839, and after a period of wandering he settled in the city between 1842 and his emigration to Western Europe in 1847.

Herzen was to find that the intellectual world he had left behind had changed significantly in his absence. His own circle had broken up, as had Stankevich's group, which during the 1830s had included such radical figures as Vissarion Belinsky and Mikhail Bakunin. Nikolai Stankevich was a young aristocrat who brought together a group of disciples to read and discuss recent German thought, in particular the works of Hegel. Stankevich died of tuberculosis at the age of twenty-seven, after which the members of his group went their separate ways.

Belinsky was the son of a provincial doctor who had moved to Moscow in 1829 to attend university. Expelled for writing a play critical of serfdom, he took up a series of writing and teaching jobs while at the same time attending Stankevich's discussion group. Unlike most of the radical thinkers of the period, Belinsky's relatively humble origins meant that he did not have a private source of income and he spent much of his life working as a literary critic for the periodical press. For several years during the 1830s he lived on Rakhmanovsky pereulok, a small street that cuts between the Petrovka and Neglinnaya within the Boulevard Ring, in rooms above a blacksmith and next door to a laundry where there was an ever-present smell of wet linen and soap. Belinsky moved to St. Petersburg in 1839, but he remained in contact with Muscovite debates, carrying out a regular correspondence with Herzen during the early 1840s.

Mikhail Bakunin spent much of his life travelling around Europe fomenting revolution in different countries, but he, too, spent a short period living in Moscow during the later 1830s, during which time he attended Stankevich's circle and sponged off his friends. He left Moscow after Stankevich's death, travelling to Germany in order to study in Berlin—a move partly funded by the ever-generous Herzen.

Scandal hit radical circles in Moscow in 1836 when the writer and philosopher Pyotr Chaadaev was officially declared insane after writing in his First Philosophical Letter that Russia existed in a cultural vacuum, "outside of time, without a past or a future", having cut itself off from the main course of western European civilization:

Alone in the world, we have given nothing to the world, learned nothing from the world and bestowed not a single idea upon the fund of human ideas. We have not contributed in any way to the progress of the human spirit, and whatever has come to us from that progress we have disfigured.

The journal in which the letter was published, the *Moscow Telescope*, was closed down and Chaadaev was placed under house arrest for over a year. He died twenty years later, in 1856, and his grave can be found in the cemetery of the Donskoi monastery.

The other place in Moscow that anyone interested in the radical discussion groups of the period should visit is the house on 27 Sivtsev-Vrazhek pereulok, just off the Arbat, where Herzen settled when he returned to Moscow in the early 1840s. The house is now a Herzen Museum and was one of the places where the intellectual discussions of this period took place. The 1840s, the "Remarkable Decade", were the time when the great debates between westernizers and Slavophiles came to dominate intellectual life in both the Russian capitals. The Slavophiles reacted sharply against Chaadaev's line, arguing that he was wrong to think that Russia had no distinctive contribution to make to world civilization and that indigenous Russian culture was something to be celebrated; whereas westernizers tended to the opinion that Russia was a part of Europe and that it should follow a western line of development. Herzen himself, who is usually categorized within the westernizer camp, eventually developed a separate line of argument that said that Russia could teach the West a lesson, by developing a new and distinctively Russian form of socialism based around the traditions of the peasant commune. Herzen left Russia in 1847 and never returned: he spent much of the rest of his life in London, where he died in 1870.

1905: Krasnopresnenskaya

The Krasnopresnenskaya district to the north-west of the city centre is famed as the focal point of the events of the 1905 Revolution in Moscow. The metro stations around this area bear witness to this connection: Barrikadnaya evoking the barricades erected in the streets of this part of the city during the December uprising; Ulitsa 1905 goda or "1905 Street" and even Krasnopresnenskaya itself—the "Red" Presnya district with its industrial factories and strong socialist presence. Rochdelskaia ulitsa, which runs along the back of the White House, the main headquarters of the Russian government, was named—during the Soviet period—in honour of a group of workers from Rochdale in Lancashire who founded an early workers' cooperative in 1844. Before the twentieth century the area was simply called the Presnya district, named after the local river that has long since been diverted underground.

The 1905 revolution began in St. Petersburg after the events of "Bloody Sunday" in January, when a peaceful mass demonstration that came to present a petition to Tsar Nicholas II was fired on by tsarist troops outside the Winter Palace. Uprisings began across the empire with workers' strikes, army and navy mutinies and peasant unrest in the countryside. Middle class liberals joined forces with socialist organizations in pressing for change. By October of that year the Tsar had been forced to concede an elected parliament or Duma as well as many of the liberal demands for freedom of speech, conscience and assembly. These concessions were welcomed in Moscow by a large crowd of people who gathered outside the Bolshoi theatre to sing the *Marseillaise.*

In Moscow, the two most notable events of the revolutionary year were the Bauman funeral and the December uprising. Nikolai Bauman was a young revolutionary who was shot and then beaten to death by right-wing thugs during a demonstration that took place the day after the Tsar promulgated his October Manifesto. He became an early Bolshevik martyr and his funeral was a massive affair with an eight-hour procession of workers paying their respects to their fallen comrade. Alexander Pasternak witnessed the funeral as a child and described how

the silence of that moving mass was most menacing; it was so heavy you wanted to scream, till it was broken by voices singing the requiescat, or the valedictory hymn of that time, "You fell as victims in the fight…" Then silence fell once more.

The authorities claimed that 30,000 people had taken to the streets that day; unofficial estimates put the figure considerably higher. Photographs of his funeral can be seen in the Museum of Modern History (formerly the Museum of the Revolution) housed in the building of the old English Club on ulitsa Tverskaya. Bauman's grave is to be found in the Vagankovskoe cemetery in the Krasnopresnenskaya district. The street and the whole area to the north-east of the city centre where Bauman was killed were renamed in his honour after the Revolution, and a bust of him can be seen at Baumanskaya metro station on the dark blue line.

The atmosphere in Moscow as winter drew on became ever more tense. Strikes and pogroms flared up across the city, and workers joined unions and formed *soviets* or councils of workers' deputies. An English journalist, Henry Nevinson, who was visiting Moscow, recalled the fear that stalked the streets at this time as random attacks became increasingly common.

People walked warily, kept one eye behind them, turning sharply round if they heard even the padding sound of galoshes in the snow. Often at night, as I went up and down the ramparts of the Kremlin and watched those ancient white temples with their brazen domes glittering under the moon, I noticed that the few passers-by skirted round me in a kind of arc, and if they came upon me suddenly they ran. My intentions were far from murderous, but all were living in that haggard element of fear.

In December 1905 the Moscow branch of the Bolshevik party called a general strike and workers across the city downed tools and built barricades out of bed frames, gates, telegraph poles and street lamps—any materials that came to hand. Trade union membership soared. The authorities were distinctly alarmed; the Prime Minister Sergei Witte demanded reinforcement troops declaring that "if Moscow falls into the hands of the revolutionaries, it would be such a blow to the government of His Majesty that it could have incalculably harmful consequences." Armed clashes followed between workers' militia

organizations and tsarist troops and a local soviet was formed that took control of the Presnya district. A pitched battle followed as the Presnya was surrounded by troops who bombarded the revolutionaries into submission. A newspaper report from 18 December described how

> *in the battle hundreds have fallen and there are perhaps thousands*
> *of victims; in all streets, bodies are scattered about, the cemeteries*
> *and hospitals are overcrowded, and the end of the battle is still not*
> *in sight… Barricades increase as though by the wave of a wand.*

Boris Pasternak, who was fifteen at the time, wrote of how at the end of 1905, "the nights were frosty; the pitch-black city was lit by bonfires. Stray bullets whistled down the empty streets, and mounted patrols charged with soundless fury over the untrodden snow."

The little eighteenth-century Gorbaty bridge just to one side of the White House, which once spanned the Presnya river, bears a sign telling visitors of how "here, in December 1905, bitter fighting took place between the workers' militia of Presnya and the tsarist forces." A monument to the revolutionaries stands close by. Over a thousand people were estimated to have been killed in the fighting here, and the unrest provoked ferocious reprisals from the authorities. Hundreds of people were arrested on suspicion of participating in the uprising, and the events of December 1905 split the opposition to the Tsar as moderate liberals became more cautious in their approach.

War, Revolution and Civil War

The First World War is not commemorated in Russia. There is no memorial to the millions of men who died in the fighting at Tannenburg, the Masurian Lakes and other battlefields across Poland, Galicia and the Carpathians. Patriotic enthusiasm at the outbreak of war in 1914 swiftly turned to disillusionment as Russian defeats mounted. People took to the streets in the summer of 1915 as a wave of anti-German feeling swept the city. Mobs attacked anyone who was thought to be German; they broke into music shops and smashed up Bechstein pianos and mass demonstrations called for the "German woman", the Tsarina, to be sent to a nunnery. Boris Pasternak was working for a German merchant in Moscow at this time; the house where he was living was ransacked and many of his manuscripts were destroyed.

In Moscow, the population was increased by the influx of refugees from the western provinces of the empire as well as by the staff of factories that had been evacuated from the front line. New metal-working factories were built and older ones expanded to meet the demand for munitions and war materiel at the front line. An army garrison was established in the city, and wounded soldiers filled the hospitals. By 1917 the population reached a new height of two million people. Alexander Pasternak remembered living on ulitsa Volkhonka, near the Cathedral of Christ the Saviour, during the war.

The high expectations of the past dwindled; all one could hope for was to stop the cracks that had already appeared. With extraordinary speed our preconceptions of the necessities of life were abandoned. Values dropped and money (which itself became devalued) was desperately needed. Many of our possessions were sold for absurdly little...Denial after denial drove each Moscow family back to a primitive existence, huddled in the lair of a single, barely heated room within the inimical chill of the surrounding flat.

By early 1917 food shortages in Moscow were serious and workers were becoming restless. Even the tsarist secret police began to experience anxiety: in a report on the strike movement that was taking hold of the city in January-February 1917 it was feared that:

the state of extreme agitation of the working mass and in social circles, the aggravation of the bread shortage in Moscow and the activities of revolutionary circles could create, under a new onslaught of strikes and demonstrations, a much more serious threat to official order and to public security.

In the midst of this gathering crisis in Moscow, bread riots in the capital—now renamed Petrograd to make it sound less German—brought the toppling of the autocracy. Nicholas II abdicated on 2 March following days of unrest in the capital and the refusal of troops from the Petrograd garrison to fire on demonstrators. In Moscow, news of the turbulent events in Petrograd brought workers onto the streets in ever greater numbers and by 28 February a general strike was beginning to take hold of the city.

Robert Bruce Lockhart, the acting British Consul-General in Moscow witnessed the scenes that took place outside the City Duma, next to the Historical Museum just a stone's throw from Red Square, at the time of the February Revolution. One of his most vivid memories was of

the warmth of the surging mob before the Town Duma. There was no hooliganism… Inside, the rooms and passages of the huge Town Hall were thronged with bands of students and soldiers—the soldiers hot, greasy and officious, the students raucous and exultant.

It was all over very quickly: a handful of street skirmishes and nothing more. A Moscow businessman, P. A. Buryshkin, summed up the events of February-March 1917, noting that "there was no shooting in the streets, no barricades. The old regime in Moscow in truth fell all by itself, and no one defended it or even tried to."

On 1 March, two bodies were set up that would quickly restore order to the streets. A Committee of Public Organizations was formed by moderate Duma politicians to fill the vacuum of power at the centre and take charge of running the city; it was forced to share power with the reincarnated Moscow Soviet of Workers' Deputies which claimed to speak for the city's working masses. Members of the Soviet held discussions on the issue of whether to try and take over control of the Duma's responsibilities, but they rejected this idea on the grounds that running the day-to-day life of the city would be an impossible burden to shoulder. It was feared that taking over responsibility for the condition of the pavements would detract attention from the more important business of fomenting revolution.

Worsening economic conditions over the months that followed, as the food supply problems continued and prices began to rise, led to socialist deputies winning a large majority of the votes in elections to the Municipal Duma in June. Although Bolsheviks were vastly outnumbered by members of other socialist parties, they polled strongly in southern and eastern districts of the city, the working-class suburbs beyond the Garden Ring. The party's popularity increased still further over the summer as bread rations were cut and the war seemed to be dragging on with no hope of an end in sight. An attempted right-wing coup by General Kornilov in Petrograd that was strongly opposed by the Bolshevik forces brought a further surge in popularity for the party and by September it had taken control of the Moscow Soviet. The food situation became still more critical over the late summer and early autumn, and cuts in the bread ration caused increasingly serious worker discontent.

As had been the case back in February, events in October followed the lead given by Petrograd. On 25 October Lenin ordered the takeover of key strategic points in the capital by Bolshevik militias— bridges, telegraph offices, stations and the like—and took control of the city in the name of the Petrograd Soviet. The Provisional Government in Petrograd swiftly collapsed. The historian Yury Gote, who was living in Moscow at the time, noted in his diary for 26 October that "there is no precise news from Petrograd, all kinds of rumours are circulating, but which of them correspond to the truth and which don't you can't tell." The Moscow Soviet moved to set up its own Military Revolutionary Committee to mirror the one led by Trotsky in Petrograd; defenders of the previous order in the city Duma organized themselves into a Committee of Public Safety and took control of the Kremlin.

Street fighting began with an exchange of fire in Red Square on 27 October. Reports from people living in central Moscow at the time told of how people were too frightened to leave their houses: an English governess in Russia who was living in a house off the Arbat recalled how the family she worked for stayed in the windowless vestibule of their apartment for six whole days. Alexander Pasternak and his family had a similar tale to tell:

> *The fighting lasted many days... You couldn't think of going onto the street. The telephone was silent. The lamps didn't burn... Water in the taps was equally uncertain... The days passed so monotonously that we lost all sense of how long we had waited in our besieged lair, and how much longer we should still be there.*

In his brother's fictional account of those days in *Doctor Zhivago*, Yury's Uncle Kolya bursts into the family's rooms to announce:

> *They're fighting in the street. The Cadets are fighting for the Provisional Government against the garrison soldiers who are backing the Bolsheviks. They're skirmishing all over the place... I got into trouble coming here—once at the corner of Bolshaya Dmitrovka and once at the Nikitskye vorota... Come on, Yura, put your coat on and come out. You've got to see it. This is history. This happens once in a lifetime.*

The battles continued for ten days. House to house fighting took place along the Arbat, and the Bolshevik forces shelled the Kremlin from their strongholds south of the river. Wild rumours reached John Reed in Petrograd of the damage being done in the heart of Moscow; travellers told exaggerated stories of how St. Basil's had been reduced to a smoking ruin, Tverskaya and Kuznetsky Most were in flames, and the Duma building had been burnt to the ground. (Reed was able to confirm for himself that these reports were untrue on his visit to Moscow shortly after the transfer of power.) On 3 November the Red Guards took control of the Kremlin and the last of the opposing forces gave themselves up. Photographs from the time on display in the Museum of Modern History depict the damage done to St. Basil's cathedral during the bombardment as well as some of the street barricades and mass demonstrations from the time.

The comparison with the events in Petrograd where the new government had taken control with remarkably little blood spilled was stark. The Moscow Bolsheviks claimed that one thousand people had been killed in the fighting; this included the 238 martyrs of the

Revolution who were buried with full revolutionary honours in two mass graves by the Kremlin wall on 10 November. Factories were closed for the funeral, which became a major public event with a procession, banners and speeches from Bolshevik dignitaries. John Reed was present at the occasion and described in *Ten Days that Shook the World* how he saw workers digging the two massive pits for the graves on the evening before the funeral. On the day itself, "through all the streets to the Red Square the torrents of people poured, thousands upon thousands of them, all with the look of the poor and the toiling." Workers arrived from their factories, carrying their dead:

> *They could be seen coming through the Gate, the blare of their banners and the dull red—like blood—of the coffins they carried. These were rude boxes, made of unplaned wood and daubed with crimson, borne high on the shoulders of rough men who marched with tears streaming down their faces, and followed by women who sobbed and screamed, or walked stiffly, with white, dead faces.*

The Bolshevik position in power was by no means secure and the next four years brought massive upheavals for Muscovites as they sought to consolidate their position in the country. In the months immediately following the Revolution strikes broke out all over the city: teachers, doctors, civil servants and bank clerks all came out to express their opposition to the new order. The Bolsheviks responded by taking the opportunity to sack large numbers of bureaucratic staff. Mikhail Bulgakov wrote to his sister Nadezhda at the end of December 1917, describing the situation he saw around him:

> *On my recent journey to Moscow and Saratov I saw with my own eyes things that I hope never to see again. I saw crowds smashing the windows of trains, and saw people being beaten. I saw ruined and burnt-out houses in Moscow... I saw hungry queues outside the shops, hunted and pitiful officers, and I saw news-sheets where in effect they write about only one thing: about the blood that is flowing in the south, in the west and in the east.*

When Bruce Lockhart returned to Moscow in March 1918 he was surprised by the behaviour of middle- and upper-class Muscovites who were hoping for a German victory that would bring an end to the revolutionary escapade. "The city... was abnormally gay with a gaiety that shocked me," he wrote. "The bourgeoisie was awaiting the Germans with impatience and was already celebrating in advance the hour of its relief. Cabarets flourished." These middle-class optimists were soon to be bitterly disappointed. The new government agreed a peace treaty with the Germans at Brest-Litovsk in March and pulled out of the war altogether. Civil war soon followed.

The food situation deteriorated still further, and during the Civil War (1918-21) many Muscovites fled the city in search of food. One piece of graffiti that appeared on a city wall in January 1918 commented ruefully that "No hour passes without a soviet. No day without a decree. But there is no bread as yet." March was a month of great upheaval in the city as the Soviet government uprooted itself from Petrograd and moved to Moscow. Lenin himself arrived on 11 March and moved into the National Hotel on Manezhnaya ploshchad. He stayed here for a week before moving into his Kremlin apartment. Other central hotels including the Metropol were taken over for government use, as were most of the significant buildings in the city centre: the Middle Trading Rows, the Foundling Home, the Nobles' Club and many others. These became the offices of party and government agencies and institutions. Some Bolsheviks had mixed feelings about ruling from the Kremlin, the former seat of the Tsars: Trotsky thought it "an utter paradox as a fortress for the revolutionary dictatorship", but security considerations prevailed.

Symbols of Revolution

Although the truly radical reshaping of the centre of Moscow was only undertaken more than a decade after the Revolution had occurred, some early steps were made to change the appearance of the city. Romanov double-headed eagles were removed from the fronts of buildings and monuments to members of the royal family were pulled down; the enormous statue of Alexander II in the Kremlin was an early casualty, so too was the statue of Alexander III that stood before the Cathedral of Christ the Saviour. Lenin himself helped to demolish the cross put up in the Kremlin to commemorate the assassinated Grand Duke Sergei Alexandrovich. New monuments were erected in their place as part of the government's drive to create shrines to the

Revolution and to teach people in as simple, direct and visual a way as possible about the new revolutionary and socialist values. Lenin set out his aims in a letter to his Commissar of Enlightenment:

> You remember that Campanella in his City of the Sun speaks of frescoes on the walls of his fantastic socialist city, frescoes that were to serve as graphic lessons in natural science, history... I think that this is by no means naïve and with certain modifications could be assimilated by us and realized right now.

Statues of Marx, Engels, Herzen and Robespierre were included among the first wave of revolutionary monuments, and the Romanov obelisk in the Alexander Gardens was converted into a revolutionary totem pole. The equestrian statue on Tverskaya ploshchad of General Skobelev, hero of the wars in Central Asia in the 1870s who apparently died of a heart attack in 1882 while being whipped by prostitutes, was torn down and replaced with an obelisk intended to symbolize liberty. This Liberty Obelisk, which became the symbol of the city for a time and appeared on Moscow's coat of arms, was torn down in 1941 and during the 1950s it was replaced by the statue of Yury Dolgoruky which stands there to this day.

Most of the first wave of revolutionary statues did not last long. Quickly constructed by inexperienced sculptors, often from poor materials, they crumbled away when placed at the mercy of the elements. Some were deeply unpopular with the public and with critics; the modernist sculpture of Bakunin by Boris Korolev was described in one newspaper as follows:

> The statue is not exactly just a narrow slab of stone, and it's not exactly the remains of some kind of ugly tree, but one thing's certain—it's a scarecrow... Workers and Red Army men are surprised and outraged when they find out that the monument is about to be unveiled.

This particular monument did not last long in fact; it was rapidly removed and broken up. Rumour had it that the statue of Robespierre in the Alexander Gardens was blown up by mysterious protestors. Other statues were criticized on the grounds that their subjects were unrecognizable and in general there were feelings of considerable public resentment at the sums of money being invested in the whole project at a time of food shortages and widespread poverty.

Another way in which the revolutionary authorities sought to create distance between the new Moscow and the old was by renaming the streets and squares of the capital. Names with religious or monarchist associations were the first to go: for example, Voskresenskaya ploshchad (Resurrection Square) became ploshchad Revoliutsii (Revolution Square) and in this particular case the name has stuck. Other streets were named after revolutionary luminaries and members of the party: Herzen, Marx, Kropotkin, Gorky, Kirov, Sverdlov. Most of these have now reverted to their original names although the Soviet names of metro stations (Marksistskaya, Mayakovskaya, Ploshchad Ilicha) have often remained unchanged.

Major ceremonial events and festivals offered an opportunity to the regime to showcase its achievements, propagate its slogans and project its ultimate mission of building a new society to mass audiences. Early public events in Moscow included the burial of the Martyrs of the Revolution in November 1917 as well as the celebrations of May Day and the anniversary of the October Revolution, which became annual festivities. Although these celebrations ultimately became routine, with serried ranks of marchers obliged to process across Red Square saluting their political leaders as they went, they began in a far less regimented fashion. In the very early years of Soviet power, before the trend towards grandiose pomposity in public events had become institutionalized, revolutionary festivals could take on something of a carnival atmosphere.

Futurist artists had a field day on 1 May 1918. Given free rein by the Commissar of Enlightenment, Anatoly Lunacharsky, to decorate the city as they wished as part of the celebrations, they painted murals on buildings and even spray-painted the trees and the grass on Teatralnaya ploshchad in front of the Bolshoi Theatre. The writer Ilya Ehrenburg described how "demented squares battled with rhomboids on the peeling facades of colonnaded Empire villas [and] faces with triangles for eyes popped up everywhere." Lenin was dismayed by the artists' over-enthusiastic response and demanded that the paintings be taken down and the trees be washed clean. This was not possible in all cases, and Arthur Ransome found that the remains of the revolutionary murals were still visible when he visited Moscow in the spring of 1919:

> *Though the weather had damaged many of their paintings, enough was left to show what an extraordinary carnival that had been. Where a hoarding ran along the front of a house being repaired the painters had used the whole of it as a vast canvas on which they had painted huge symbolic pictures of the revolution. A whole block in the Tverskaya was so decorated...*

The first anniversary of the Revolution was celebrated in style with music, fireworks and the burning of effigies of the leaders of the Entente—Woodrow Wilson, Lloyd George and Clemenceau—who had recently ordered Allied troops into Russia to attempt to dethrone the new Bolshevik government.

Red Terror

Not everyone was in the mood to celebrate, however, and it was not just members of the former ruling classes who felt dismayed about their new rulers. In July 1918 a group of non-Bolshevik left-wingers, the Left Socialist-Revolutionaries, outraged by the decision to make peace with Germany, staged a bungled coup attempt by assassinating the German ambassador to Moscow and arresting the head of the Cheka, the secret police. They had hoped by their actions to provoke the Germans into renewing the war and to spark a popular revolt against the new regime. The attempt failed due to incompetent planning, but a month later another Socialist Revolutionary activist renewed the attempt to unseat the Bolsheviks by trying to assassinate Lenin.

This drama took place on 30 August outside the Michelson arms factory on Bolshaya Serpukhovskaya ulitsa, beyond the Garden Ring to the south of the city centre. Lenin had been addressing a workers' meeting at the factory, and on his way out he was shot at with a pistol by Fanya Kaplan, herself a former anarchist turned Socialist Revolutionary. One bullet, said to have been dipped in curare, lodged in his neck and it was unclear for several days whether he would recover. Kaplan, whose responsibility for the deed has been doubted by some historians on the grounds that her sight was very poor, was bundled away and executed four days later. This event marked the starting point for two phenomena: the Lenin cult of veneration for the great leader, and the Red Terror.

Thousands were arrested in the wake of the attempt on Lenin and mass executions took place across the city, at Khodynskoe field, Petrovsky park and the Butyrki prison, all in the north of the city, as well as in the Cheka headquarters at the Lubyanka. (For anyone wishing to visit these sites with their macabre connections, Petrovsky park is near Dinamo metro station as is Khodynskoe field, while the Butyrki is near Savelovskaya station.) The bodies of those who were shot at this time were mostly dumped in the Kalitnikovskoe cemetery near Proletarskaya metro; this cemetery's association with Terror victims would continue on into the 1930s. Forced labour camps were created for political prisoners, sometimes housed in monasteries: the Novospassky and the Andronikov monastery as well as the Ivanovsky convent near Kitai gorod metro were all used for this purpose.

The rationale behind the operation was to terrorize all opposition, real and potential, to the new authorities and render it impotent. The strategy worked. In telegrams exchanged between members of the opposition armies fighting against the Bolsheviks in September 1918 one report stated that:

> *The position in Moscow is desperate. Not only is the city out of bread, but there is not even dried fish. There are not many of the*

Bolshevik army in Moscow. It would not be difficult to overthrow Soviet power, but systematic terror has robbed the Muscovites of any power to act.

It was not just terror that had robbed Muscovites of the power to act. Hunger and disease stalked the capital, and the lack of fuel meant that heating homes in the winter months became a major preoccupation for families. People pillaged wood for their stoves from abandoned houses and churches, pulling the buildings to pieces in their search for fuel. Those who could left the city. An account of Civil War Moscow by an English governess gives some sense of the mood of the times:

We drank to 1919 rather dispiritedly... Last night an unfortunate woman threw herself from a seventh story window of the house opposite on to the pavement... There are cases of small-pox; typhus goes on... More and more people are dying from heart failure caused by attenuation.

The population of Moscow slumped. From a total of just over two million people in 1917 it had dropped by more than half by the summer of 1920 as people died, fled abroad or returned to their villages in search of food. Party agencies shut down the main food markets in their battle against private trade, although the Sukharevka, near the metro station of that name, kept going until December 1920, providing families who could raise the money with a source of food when rations failed. In *Doctor Zhivago*, Tonya goes searching for food:

She wandered about the alleys in the neighbourhood where you could sometimes catch a peasant from one of the villages outside Moscow selling vegetables and potatoes... In the main streets, peasants with loads were liable to be arrested.

The early months of 1921 witnessed a renewal of workers' protests in factories across the city. Triggered by the food shortages, the campaign culminated in a 10,000-strong protest march on 23 February, prompting the authorities to declare martial law. Demonstrations like these, as well as incidents in other cities, forced a crucial policy rethink, and in 1921 Lenin opted to take "two steps forward, one step back" and introduced a package of economic reforms designed to help rebuild the shattered economy. Private commerce was made legal once more and small-scale capitalism flourished. The New Economic Policy (NEP) brought about the liberalization of private trade that would last until the end of the 1920s.

New Economic Policy

Moscow under the early months of the New Economic Policy was a very different place from Civil War Moscow. Once the food supply problem had been resolved and the population began to return, prices quickly spiraled out of control. The writer Mikhail Bulgakov wrote to his mother in November 1921 about conditions in the capital:

> *A furious battle is going on for survival and to adapt to the new conditions of life... it's possible to survive in Moscow only through private enterprise or through trading... the prices are rising and rising! The shops are full of goods but what can you buy! In Moscow there is everything: shoes, cloth, meat, caviar, preserves, delicacies, everything! Cafés are opening, they're sprouting like mushrooms... There is the buzzing of a wave of speculation.*

Buildings that had fallen into disuse and dilapidation during the Civil War were refurbished and thousands of shops and market stalls reopened across the city. Walter Benjamin, who visited Moscow in 1926, was very struck by the number of small shops and private traders in operation across the city. "There are conveniences here unknown to Western Europe," he noted, "the state grocery stores remain open until eleven at night." The population of Moscow rapidly recovered to its pre-war levels and continued to grow as new migrants moved in.

In the arts and in society at large, radical activists continued to push the boundaries of what was acceptable. Radical students sought to cast off bourgeois social restraints and sought sexual liberation with their peers; nudists from the "Down with Shame" movement paraded through the streets of Moscow to demonstrate the egalitarianism of their approach to daily life. Constructivists designed new kinds of living space, film directors used montage techniques to create striking and often disconcerting associations between images, and composers experimented by introducing sirens and factory whistles into the symphony orchestra. Self-styled "proletarian" writers and artists, rarely from the working classes themselves, set about the curious task of aiding the proletariat in the spontaneous generation of its own culture. But this wave of radical experimentation would not last for long.

Chapter Four
RED MOSCOW—CITY OF SOVIETS AND
SINCE

Musing towards the end of the Civil War on the future of his adopted city, the writer Ilya Ehrenburg anticipated that "a new and extraordinary city would grow up in the place of the crooked little wooden houses familiar to me since childhood." He was right. The Soviet period had a profound impact on the city of Moscow, reshaping its population, its streets, its monuments and its memories. The experience of living through the Revolution, the Stalin period and the Second World War transformed the lives of Muscovites, while the stagnation of the Brezhnev era is now a time that many older residents of the city look back to with nostalgia as an era of stability.

Lenin died in 1924 and the later 1920s witnessed the climax of the power struggle over his succession. Matters came to a head in the debate over the future of the New Economic Policy and in the end, Stalin was able to outmanoeuvre his rivals and led a radical shift to the left, bringing about the abandonment of the NEP and the introduction of state economic planning. The years of the first Five Year Plan at the end of the 1920s saw a huge influx of new migrants into Moscow, peasants who were fleeing the newly collectivized villages and seeking work in the factories and construction sites that were being created in the capital. Moscow offered all kinds of modern facilities—shops, parks and cinemas—for the newcomers to enjoy, if they had the time and the energy available. One former peasant who moved to the capital in 1937 described his impressions:

> *Electric lights shone in every building along the street. I had never seen such electric lights before—I liked them so much! ... I liked Moscow so much that I think I would have sold my soul to stay in Moscow. Why? Because Moscow is a beauty. And when I went to Red Square, oh, I liked it, especially the Kremlin.*

The rapid growth of the city prompted the authorities to take the whole business of town planning very seriously indeed.

The General Plan

In June 1931 Lazar Kaganovich, the Moscow Party chief, put forward his proposals for the reconstruction of Moscow, declaring proudly "I consider that Moscow should be and will be a laboratory to which people from all over the Union will flock to study its experience." The plan encompassed many and various aspects of the city's life—housing, transport, sanitation, public spaces—and sought to achieve both the decisive modernization of the Soviet capital and to transform the appearance of the city centre. The ultimate aim, as Kaganovich himself put it, was to create "a capital worthy of the proletarian state" that would win international admiration and demonstrate what the socialist workers' state could achieve.

Some of the projects outlined by Kaganovich got underway immediately: work on building the metro began in 1932 as did the construction of the Moscow-Volga canal, a massive project built largely by prison labour. Planning for the new Palace of Soviets had already been started. It was not until 1935, however, that the definitive General Plan for the reconstruction of the city was published. Architects and town planners had been hard at work in the early 1930s putting forward possible designs for what the future city should look like, some proposing widespread demolition and rebuilding, others focusing on a garden city approach with green spaces integrated into the overall design. The eventual plan adopted by the Party leadership looked to a city of five million inhabitants and sought to provide for their needs through a structured approach to town planning. Streets would be widened in the city centre to aid the movement of traffic; and urban services would be brought up to the highest possible standards.

Plans to open up the centre of Moscow in order to facilitate the circulation of traffic required considerable changes to the existing layout. The narrow medieval streets and city walls complicated the process of modernization and some very drastic decisions were taken in order to surmount these problems. The old Kitai gorod wall, which had surrounded the settlement to the east of the Kremlin since the sixteenth century, was destroyed in the early 1930s together with its gateways; 1934 saw the pulling down of the Sukharev Tower on Sukharevskaya ploshchad. A year later the massive project of widening ulitsa Tverskaya, or ulitsa Gorkogo (Gorky Street), as it was renamed, was begun. The Kazakov building occupied by the Moscow Soviet, the former house of the Moscow Governor on Tverskaya ploshchad (renamed Sovetskaya ploshchad), was moved backwards by about fifty feet and the building itself was extended. The American émigré Margaret Wettlin witnessed the beginnings of this whole process:

> *Horse-drawn carts and carriages passed us on our walks, rarely an automobile. But Moscow was preparing for the automobile age. Its cobblestone streets, which were filing off the soles and nibbling into the uppers of my American shoes… were being asphalted, and the steep Tverskaya… was being graded. The only big buildings on Tverskaya were the Central Telegraph and the National Hotel, which reared like mother hens surrounded by broods of one- and two-story chicks; but a yawning excavation opposite the National proclaimed that a modern skyscraper of at least fifteen stories was under construction.*

A famous painting by Yury Pimenov entitled *New Moscow* depicts the back of a girl's head as she drives her car through the centre of the modernized city in 1937. It can be seen in the New Tretyakov Gallery.

Andrei Platonov's unfinished novel *Happy Moscow* takes as its theme the changes taking place in the city during the 1930s and in particular the discrepancy that he perceived between official declarations that life was getting better and happier, and real life as it was experienced by the majority of ordinary people. Platonov, who had already been the target of considerable criticism for writing a series of satirical works on the communist project, must have realized that this novel was unpublishable and he abandoned it towards the end of the 1930s.

The 1930s saw many more of Moscow's ancient landmarks disappear. The Triumphal Arch, built by Bove on the road leading out to St. Petersburg to commemorate the war against Napoleon was pulled down; this monument was reconstructed in the late 1960s but this time it was placed on Kutuzovsky prospekt near the Borodino Panorama museum and the spot that had been designated for the new Victory Park. Massive changes took place in and around the very heart of the city. The Church of the Saviour in the Woods and the Red Staircase in the Kremlin were both destroyed, as were the Voskresenskie gates, the Iverskaya chapel and the Kazan Cathedral on Red Square. The Romanov eagles on the Kremlin towers were finally removed and replaced with stars, initially made of metal but later replaced by red glass. Several of the capital's ancient monasteries were also destroyed either in whole or in part: the Strastnoi Convent on the site of what is now the Rossiya cinema on Pushkinskaya ploshchad was dismantled and many of the buildings of the lovely Simonov monastery on Simonovsky Val, south-east of the centre, were blown up in order to provide extra space for the nearby car factory and workers' club.

The Cathedral of Christ the Saviour

One of the most spectacular demolitions of the Soviet period was the destruction of the grandiose Cathedral of Christ the Saviour on ulitsa Volkhonka near Kropotkinskaya metro station. The cathedral had been proposed by Alexander I as a monument to commemorate the Patriotic War of 1812 and to thank God for saving Russia from Napoleon; it took many years to raise the money to build it and it was completed only in the 1880s, funded in part by popular subscription. The construction of the cathedral, to a design by Konstantin Ton, required the relocation of a medieval monastery to make space for it; when it was eventually finished the cathedral was the largest religious building in Russia and dominated the skyline for miles around. It was not the world's most attractive work of religious architecture, but its size and scale gave out a clear message to visitors—especially foreign ones—about the supremacy of the Russian state. A statue of Tsar Alexander III was unveiled in 1912 next to the building, the work of sculptor Alexander Opekushin who was also responsible for the much-loved Pushkin statue and the monument to Alexander II in the Kremlin.

The Opekushin statue was destroyed in 1918 but the cathedral itself survived the first decade of Soviet power. The decision to pull it down was taken only in 1931, after the riverside site had been earmarked by Stalin as a suitable position for his new Palace of Soviets. The bells and the gold leaf from the cupolas were removed and then in December 1931 the cathedral was blown up with dynamite; it took three massive explosions to raze the entire building to the ground. Rumour had it that the iconostasis ended up in the hands of Eleanor

Roosevelt, who donated it to the Vatican. It took many months of labour before the site could be completely cleared and work could begin on the Palace of Soviets. Orthodox believers regarded it as an act of sacrilege and considered the cathedral as a martyr in the Soviet war against religion. The fact that both Kaganovich and Boris Iofan, the architect of the proposed new Palace, were Jewish helped to fuel conspiracy theories among anti-Semites.

This Palace was to have served as a monument to Soviet power and as the focal point of the new Moscow, its Great Hall earmarked to provide space for Party congresses and other political extravaganzas. An open competition was held to design the new building; several of the proposals put forward approached the project from a modernist perspective and a significant proportion of the entries came from foreign architects including Le Corbusier and Walter Gropius. The plan that was eventually chosen was created by Boris Iofan and would, if it had ever been built, have been the tallest building in the world, higher even than the Empire State building in New York. The design was for a monumental tower, rising in tiers and topped by a vast statue of Lenin, his arm outstretched in greeting to the inhabitants of the first socialist city. In addition to the Great Hall, the building would have housed several other meeting spaces, a Museum of World Revolution, an Institute of Marx-Engels-Lenin and a radio mast. A thirty-foot-high model of the design went on display at the 1939 World's Fair in New York.

Although work began on laying the foundations for the Palace of Soviets in 1935, the building project was beset with problems. Water kept seeping into the foundations, holding up the construction, and old ladies whispered that this was God's revenge on the heathen socialists. Work on the Palace was halted altogether during the Second World War. Although some efforts were made after the war to continue work on the project, the plans were scaled down considerably and by the late 1950s the idea of building on this site was abandoned. A vast open-air heated swimming pool, the

Moskva, was installed instead, where swimmers could bathe even in the winter months when the snow was falling. Some Orthodox believers maintained that anyone swimming in the pool would undergo involuntary baptism, such was the religious significance of the spot.

The rebuilding of the cathedral in the mid-1990s was one of Mayor Yury Luzhkov's major prestige projects. Religious nationalists had been campaigning for its resurrection ever since the inauguration of *glasnost* had opened up opportunities for public debate. President Yeltsin offered his public support, declaring that "it is a Russian national sacred place and must be reborn. With it, it will be easier to find the path to social accord, the creation of goodness, and a life in which there will be less room for sin."

Funding for the project, which includes such inauthentic touches as a car park as well as church offices in the basement, was raised from private donations encouraged by generous tax breaks but the costs quickly spiraled to a figure of over US$350 million. Although the decision to rebuild the cathedral was welcomed by Church leaders, critics felt that the money could have been better spent elsewhere.

The Moscow Metro
The metro system is one of the glories of Moscow; fares have gone up sharply since the collapse of communism, but they still remain significantly lower than those charged for urban public transport in the west; it also remains fantastically efficient with trains running every minute during peak times. It is not all that easy for a non-Russian speaker to use the metro, particularly if you need to change trains, although some of the maps in the trains are now transliterated and announcements identify the names of the stations as you arrive. The stations themselves are often extraordinarily grand, with marble halls, stained glass, statues and mosaics decorating these "Palaces of the People". Initially known as the Kaganovich metro after its founder, the name was later changed to the Lenin metro; today it is simply the Moscow metro. Nowadays advertising is commonplace in the trains and at the stations and the underpasses are full of stalls selling newspapers, soap and icons; musicians and beggars are another common sight.

Construction work began in the early 1930s and the tunnels were built deep into the ground, partly so they could double as air raid shelters; the escalators are therefore often extremely long. Workers were brought in from outside Moscow to participate in the excavation and thousands of members of the Young Communists' organization, the Komsomol, volunteered to play their part in helping to build the new transport system. Many were killed or seriously injured in the work and at the end of their labours the non-Muscovites in the construction team were unceremoniously expelled from the city. The group of British observers led by the liberal MP Sir E. D. Simon who visited Moscow in 1936 questioned the decision to build a metro system when housing was arguably a more pressing need; they were informed that the traffic congestion was just as urgent a problem, but also "that the Metro was a symbol, an expression of the power of the people to create gigantic and beautiful things, a foretaste of the wealth to be at the command of all as the successive plans unfolded."

Certainly part of the reason for expanding the public transport network was connected with the expansion of the city. With ever more workers flooding into the outlying districts, transport links to enable them to get between their homes and places of work became increasingly vital. Government paranoia about worker lateness and absenteeism became heightened as the decade wore on, and by 1939 it had decreed that being twenty minutes late to work was a criminal offence that could bring instant dismissal. The metro was not much help, at least not to begin with, as the initial stretches did not reach beyond the central areas of the city. The first line, today's red line, was opened in 1935 and reached from Park Kultury (Gorky Park) in the south-west to Sokolniki in the north-east, allowing easy access between two of the city's leisure parks and the centre as well as taking in Komsomolskaya ploshchad with its three main line stations.

Yelena Bulgakova, Mikhail Bulgakov's third wife, was very impressed by her first trip on the metro. "It's been wonderfully done!" she confided in her diary. "It's comfortable and clean and there's plenty of air. I very much liked the escalator, it's such fun to stand on a step and slowly be carried upwards." Stalin himself went for a ride when it was first opened; his unexpected appearance at Okhotny Ryad caused a crush as enthusiastic Muscovites crowded around, hoping to catch a glimpse of him. Even the Simon commission members were impressed by the rapid service, reasonable fares, splendid architecture and the evident fondness that Muscovites had for their new transport system.

The travel writer Martha Gellhorn, who visited Moscow in 1972 and included a description of her trip in a book subtitled "Five Journeys from Hell", had this to say about the Moscow metro:

The Moscow subway stations resemble vast subterranean Turkish baths, with a touch of old-time Roxy movie palaces. Giant murals in mosaic and brilliant paint; statuary in niches, many-coloured marble, pillars and arches. It is the most sumptuous public transport system in the world. Stupefying. Why this opulence below ground when above ground all amenity is lacking?

Some of the most lavishly decorated stations are on the circle line, the brown line that roughly follows the course of the Garden Ring. Kievskaya metro has mosaics on the ceiling showing happy Ukrainians joyfully welcoming their Russian brethren; white medallions adorn the walls of Park Kultury depicting the kinds of activities that people can enjoy in Gorky Park; Komsomolskaya contains mosaics depicting Russia's military heroes and Novoslobodskaya is distinguished by its decorative features made of stained glass. Ploshchad Revoliutsii in the city centre contains a whole series of life-sized bronze statues of Soviet heroes: the idea is that as you walk along the platform, the statues move forward chronologically, from revolutionary partisans through to the builders of industry and then on to younger Soviet citizens taking part in educational and leisure activities. Less extravagant, but no less impressive designs with clean lines and soaring arches can be found at Kropotkinskaya—originally Dvorets Sovetov (Palace of Soviets) station—and at Mayakovskaya, the station where Stalin famously delivered his speech on the eve of the anniversary of the Revolution in 1941. The marble used to build many of the stations was recycled from the Cathedral of Christ the Saviour after its demolition. Expansion of the metro system continued in the post-Stalin era, although the more recent stations are far less opulent in their decoration. Car ownership very gradually increased from the Brezhnev period onwards but little attention was paid to road building until after the collapse of communism.

The Great Terror: the Solovetsky Stone

If you were to stand in the middle of the traffic roundabout where the statue of Felix Dzerzhinsky was once to be found, facing the Lubyanka, the large yellow building of the secret police headquarters on Lubyanskaya ploshchad, directly to your right you would be able to see a stone surmounted by lump of granite. Leaping across Russian roads is not recommended at the best of times, and you would be advised to use the underpasses beneath the square, but it is useful to have some indication of where you are headed as the stone is quite small and could easily be missed. This stone is a monument that was established in 1990 by the Memorial organization, a society dedicated to remembering the victims of political repression during the Soviet era. The inscription on the stone informs you that it comes from Solovetsky island in the White Sea, the site of a monastery where the Soviet regime set up one of its first prison camps, and that it was erected by Memorial in memory of the millions of victims of the totalitarian regime. A stand nearby gives further details, informing you that 40,000 people were shot in Moscow during the terror and were buried in the cemetery of the Yauza hospital, in Vagankovskoe cemetery, in the Donskoi crematorium and in two secret police execution sites a short distance outside Moscow, at Butovo and Kommunalka.

Memorial was one of the many organizations set up during the *glasnost* era that worked to open up public debate. It concentrated its work in lobbying for public memorials to be set up to the victims of the Soviet era, setting up research centres and carrying out oral history interviews with survivors from the labour camps. Leading members of the organization included high-profile dissidents, artists and public figures such as Andrei Sakharov, Bulat Okudzhava and Boris Yeltsin. The group played a crucial role in stimulating public interest in recent history during the Gorbachev era and its petitioning for a public memorial in Moscow was ultimately successful: the stone was erected on 30 October 1990 on the Day of Remembrance of Political Prisoners.

Political arrests were not limited to any single period in Soviet history, but undoubtedly the worst time of all came during the 1930s. People who were aware of being at risk of arrest would lie awake at nights listening to hear whether the lift would stop at their floor. Some even kept a small suitcase packed and ready in case the secret police came calling for them. During the "Great" Terror of 1937-8 Party members working in political or administrative roles were most in danger, as were army officers, non-Russians and the "usual suspects", principally religious believers and members of the former ruling classes. The torture and execution of those arrested took place in the Lubyanka itself or in other secret police buildings nearby. Those who escaped execution would be held in one of the transit camps in and around the capital before transportation to the Gulag. Relatives of those arrested queued for hours to try to find news and send parcels and letters to those who had been taken; one young man who waited in line at the information office on ulitsa Petrovka for several days hoping for news of his mother described how an old woman of about seventy was finally able to approach the window:

> She braced her arm on the sill so as to stand up taller and her toothless old gums mumbled out the names of her sons, the first, the second, the third. It turned out they all had been sent into exile. Two big yellowish drops appeared in the corners of her eyes, trickled down her wrinkled cheeks and fell onto the dirty floor, disappeared in the dust and mud… No one paid any attention to the weeping old woman. She's not the first and she's not the last either.

Among the political leaders to be arrested were several figures who had been rivals to Stalin for the Party leadership during the 1920s. These men—Grigory Zinoviev, Lev Kamenev, Nikolai Bukharin—were tried publicly on outlandish charges of treason, conspiracy and espionage in the Moscow show trials, held in the former Nobles' Club on Okhotny Ryad. Transcripts of the trials were published daily in the press beneath headlines calling on the authorities to "Shoot the Mad Dogs!" All of the defendants at the show trials were found guilty and most were executed.

Mass graves of those executed in Moscow can be found in the cemetery of the Donskoi monastery where a few memorial stones have been put up. Blue fir trees line the alley leading from the entrance gate to the crematorium where so many of the victims' bodies were incinerated. Victims of the Terror also lie in other Moscow cemeteries—Vagakovskoe, Rogozhskoe and Kalitnikovskoe among them—and in other sites as well. Foreign communists who were shot in 1937-8 were buried along the steep banks of the wall of Novospassky monastery as it rises up above the pond at the back of the complex.

An imposing statue of the founder of the Soviet secret police, Felix Dzerzhinsky, used to stand in the middle of Lubyanskaya ploshchad facing the Lubyanka building. Erected in 1958, three decades after Dzerzhinsky's death, the statue reminded passers-by of the purpose of the building and its grim history. It was hardly surprising that during the *glasnost* era the statue became a focus for opposition pressure and in the aftermath of the failed coup of August 1991 it was toppled amid scenes of popular rejoicing; thousands of Muscovites determined to stay outside late into the night and watch until the statue was finally removed from its pedestal. Attempts by demonstrators to pull the statue down with their bare hands sparked fears about safety and persuaded the city authorities to send for a crane—borrowed from the American Embassy—to bring it down. Dzerzhinsky now stands in the sculpture park at the back of the Central House of Artists on the south bank of the Moskva River along with other fallen idols: Stalin sculpted out of pink granite and with his nose broken off stands alongside Marx, Brezhnev and several Lenins. They share the space with a rose garden and works of contemporary sculpture including a 1998 piece by Evgeny Chubarov representing Terror victims.

Dzerzhinsky's fate is still contested, however. In 1998 members of the State Duma approved a resolution calling on the Moscow authorities to restore the statue to its former spot. The leader of the Agrarian bloc said that it would act as a symbolic deterrent against crime and pronounced Dzerzhinsky—a man whose ruthless reputation earned him the nickname "Iron Felix"—to be a man of "fiery heart, cool head and clean hands". Although nothing has—as yet—been done to move the statue, his former position outside the Lubyanka still remains vacant. In 2002 Mayor Yury Luzhkov gave an indication of his own support of the scheme to return Dzerzhinsky to his former home; some people speculated that this was part of an attempt to ingratiate himself with President Putin, himself a former member of the KGB and the ex-head of its successor organization the FSB or Federal Security Service. Supporters of Dzerzhinsky tend to emphasize the role that he played in setting up children's homes and orphanages after the Civil War: it is not for no reason that the children's department store Detsky Mir (Children's World) was built just across the street from the Lubyanka.

The Great Patriotic War, 1941-45: The Moscow Panic

There is no one obvious site around which to centre a discussion of the events of 15-19 October 1941. Perhaps the Zhukov statue in Manezhnaya ploshchad, honouring the military hero of the Battle of Moscow, or the barricades left on the roadside up at Khimki on the road to Sheremetyevo airport to mark the furthest point of the German advance. I prefer here to focus on Komsomolskaya square and to imagine the scenes around Kazan Station during the October days when the whole of Moscow was in uproar with people desperately trying to escape the city by any means they could find. News that the German Army Group Centre had broken through the main line of the city's defence and was advancing on the capital reached Muscovites on 15 October and, as the American émigré Mary Leder recalled, "no one who lived in or near Moscow will ever forget that day. Panic gripped the city."

As officials made rapid plans to evacuate the government to Kuibyshev (now reverted to its older name of Samara) on the Volga and ordered factories to start putting in train the "scorched earth" policy of destroying any machinery that could not be moved eastwards, ordinary people flooded the stations in the hope of finding some way of escape. One doctor who was working for the ambulance service at the time observed in his diary that "the squares in front of the railway stations are crowded to overflowing, impassable." Mary Leder herself tried to leave by train only to be told that her ticket was not valid because all the trains had been commandeered by different organizations for their employees. Eventually she managed to become included in the evacuation of the publishing house where her husband had worked before the war and was able to board a train heading east. Not everyone was so lucky. As she remarked: "The organized evacuees departed by train. The unorganized took what they could carry, and walked or hitched rides whenever and by whatever means they could. For days, a stream of Muscovites moved eastward along the Highway of Enthusiasts, one of Moscow's main roads."

One can only imagine the panic and terror that must have been felt by those left behind. No one was under any illusions as to the German attitude towards the "subhuman Slavic race". Writing later, the poet Konstantin Simonov described how "the memory of Moscow was unbearable. Like the face of a person you love distorted by fear." Law and order broke down in the streets and reports flooded in to the authorities of riots and looting taking place all over the city.

Further measures taken by the authorities in the face of the German threat included burning crucial documents to avoid having them fall into enemy hands; reports told of bonfires being lit all over the city. I myself discovered, when doing research in Moscow on one occasion, that a set of documents from the 1930s that I wanted to consult in the Central Party Archives did not exist because they had been destroyed during the Moscow panic. Lenin's body had already been evacuated to Siberia back in July, not long after the German invasion. Some prisoners were evacuated, others were simply shot. Alexander Shcherbakov, the Moscow Party chief, tried to rally Party workers to the defence of their city:

> We shall fight resolutely, desperately, to the last drop of blood... Comrade Muscovites! Let each one of you, whatever your past, whatever your work, be a soldier in the army defending Moscow from the fascist aggressors!

No one was sure if Stalin would abandon Moscow, not even the man himself. Some of his apparatchiks advised him to leave; the secret police chief Lavrentii Beria argued: "Moscow is not the Soviet Union. Defending Moscow is useless. Staying in Moscow is dangerous, they will shoot us like sitting ducks." On 16 October Stalin announced to his lieutenants that they should evacuate the city without delay and that he himself would leave the following morning. He did not leave then, nor on the following day and it seems that it was only on the evening of 18 October that he finally made his decision not to join the great exodus. He had already discussed the situation with Zhukov and had been assured that the general was confident that he could hold the city. On 19 October Stalin's war cabinet declared a state of siege in Moscow. A curfew was imposed and a harsh police crack-down restored some semblance of order to the beleaguered city. Looters and panic-mongers were to be shot.

On 7 November, the anniversary of the Revolution, Stalin ordered that the traditional military parade on Red Square should take place. On the eve of the demonstration he gave a rousing public speech on the platform at Mayakovskaya metro station in which he rallied Muscovites proclaiming:

> *It is these people without honour or conscience, these people with the morality of animals, who have the effrontery to call for the extermination of the great Russian nation—the nation of Plekhanov and Lenin, of Belinsky and Chernyshevsky, of Pushkin and Tolstoy…of Suvorov and Kutuzov… If the Germans want to have a war of extermination, they will get it.*

Suvorov and Kutuzov were both generals who had fought against Napoleon, and parallels with the earlier Great Patriotic War of 1812 became a constant refrain with Soviet propagandists throughout the 1941-5 war. The following day on Red Square, Stalin continued his theme of invoking Russia's heroic ancestors to rouse the people to advance the struggle: "let the manly images of our great ancestors—Alexander Nevsky, Dmitry Donskoi, Kuzma Minin, Dmitry Pozharsky, Alexander Suvorov and Mikhail Kutuzov—inspire you in this war." The tanks rolled over the cobblestones and then headed straight up Tverskaya—Gorky Street as it was then—for the front.

A second German offensive in late November met with stern resistance from the Russians and on 6 December the Red Army launched a mighty counter-offensive against the Wehrmacht, which drove them back from Moscow. The coming of the harsh Russian winter played its part in throwing back the poorly prepared invaders, as it had done before in 1812, but overstretched German supply lines and the ability of the Russians to bring in reinforcement troops from Siberia also played their role. Ultimately, perhaps, Hitler's key strategic mistake was to have launched Operation Barbarossa, the invasion of the USSR, too late in the year. If Moscow could not be taken quickly, by *blitzkrieg* methods, then arguably it could not be taken at all. Certainly, never again would the Germans come so close to capturing the city.

The story of the Moscow panic was written out of official Soviet versions of the history of the war. An unedifying episode, it was felt that the rush to abandon the city by officials and populace alike did not present an appropriate picture of staunch patriotism and resolution in the face of danger. Heroism was preferable to defeatism and cowardice in the official narrative of the war.

Victory Park

Poklonnaya Gora, the Victory Park stretched out along Kutuzovsky prospekt to the west of the city (metro Park Pobedy) was the spot where Napoleon is said to have stopped, cast his eye over the city and waited for a non-existent deputation to be sent out to meet him. As Tolstoy pictured it:

> At ten in the morning on the 2nd of September, Napoleon was standing among his troops on the Poklonny Hill looking at the panorama spread out before him... The brightness of the morning was magical. Moscow, seen from the Poklonny Hill, lay spaciously spread out with her river, her gardens and her churches, and she seemed to be living her usual life, her cupolas glittering like stars in the sunlight.

A Soviet-era museum containing a panoramic depiction of the battle of Borodino can be found along Kutuzovsky prospekt, as can a more recent equestrian statue of General Bagration and the relocated Triumphal Arch. It was this spot, full of associations with the earlier Patriotic War of 1812, which was chosen by the Soviet authorities in 1957 as the site for a grand memorial complex to honour the victory in the war with Germany in 1941-5 and pay tribute to those who had died.

In the final scene of the 1957 Mikhail Kalatozov film *The Cranes are Flying*, there comes an unforgettable sequence. It is Victory Day, 9

May 1945, and the young heroine, Veronika, searches through the crowd for her fiancé Boris, unaware that he has been killed at the front. She finally learns of his fate when shown a photograph that was found on his body and continues her walk through the crowd, tears streaming down her face and giving away the flowers she has brought for Boris to happier couples now reunited with one another. The journalist and writer Alexander Werth, who was also in Moscow on that day, left the following description of the celebrations:

> *The spontaneous joy of the two or three million people who thronged the Red Square that evening—and the Moscow River embankments, and Gorky Street, all the way up to the Belorussian Station—was of a quality and a depth I had never yet seen in Moscow before...* [Muscovites had] *thrown all reserve and restraint to the winds. The fireworks display that evening was the most spectacular I have ever seen.*

The commemoration of the Second World War in Russia has been a very politicized issue. The status of Victory Day was downgraded soon after the war and it was not reinstated as a national public holiday until 1965, when the Brezhnev regime decided to try and harness the positive emotions felt about the Soviet victory to the service of the state. While Stalin was still alive, the victory had largely been attributed to the Soviet leader's brilliance; in 1956 in his Secret Speech, Khrushchev dethroned his predecessor, detailing his various failings as a military leader and the many needless deaths that had followed as a result. In Khrushchev's words, the victory had been won thanks to "the magnificent and heroic deeds of hundreds of millions of people". The official version of history as told during the Brezhnev period raised the Party to new heights: it was the Communist Party, apparently, which had united the people and led them together to the ultimate victory. War memorials were built across the USSR during the 1960s, including the Tomb of the Unknown Soldier in Moscow, and an annual minute of silence was introduced out of respect to the dead.

Gorbachev set a very different tone in his comments on the forty-fifth anniversary of the 1945 victory. He had already been instrumental in helping to fill in some of the "blank spots", those elements of the Soviet past such as the Nazi-Soviet non-aggression pact of 1939 which had provided for the carving up of Eastern Europe between Russia and Germany and which the authorities had sought to erase from the historical record. Now he spoke about ordinary citizens and their sufferings during the war; about the enormous loss of life—Soviet losses are estimated at around twenty-seven million people or one in seven of the pre-war population—and about "those about whom there was silence for long decades, who had been illegally stripped of their honourable names and their citizenship rights, and locked up in the camps." He hardly mentioned the Party at all.

The Victory Park is a curious amalgam of past and present ways of commemorating the Soviet war experience. As noted above, the site was chosen as far back as 1957 although work on the project did not begin until 1984. The upheavals of the Gorbachev era meant that work was soon shelved only to be revived again in the early 1990s with considerable input from Yury Luzhkov: the park was officially opened on Victory Day 1995. Although Soviet symbols have been avoided and religious buildings are included in the complex, the ponderous monumentalism of the design concept gives a very Soviet feel to the place. The design of the complex was put out to competition more than once during the late Soviet period but no overall winner emerged. Arguments raged over what the central monument should look like; after the collapse of communism in 1991 the idea of a red stone banner depicting Lenin's profile being raised by Soviet workers and soldiers was rejected. A later proposal for the figure of a woman symbolizing Mother Russia drew the wrath of veterans' groups and in the end Luzhkov's old friend Zurab Tsereteli was brought in to do the design. He chose an obelisk surmounted by the winged figure of the goddess of victory, Nike, and two angels, at the base of which the mounted figure of St.

George slays a dragon covered with swastikas. Carved into the obelisk are the names of the crucial battles of the war. The heroic message is very much in line with earlier Soviet war memorials, even though the use of religious symbolism is a new departure, and one correspondent with a national newspaper felt that it was designed to offer a particular, heroic narrative of the war and to downplay the suffering that people had undergone:

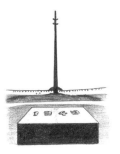

> *There's no respect for the sorrow, deaths, hardships of the war. From the very beginning, this was conceived of as a monument to the generals' war. The goal was to draw attention to the CPSU* [Communist Party of the Soviet Union], *its leadership and to hide the truth about the people's tragedy.*

Other monuments in the complex include three religious buildings, positioned around the park according to a strict spatial hierarchy: the Russian Orthodox church stands in the main part of the site, obvious to all visitors, whereas the synagogue and the mosque are hidden away from view. A further Tsereteli monument, a sculpture of emaciated human figures entitled *The Tragedy of the Peoples* does explore the theme of genocide and human suffering, but it was moved to a less visible part of the complex after Luzhkov decided that it was too depressing. The park is best visited on Victory Day, 9 May, when veterans congregate here to sing, dance and reminisce and Muscovites come to lay flowers. The evening invariably ends with a magnificent fireworks display. Unlike most of the other Soviet era public holidays, Victory Day is a genuinely popular and emotionally charged event and nowadays is much more of a significant date in the Russian calendar than the May Day holiday a week earlier.

Trophy Art at the Pushkin Museum
Victory in the war brought the Soviet Union a superpower status that it would eventually prove unable to sustain. It also brought a large number of items of cultural value into the country, many of which ended up in Moscow, and the Pushkin Fine Art Museum on ulitsa Volkhonka is currently home to an impressive collection of trophy art. Special "Trophy Commissions" of Red Army troops were set up at the end of the Second World War to oversee the removal of valuables from museums and private collections and take them back to Moscow as a form of compensation for the devastation wrought by the German invasion. The Germans themselves had taken, and often destroyed, countless Soviet treasures during the years of the war. Items seized from Germany in this way included art works by Degas, Rubens, Manet, Renoir and Matisse, rare books including a Gutenberg Bible from Leipzig, archival documents and the collection of gold treasures discovered by Heinrich Schliemann in his excavation of Troy in the 1870s.

Most of these treasures were deposited in secret museum vaults, and the Soviet authorities spent the next fifty years denying their very existence. Many of the works were not stored in appropriate conditions and consequently suffered significant deterioration. During the *glasnost* era, the whole issue was reopened when Gorbachev signed a Treaty of Good Neighbourhood and Cooperation with the German Chancellor, a treaty that included a clause stating that "lost or unlawfully transferred art treasures... will be returned to their owners or their successors." Members of the State Duma have proved unenthusiastic about the whole idea of restitution and in 1998 a law was forced through declaring that war trophies were Russian national property, in defiance of the presidential veto. Since the 1990s some of the works seized have been exhibited in Russian museums, including the Pushkin Museum where the Schliemann gold has been put on display. The issue has clouded Russo-German relations for many years now, and the emotions that it stirs make it unlikely that it will be resolved any time soon.

Stalin's Death

Stalin died in his dacha at Kuntsevo, a suburb of western Moscow, at the beginning of March 1953. His body lay in state in the Columned Hall of the House of Unions—the former Nobles' Club—on Okhotny Ryad while hundreds of thousands of people queued in line to file past. On the final day of the lying-in-state, hundreds of Muscovites were killed, trampled to death or asphyxiated amid scenes of crowd hysteria. On 9 March the coffin was taken on a horse-drawn hearse to Red Square where Stalin's name had already been carved into the marble front of the Mausoleum below that of Lenin. His successors to the Party leadership—Malenkov, Molotov and the soon-to-be-arrested secret police chief Beria—gave orations and the embalmed body was laid to rest alongside Lenin. Workers' meetings were held all over Moscow, as in the rest of the country, as people got together to profess their collective grief and write tributes to the dead leader. Letters poured in to the authorities suggesting ways of commemorating him: particularly popular was the idea of some kind of pantheon, a much more impressive building than Shchusev's mausoleum, and ideas for the design of such a monument were submitted although never followed through.

Stalin's official fall from grace came in 1956. In a speech, the famous "Secret Speech", given to a closed session of the twentieth Party Congress, Khrushchev denounced his predecessor in no uncertain terms. Stalin had, he said:

> *used extreme methods and mass repression...* [He] *showed in a whole series of cases his intolerance, his brutality and his abuse of power. Instead of proving his political correctness and mobilizing the masses, he often chose the path of repression and physical annihilation, not only against actual enemies, but also against individuals who had not committed any crimes against the Party and Soviet government...*

This speech set the tone for de-Stalinization: the wholesale rejection of the cult of personality, the relaxation of police terror and a lessening of state censorship during what became known as "the Thaw". In 1961 Stalin's body was removed from the Mausoleum and reburied a few feet away in the Kremlin wall; people joked that Khrushchev had resettled Lenin's communal apartment.

KGB Agents and the Cold War

The Soviet Union may have won the war, but any hopes that the victory might usher in a new age of peace and international cooperation were to be disappointed. Mutual suspicion between the erstwhile Allies brought a rapid deterioration in their relationship and plunged the world into the Cold War, an ideological and geo-strategic conflict that was the dominant issue in international relations for the next forty years. The United States and the Soviet Union sought to outdo one another in the race to acquire a nuclear arsenal, and great efforts were made by each side in trying to gain intelligence about what the other was getting up to.

Moscow became the final home of three of the Cambridge Spies, the British establishment figures who were recruited to work for the KGB during their student years in Cambridge and who passed on valuable secrets to the Russians during the war years and beyond. During the 1930s, a time when the western world was mired in economic depression, many left wing intellectuals took an optimistic attitude towards the Soviet experiment and looked to the USSR as the great hope for the future. Guy Burgess and Donald Maclean were both diplomats who had worked at the British Embassy in Washington after the war, passing secrets on to their contacts in Moscow. On learning that their cover had been blown and that they were under suspicion, they defected to Moscow together in 1951. Khrushchev denied that they were in Russia and it was only five years later that they came out into the open, giving a press conference to western journalists. Burgess lived in the Moskva Hotel with a state-approved male lover until his death in 1963; it is said that he continued to order his suits from a tailor in Saville Row. Maclean, by contrast, sought to integrate himself into Soviet life, learning Russian and working as an advisor on British affairs. His American wife Melinda and three children came out to join him in 1953 although the marriage did not survive. He died in 1983 and, like Burgess, left a final request that his ashes be returned to Britain.

Kim Philby's defection came in 1963. A member of the British intelligence services, he too had worked in Washington during the late 1940s but was recalled after the defection of Burgess and Maclean. Finally uncovered as a double agent by the British authorities while he was undertaking freelance intelligence work in Lebanon, he fled to Moscow and lived there until his death in 1988, working as a consultant to the KGB. Philby married his fourth wife, Rufina Pukhhova, in Moscow and wrote memoirs entitled *My Silent War*. He is buried in Kuntsevskoe cemetery, which is something of a trek to visit by bus from Kuntsevskaya metro.

At the time of writing this book in 2005, another British spy who was not part of the Cambridge circle, George Blake, is still alive and living in Moscow. He came from a cosmopolitan background, was active in the Dutch resistance during the war and was recruited by the KGB during his period of captivity in Korea where he had been working for British intelligence. After his release he continued to work for the British Secret Service, all the while passing secrets to the Russians; he was eventually uncovered and arrested. Charged under the Official Secrets Act, he was sentenced to forty-two years in prison by the trial judge in 1961. Blake served only five years before escaping from Wormwood Scrubs and defecting to Moscow where he has lived ever since. In a recent interview he described his years spent in Russia as "the happiest of my life".

The Exhibition of Economic Achievement

Another feature of the Cold War rivalry was enthusiastic self-promotion by the Soviet authorities of their achievements in many different spheres of life. Soviet citizens had to understand how superior their way of life was to that endured by the exploited peoples of the capitalist West. Trumpeting Soviet achievements was, of course, not a new phenomenon: in 1939 an All-Union Agricultural Exhibition had opened in Moscow dedicated to showcasing what had been achieved in ten years of collectivized agriculture. The exhibition was held at Ostankino in the north of the city in a special park. A vast statue of Stalin was put up inside the exhibition and the famous Vera Mukhina statue of the *Worker and Collective Farm Girl*, he holding a hammer aloft and she a sickle, was placed outside the main gates. This statue would become familiar to all Russians as the symbol of Mosfilm, the state film company. The exhibition was revived in the 1950s and in 1958 it was broadened out and renamed the Exhibition of the Economic Achievements of the USSR. The acronym VDNKh remains the name of the nearest metro station on the orange line. More than seventy pavilions, built in many different styles, exhibited the achievements of Soviet planning in fields such as atomic energy, electrical engineering, coal and grain production. Fountains and statues adorned the park, including the Fountain of the Friendship of the Peoples in which golden statues of women representing the different republics of the USSR stand in a circle gazing outwards, while in the centre, water spouts from a golden wheatsheaf.

The park is still open today and the pavilions and fountains are still there, although the exhibits have mostly gone. After the demise of communism the government cut off funding to the attraction and in 1992 its name was changed to the All-Russian Exhibition Centre (VVTs). In order to raise the capital to keep the site open, the park has diversified. Trade fairs are now held here, and most of the pavilions now contain shops selling a diverse range of goods: computers and cars as well as houseplants and honey. It is a popular spot for family outings in the summer and a fun-fair has opened here as well, including a ferris wheel erected for the celebrations of the 850th anniversary of the founding of Moscow in 1997.

On the other side of the main gates from the Mukhina statue stands the Space Obelisk, an extraordinarily phallic monument erected

in 1964 to commemorate Yury Gagarin's orbit of the earth, one of the proudest achievements of Soviet technology during the Cold War era. The first Soviet sputnik had circled the earth in 1957 and the twenty-seven-year-old Gagarin followed this up with a manned flight on 12 April 1961. He was welcomed back to earth as a hero and was cheered by crowds when he entered Moscow. Another statue of him was erected in 1980 in the south of the city, outside Leninsky Prospekt metro station on the orange line at the major traffic intersection at ploshchad Gagarina, named in his honour. Gagarin died tragically young in an air crash in 1968 and was buried in the Kremlin wall.

The Late Soviet Era

Khrushchev was ousted from his position as Secretary General of the Communist Party by his colleagues in 1964—and hence was deprived of a prized position in the Kremlin wall after his death—and Leonid Brezhnev took over. The long Brezhnev period, 1964-82, was a time of economic stagnation, and life for ordinary Muscovites involved a great deal of queuing. Amid conditions of near-universal shortage of consumer goods, standing in queues became a way of life and people habitually joined queues without even necessarily knowing what they were queuing for. One joke from the 1970s went as follows:

A Muscovite goes shopping for bread, but as he approaches the bakery, he sees that the queue is one block long. Discouraged, he decides to go and buy potatoes instead, only to discover that the queue for potatoes is even longer. He checks out the butcher's shop but the queue there is longer still. Infuriated, he decides that it is all Comrade Brezhnev's fault, gets a sharp knife and heads for the Kremlin in order to kill him. As he approaches, he notices a queue there that is even longer than any of the previous queues he has seen that day. Out of habit, he joins it anyway and after a minute he asks the man ahead of him: "What's this queue for?" The man replies: "We're all queuing to kill Comrade Brezhnev!"

People also used informal methods of exchange through personal networks of friends and acquaintances as a means of acquiring goods and services: some swapped goods stolen from factory workplaces in return for plumbing skills or whatever. This system—known as *blat*—became quite ubiquitous in the late Soviet era and beyond, as a practical way of dealing with conditions of extreme shortage. Another Brezhnev era joke plays on this theme of scarcity:

A man goes into a shop and asks the assistant: "Don't you have any meat?" "You must be in the wrong shop," she replies. "This is the shop where we don't have any fish. The shop where they don't have any meat is just across the street."

The Brezhnev period was a time when the gap between the privileged elite—and few were more privileged than Brezhnev himself—and the mass of ordinary people became ever more apparent. Members of the Party leadership, the *nomenklatura* as they became known, enjoyed access to better housing, medical care and consumer goods than anybody else, as well as chauffeur-driven cars, foreign holidays and luxury dachas in the countryside.

The position of this elite and the Soviet regime as a whole did not go uncontested, however. From the late 1960s onwards groups of intellectuals began to play an increasingly significant role in public life, in particular through the dissident movement. Despite vicious persecution by the secret police, internal opponents of the regime campaigned on human rights issues and circulated banned works of literature among themselves by means of *samizdat* or self-publishing. *Samizdat* involved members of a dissident circle making carbon copies of illegal works in order to pass them on to their friends. Pasternak's *Doctor Zhivago* was first circulated in this way, as was Venedikt Yerofeev's novel *Moskva-Petushki*, sometimes translated as *Moscow to the End of the Line*, a work dating from 1970 about a drunken intellectual's train journey and the people he meets along the way. Western critiques of the Soviet system also became the subjects of *samizdat* publishing: Arthur Koestler's *Darkness at Noon*, George Orwell's *1984* and other illegal works of this nature thus became available to Soviet dissident groups. A Muscovite friend of mine has a copy of Solzhenitsyn's *Cancer Ward*, painstakingly copied out by hand, in a cupboard at home.

Andrei Sakharov was a prominent dissident during the late Soviet era. Muscovite-born and a nuclear physicist by training, he worked for many years on the Soviet nuclear arms programme before coming to the conclusion that the dangers posed by the new weapons meant that it was essential to work for international cooperation. In his *Manifesto on Progress, Co-existence and Intellectual Freedom* issued in 1968 Sakharov called for world cooperation to transcend national and ideological borders in order to avert the threat of nuclear war. In 1975 he was awarded the Nobel Peace Prize for his efforts to promote human rights in the USSR; like Pasternak, he was refused permission to go to Oslo to accept his award. Sakharov's repeated high-profile criticisms of the authorities meant that he was regarded as a threat and after he publicly protested against the Soviet invasion of Afghanistan in an interview with an American television station in 1980, the government was spurred into action. Sakharov and his wife, Yelena Bonner, were sent into internal exile in Gorky, a city on the Volga that has now returned to its previous name of Nizhny Novgorod. He was only permitted to return to Moscow in 1986 after Gorbachev had taken over the Soviet leadership; the street, stretching between Turgenevskaya and Komsomolskaya metro stations, where he lived for the last three years of his life, has been renamed prospekt Akademika Sakharova in his honour.

Sakharov died in 1989 at the age of 68 and his open air "civic funeral" became a mass affair: tens of thousands of people came out to the Luzhniki stadium near Novodevichy monastery to pay their respects to him. Dmitry Likhachev, a veteran of the Gulag and respected literary scholar, gave a short address at the funeral in which he described

Sakharov as a "prophet in the ancient, time-immemorial sense of the word". He was buried in a quiet ceremony at Vostryakhovskoe cemetery in the south-west of the city, not far from Yugo-Zapadnaya metro station. A Sakharov Museum has been set up on Zemlyanoi Val, the eastern section of the Garden Ring, which contains exhibits about the Gulag, and on Sakharov's life and work.

In the summer of 1980 Moscow played host to the Olympic Games. It was a controversial episode: the United States first asked for the Games to be moved and then led a boycott in protest at the recent Soviet invasion of Afghanistan. Other countries followed the American lead, with Japan and West Germany similarly refusing to send teams to Moscow. The Games went ahead nonetheless and considerable resources were pumped into making improvements to the city in advance of the influx of visitors. Buildings were spruced up, an Olympic Village was created in the south-west of the city, new hotels were erected and a new terminal building at Sheremetyevo airport—the international terminal with the interesting upside down cake-tin effect on the ceiling of the arrivals hall—was opened. The police sought to sweep the city clean of disreputable elements: political dissidents were kept well away from the main events, petty thieves were given draconian sentences and locked up and gypsies were rounded up off the streets. Another Brezhnev joke, playing on his increasing ill health and incapacity (he had already suffered at least one stroke) went as follows: "At the 1980 Olympics, the crowd fell silent as Leonid Brezhnev stood up and started his opening address: 'Oh-Oh-Oh- Oh...' he began. At the fourth 'Oh', an aide tapped him on the shoulder. 'Don't read that bit, it's the Olympic logo.'"

Brezhnev died in 1982 following a long illness, to be followed in rapid succession by two equally elderly and unfit Party leaders, Yury Andropov and Konstantin Chernenko. It was only with the coming to power of Mikhail Gorbachev in 1985 that things began to change. Gorbachev's policy of *glasnost* or openness was launched in order to prepare society for change, to win support for his reform programme and to bring a more energetic tenor to Soviet public life. If people were given more information about their society's past and present, he surmised, they would be better equipped to participate in changing it for the better.

Signs of Change

The late 1980s in Moscow witnessed an explosion of interest in public affairs. Newspapers began to publish stories about social problems—alcoholism, the housing crisis, abortions—that had never previously been acknowledged; the artistic world enjoyed the lifting of censorship, and works by discredited writers including Solzhenitsyn, Mandelstam and émigrés such as Vladimir Nabokov were finally published. The authorities stopped jamming foreign radio broadcasts, and information from the West became freely available. Militant environmentalists began to publicize some of the city's worst ecological problems: industrial pollution from factories was being dumped in the Yauza river and radioactive waste sites were located within built-up areas of the city.

In 1987 Gorbachev delivered an address on the anniversary of the October Revolution which served as the starting pistol for a wave of interest in the Soviet past. "If today we look into our history with an occasionally critical gaze," he declared, "it is only because we want to get a better, a fuller idea of our path into the future." He demanded an end to the "blank spots" in history, those episodes that the regime had thought it best to keep quiet about. New organizations were set up, such as Memorial, which worked to uncover some of the less salubrious aspects of the Soviet past, while other groups worked for the restoration of church buildings. These attempts to come to terms with the recent past proved distressing for many Russians as mass graves were uncovered and the whole country was invited to confront a past that was by no means as glorious or uplifting as they had previously been led to believe.

Anger against a political system that had repeatedly lied to people over the years fed the reformist movement of those who felt that Gorbachev's efforts did not go far enough. Others held a very different view of what Gorbachev was trying to achieve. As his attempts at economic reform gave rise to inflation and unemployment, and as people in the non-Russian republics began to call for independence, many conservatives in the Party leadership rallied to the opposition and demanded that reform be rolled back. Matters came to a head in August 1991.

The White House

The Russian White House, the parliament building, stands overlooking a bend in the river to the west of the city centre, just beyond the Garden Ring. Built in the early 1980s as government offices, it is closely associated with two key events of the early 1990s: the coup against Mikhail Gorbachev in August 1991 and the bloody stand-off between President Yeltsin and the Russian parliament of October 1993. The image that most readily springs to mind from the first of those events, the August coup, is that of Boris Yeltsin, recently elected President of the Russian Republic, standing on top of a tank outside the White House and rallying the popular opposition to those who had sought to oust Gorbachev in an illegitimate seizure of power. This heroic image of the brave and defiant leader was sadly tarnished two years later by the broadcast images of the building in flames, after having been shelled by Russian tanks on Yeltsin's orders.

The first most Muscovites knew of what was going on that August day in 1991 was when they turned on their television sets that morning only to find that normal broadcasting had been suspended and all channels were showing the Tchaikovsky ballet *Swan Lake*. It was clear that something momentous must have occurred. Early in the morning of 19 August a state of emergency was announced and the eight conspirators—conservative opponents of Gorbachev's liberalizing policies who had significant vested interests to defend—announced that Gorbachev, who was on holiday in Crimea at the time, was ill and could no longer take charge of the country. Political parties were suspended, strikes and demonstrations banned, the media silenced and tanks were sent onto the streets of Moscow.

But the plotters had underestimated the strength of popular opposition to their moves. Gorbachev's policy of *glasnost* had opened a floodgate in Russian society that could not be slammed shut. People were simply not prepared to be fobbed off any longer with a lack of information alongside the old clichés about Soviet patriotism; and crowds came out onto the streets to help defend the White House from the advancing tanks. Three people were killed on the night of 20-21 August before the coup conspirators, mostly incapacitated by heavy drinking, gave themselves up. They had utterly failed in their project: the party in whose name they had claimed to act was promptly declared illegal on an order from Yeltsin, and the Union that they had sought to preserve would be destroyed within the year. Gorbachev returned from Crimea, where he had been held under house arrest, but from now on Yeltsin had seized the initiative and dictated the speed and course of events. By the end of the year it was all over. The Soviet Communist Party had been disgraced and was declared illegal, and the Union of Soviet Socialist Republics had broken up, with the republics falling over one another to declare their independence from Moscow. Gorbachev found himself stranded, left without a country to lead now that the state he had governed for the last six years was in pieces, and he resigned on 31 December 1991.

A small stone memorial to those killed in these events stands at the western end of Novy Arbat just above the entrance to the traffic tunnel on the Garden Ring. Their funerals were a major state occasion preceded by a rally with speeches from Gorbachev and Yeltsin, the whole thing broadcast on national television. The inscription on the stone here reads:

In August 1991, defenders of democracy in Russia were killed here:
Dmitry Alekseevich Komar
Ilya Maratovich Krichevsky
Vladimir Aleksandrovich Usov

A Russian tricolor flag flies alongside. Another memorial to the victims can be seen in the Vagankovskoe cemetery.

Memorials and "Patriots"

Walking around the back of the White House one comes across a little park and beyond it lies waste ground where a series of curious memorials has been erected: a makeshift barricade made of mattress springs and metal piping, a tall red post with black and white photographs of people stuck down its centre and a little wooden shrine surrounded by plastic floral offerings. Glass-fronted billboards tell the story—from the point of view of the defeated parties—of the events of October 1993. In words and pictures they tell of how, in their words, "the patriots of Russia, who dreamed of the flourishing and unity of our motherland, were killed here under tank fire." Photographs show images of the White House being destroyed by heavy shelling, of corpses; there are copies of government resolutions and newspaper reports from the time and brief biographical details of the 145 victims. A shrine close to the White House itself reads simply "Patriots were killed here." The imagery on the various memorials offers an eclectic mix of the traditional Soviet red flags, red stars and plastic flower arrangements depicting the hammer and sickle sitting cheek by jowl with religious symbols such as crosses and icons.

The events that these memorials commemorate came at the end of a long struggle between Yeltsin and the leaders of the largely still communist Russian parliament. Relations between Yeltsin, his vice-president Alexander Rutskoi and the speaker of the parliament, the Chechen Ruslan Khasbulatov, deteriorated over the course of 1993, worsened by parliament's failed attempt in the spring to impeach the president. Rutskoi and Khasbulatov, both of whom had stood alongside Yeltsin at the White House in August 1991, had become increasingly critical of the direction in which the president seemed to be leading the country. Ultimately the struggle boiled down to fundamental differences over the question of what the future political system should look like. On the one side was Yeltsin's vision of a presidential system in which strong authority should be invested in the head of state; opposing this, Khasbulatov aspired to a parliamentary system that could hold the government accountable for its actions, preferably with himself taking on the role of prime minister. Uneasy about the collapse of the USSR and unhappy about the direction in which Yeltsin seemed to be leading the country, parliament spent much of 1993 passing laws to obstruct the "shock therapy" policies that Yeltsin was seeking to introduce.

Events came to a head towards the end of September when Yeltsin called for new elections and a constitutional referendum. His opponents denounced him as a tyrant and Rutskoi called for a popular uprising to seize the Moscow TV tower, declaring himself Acting President. Yeltsin took the defiant actions as an excuse to attack and on 4 October he declared a state of emergency, cut off water and electricity supplies to the White House and sent in tanks to shell the building. Official figures stated that 145 people were killed in the fighting that ensued; the opposition leaders, overwhelmed by the superior force at the president's disposal, admitted defeat later that afternoon. Khasbulatov and Rutskoi were arrested, opposition newspapers suspended, a new post-communist constitution was introduced and fresh parliamentary elections were called for December.

While Yeltsin could claim that all he was doing was crushing an illegal uprising in order to destroy the last remnants of Soviet communism, many Russian democrats were shocked by his actions. The new constitution, to no one's surprise, tipped the balance between president and parliament firmly in favour of the former, giving huge powers to the president's office and heralding the way for a period of relative political stability. Yeltsin's hard-line, unconstitutional approach to dealing with a recalcitrant parliament only helped undermine his credibility with many of his erstwhile supporters and weakened his chance of imparting a sense of genuine legitimacy to the new Russia that he was seeking to construct.

Post-Soviet Moscow and Chechen Terrorism

Post-Soviet Moscow has witnessed various symbolic attempts by the new authorities to come to terms with the Soviet past. The appearance of the city has certainly changed dramatically; advertising hoardings now replace the old signs celebrating the forward march of socialism, and cafés and restaurants are now easy to find. New monuments have gone up, including the fountain by the river outside the Kiev station which includes a statue depicting the Rape of Europa; the new square here is dedicated to the ties of friendship between the European countries and Russia.

In 1996 Yeltsin sought to re-brand the old October Revolution Day holiday (which is celebrated on 7 November because Russia only adopted the Gregorian calendar in 1918), declaring that it would henceforward be know as the Day of Peace and Reconciliation. This attempt to subvert a traditionally communist festival was not a great success, and Communist Party rallies have continued to be a distinctive feature of the 7 November celebrations; in recent years it has been suggested that this particular holiday might be abolished altogether. Yeltsin's attempts to create new public holidays to mark more recent events in Russian history have similarly proved unpopular: neither Russian Independence Day on 12 June nor Constitution Day on 12 December have won any significant following and most people regard them as simply an extra day off work rather than as an opportunity to engage in public celebration.

Muscovites have been at the front line in the Chechen terrorist onslaught from the late 1990s onwards, and some terrible atrocities have been committed in the city over recent years. The origins of the Chechen conflict go back many years: the Chechens resisted the Russian expansion into the Caucasus during the nineteenth century and during the Civil War they set up their own mountain republic. In 1944 Stalin deported the entire Chechen people to Central Asia as a collective punishment for perceived collaboration with the Germans; many thousands of them died *en route* and they were only permitted to return to their homeland again after Stalin's death. When the USSR fell apart in 1991 the authorities in Chechnya, which only had the status of an autonomous republic of Russia (it was not a union republic like Ukraine or Kazakhstan) nonetheless declared its independence as well.

It was not until 1994 that the Russian government decided to step in and reassert control. Yeltsin's fears about the potential break-up of the Russian state, as well as his concern that Chechnya could act as a central point for an Islamic *jihad* and the need to secure the Caspian oil pipeline that runs through the republic prompted his decision to take action. He began the first Chechen war at the end of 1994 with the aim of restoring Moscow's authority within the errant republic: President Clinton on one occasion praised his actions, comparing Yeltsin to Abraham Lincoln in going to war to save the union. The war was a disaster for Russia. Although the Russian army destroyed the capital city of Chechnya, Grozny, and left the Chechen economy in ruins,

Chechen militants were able to inflict heavy losses on their opponents and in 1996 the troops were pulled out. An agreement gave the republic a semi-autonomous status but many issues were left unresolved.

In September 1999 terrorist bombs destroyed a pair of apartment blocks in Moscow, in the Lyublino district in the south-east of the city. Over two hundred people were killed in the blasts which occurred at night to cause maximum loss of life. Most Muscovites were convinced that the bombs had been placed by Chechen terrorists, and this incident sparked off a backlash against ethnic minorities from the Caucasus region; calls were made for all such people to be expelled from the capital. The apartment block bombings also served as justification for the renewal of Russia's war in Chechnya. Some foreign observers speculated at the time that the bombs might have been planted by the Russian secret services themselves in order to provide an excuse for a renewed crack-down. These allegations were repeated by the exiled oligarch and former Russian media-magnate Boris Berezovsky, but nothing has ever been proved.

Flowers are routinely left at the memorial stone in the underpass at Pushkinskaya metro. This marks the spot where, in August 2000, a bomb went off killing eight people and injuring many more. Further atrocities followed in subsequent years. In October 2002 Chechen terrorists staged a siege in a Moscow theatre on ulitsa Melnikova near Proletarskaya metro, taking around seven hundred audience members hostage. They were held for three days before special forces stormed the building and shot the hostage takers, using a mysterious gas to incapacitate their opponents. More than one hundred of the hostages died, most from gas poisoning.

Other attacks in Moscow have included an explosion at an open-air rock concert in July 2003 at Tushino in the north-west of the city, a suicide bomb attack outside the National Hotel in the very heart of Moscow in December 2003 and a series of suicide bombings on the metro. In the aftermath of the Beslan school siege in Northern Ossetia in September 2004 a mass rally was held in Moscow protesting against the terrorist outrages. Tens of thousands of people came out onto the streets of the city centre to express their outrage at the killing of children in Beslan, although some people avoided the rally, suspicious that it might be an attempt by the authorities to manipulate popular grief. It seems unlikely that the situation in Chechnya will be resolved at any time soon and, for all President Putin's rhetoric about the "war on terror", Moscow is certainly a less safe place as a result of Russian actions in the breakaway republic.

Chapter Five
CITY OF WRITERS

Moscow has been a city of writers for more than two hundred years and its many literary museums and statues bear testimony to the high regard with which writers have been held. Indeed, in few other cities are writers as frequently memorialized in statue form. The Chilean poet and communist Pablo Neruda, who visited Moscow several times, wrote sadly of how "The pigeons visited Pushkin and pecked at his melancholy":

> *Statues are really bitter things*
> *Because time piles up*
> *In deposits on them, oxidizing them.*

This chapter explores aspects of the lives and work of a handful of the most famous and most statue-prone Muscovite writers as well as some of those with significant connections with the city.

Alexander Pushkin

Pride of place in the annals of Russian literature must go to the poet Alexander Pushkin who shaped the Russian literary language as we know it today and who occupies a special place in the hearts of many Russians. Although Pushkin spent much of his tragically brief adult life in St. Petersburg, Moscow was his birthplace, his childhood home and the place where he was married. His imprint has been left on the city in more ways than one.

The one Pushkin site that no visitor to the city can miss is the statue of the poet on Pushkin Square where Tverskaya ulitsa intersects with the Boulevard Ring. With his back to the Rossiya cinema and the fountains and refreshment stands of the square that bears his name, this statue of the great poet is a popular rendezvous spot in the summer months. Unveiled in June 1880, it originally stood on Tverskoi Boulevard and was moved in 1950 to its present position, where the poet now stands on his pedestal gazing downwards, as if not quite wanting to raise his eyes to survey the vast McDonalds restaurant on the other side of the road. The erection of the statue was funded by public subscription and the inscription on the plinth quotes lines from the poet himself:

And long will I be honoured by the people
For awakening kind feelings with my lyre
For praising freedom, in my cruel age
And calling for mercy to the fallen.

The unveiling ceremony for this statue was a lavish affair with speeches given by two of the most prominent writers of the day, Ivan Turgenev and Fyodor Dostoevsky. "Shine forth, like him, thou noble bronze visage, erected in the very heart of our ancient capital," Turgenev beseeched the statue, "and announce to future generations our right to call ourselves a great nation, because this nation has given birth… to *such* a man!"

So who was this great man of whom they spoke in such glowing terms? Alexander Pushkin was born in Moscow in 1799 at 40 Baumanskaya ulitsa, although the house no longer exists and a school has been built on the site. A bust of the poet put in place during the Brezhnev era now marks the spot. His family moved frequently during his childhood years and in 1811 they uprooted themselves from Moscow and moved to St. Petersburg, where the young Pushkin went to school, began to write poetry and spent his young adult years living as dissolute a life as he possibly could. Exiled to the south for writing seditious verses entitled *Ode to Freedom*, his next visit to Moscow came in 1826 when he was summoned for a private meeting by no less a figure than the Tsar, Nicholas I, who had only recently ascended the imperial throne.

This famous meeting took place in September 1826 in the Kremlin while Nicholas was visiting the old capital for the occasion of his coronation. Pushkin had many friends among the participants in the Decembrist conspiracy, an attempt to oust Nicholas before he had even begun his reign, and the poet was well aware that these connections might cause serious problems for him with the authorities. A few months prior to this meeting, Pushkin had written to the Tsar, assuring him that he neither was, nor intended to become, a member of any secret society. During their meeting Nicholas made it clear that he was prepared to end Pushkin's southern exile and ominously announced that henceforth he himself would act as the poet's personal censor. Nicholas is said to have remarked later that he had just conversed with the most intelligent man in Russia.

Crossing Tverskaya and walking away from the statue along the boulevard heading south-west, the next major intersection reached is the site of the former Nikitskie gates in the Belyi gorod wall, Nikitskie vorota. Today it is a busy traffic junction with its criss-crossing trolleybus wires and an overwhelming sense of bustle and haste. Another Pushkin statue has recently been erected here, this one of Pushkin and his wife, Natalya Goncharova, whom he married at the nearby yellow, domed Church of the Great Ascension. The statues themselves, popularly nicknamed "Sasha and Natasha", are rather over-sentimental, appearing under a gold-domed rotunda set in the middle of a fountain at the edge of the traffic intersection, but the church itself is certainly worth a visit. Pushkin met the beautiful sixteen-year-old Natalya at a ball in December 1828 and fell madly in love with her. Spurned at the first attempt—her parents felt she was too young to get married—his second proposal was accepted, and in February 1831 the couple exchanged vows. One story has it that two days before the wedding, Pushkin visited a gypsy singer, Tatyana Demyanova, and asked her to sing him something to bring him luck for his wedding day.

She took her guitar and sang a song that was so mournful that Pushkin, convinced that it foretold bad tidings, burst into tears and buried his head in his hands. The bridegroom's doleful appearance at his stag party, where he read poems bidding a fond farewell to his youth, was commented on by guests.

Even the wedding itself did not avoid mishap. During the exchange of rings, one ring was dropped, a crucifix and the bible were knocked to the floor and Pushkin's candle was blown out in the general confusion. "All the bad omens", murmured the anxious poet. He was right to be concerned. Although their early married life in Moscow was idyllic—"I am married—and happy," Pushkin wrote shortly after his wedding, "my only wish is that nothing will change in my life—I could not expect better"—it was not to last. They began their lives together in the two-storey blue building on the Arbat that now houses a Pushkin museum, but the poet rapidly found his new situation rather trying. "I do not like Moscow life," he wrote. "You live here not as you want to live—but as old women want you to. Such an old woman is my mother-in-law." The couple soon moved to St. Petersburg, where Pushkin's debts rapidly spiraled out of control, and it was here that his most famous works were published: *Eugene Onegin, The Bronze Horseman* and *The Queen of Spades*.

Pushkin met his death only six years after his wedding, mortally wounded in a duel fought over his wife's alleged affair with Baron Georges-Charles d'Anthès. In a scene ominously foretold in his great poem, *Eugene Onegin*, the two arranged to meet on a snowy day in January a short distance outside St. Petersburg. D'Anthès fired first and the wound Pushkin received from this shot killed him two days later. In his last words to Natalya the poet assured his wife: "Do not worry. You are not guilty in this matter." Literary Russia was shocked by his death and Mikhail Lermontov penned a verse, *Death of a Poet* on the occasion:

> *A poet's dead—entrapped by honour,*
> *Felled by slanderous rumours spread*
> *A bullet in the breast, with vengeful anger,*
> *He bowed at last his noble head.*
> *His soul could not endure the legions*
> *Of trifling insults and their shame,*
> *He stood against the world's opinions,*
> *Alone, as always—and was slain!*

The tragic hero is a recurring character in Russian history and literature and, as we shall see, Pushkin was not the last writer to meet a violent end.

Nikolai Gogol

Two statues of Nikolai Gogol stand on the Boulevard Ring just near Arbatskaya ploshchad, the next intersection along from Nikitskie vorota if one walks south towards the river. The more obvious of the two was put up in the early 1950s in the middle of Gogolevsky Boulevard facing the square; it replaced an earlier depiction of the writer, erected to mark the centenary of his birth in 1909 and deemed too pessimistic and philosophical in its aspect for the Soviet authorities to cope with. This earlier statue now stands a short distance away in the courtyard of 7 Nikitsky Boulevard, outside the house once owned by Count Alexander Tolstoy where Gogol spent his final days. It now houses a branch of the state literary museum. Nikolai Gogol was born in Ukraine and spent most of his adult life either in St. Petersburg or on travels around Europe. His visits to Moscow were short and sporadic until the very end of his life, yet Moscow was where the writer spent his last winters and was where he died and was buried, in February 1852, a month short of his forty-third birthday.

Plagued by self-doubt throughout his life, Gogol had a tendency to destroy his manuscripts from an early stage in his writing career: on one occasion he bought up every copy of a published poem that had received a hostile review and burned them all. He also had notably itchy feet and was a frequent traveller, once writing that "travelling and change of place are as necessary to me as my daily bread." On his visits to Moscow he usually stayed with friends; the historian Mikhail Pogodin was a regular host, and the writer Sergei Aksakov organized a literary salon that Gogol often attended when he was in the city. After a short visit in the early 1830s he returned from his travels to spend two winters here in 1839-40 and again in 1841-2 when he made his home at Pogodin's estate near Deviche Pole, Maidens' Field, to the west of the city, and worked on the first volume of his projected trilogy *Dead Souls*. A wooden dacha with decorative exterior carvings on Pogodinskaya ulitsa is all that now remains of the estate. Gogol had a large room to himself at the top of the house and amused himself in the evenings by throwing pellets of bread at other guests at the dinner table. A special performance of *The Government Inspector* was put on at the Maly Theatre in his honour during his stay; at the end of the performance when the rapturous audience began calling for the author to take a bow, he crept from his box and fled the building.

During his second winter in Moscow, Gogol fell out with his host quite spectacularly over a question of publishing rights, and they ended up not speaking to one another at all and communicating only through written notes. Six months after his departure Gogol wrote to inform his old friend that "I escaped from your house as from a gloomy prison in which I had spent many years." Pogodin, not to be outdone, replied that "when you closed the door, I crossed myself and breathed freely as though a heavy load had been lifted from my shoulders."

Gogol's next stay in Moscow came towards the end of his life, from 1848 onwards. Relations with Pogodin were still difficult, as the historian had been most irritated by Gogol's recent publication of *Selected Passages from Correspondence with Friends*, a socially conservative work that attempted to set forth the religious principles that underlay all of his fictional writings. Progressive critics were dismayed by Gogol's un-reformist agenda and others disliked his preaching tone, but Pogodin had additional reason to feel incensed because one letter in the collection was entirely given over to a series of personal attacks against him. Yet relations were somehow patched up as Pogodin threw a splendid party for his erstwhile friend, and Gogol stayed with him again for a couple of months before moving in with the religious and reactionary Count Tolstoy in his mansion on Nikitsky Boulevard.

The first volume of *Dead Souls* had been published in 1842 to great critical acclaim but not of the kind that the author had hoped for. He never saw himself as a radical social critic; his intention was to promote a religious message and he struggled over writing the subsequent parts of his novel over many years. One version was cast into the flames in 1845 but he took up the task again and continued to work on it during his winter stays in Moscow at Count Tolstoy's home. By autumn 1851 he was in a state of nervous collapse; the writer Ivan Turgenev who visited him at this time was startled by the change in his appearance and described how "a sort of hidden pain and anguish, a sort of melancholy restlessness hovered over his shrewd face." In February, in the midst of a religious crisis and convinced that he had failed in his spiritual mission in life, he stopped eating almost entirely, consigned his manuscript once more into the fire and died.

Gogol's funeral was a grand affair. His body lay in state with a laurel wreath around his head in St. Tatyana's chapel at the University, on Bolshaya Nikitskaya ulitsa. Crowds queued through the night to pay their respects to the much loved writer before the coffin was carried down to the Danilovsky monastery where he was buried in the cemetery. In 1931 his remains were moved to Novodevichy cemetery and a bust of the writer was commissioned to be put above the tombstone. Part of his original tombstone can be seen here, but another section was put in storage and ended up being incorporated into Mikhail Bulgakov's grave in the same plot. The epitaph on Gogol's tombstone reads, appropriately, "And I shall laugh my bitter laugh."

Mikhail Lermontov and Fyodor Dostoevsky

Lermontovskaya ploshchad, just outside the metro station Krasnye vorota on the red line, commemorates another great poet of Russia's Golden Age. Like Pushkin and Gogol, Mikhail Lermontov lived most of his life outside Moscow but his connections with the city are nonetheless significant. The statue of the writer stands on top of a tall pedestal with his coat swaying in the wind as he surveys the traffic with a somewhat disdainful expression. The sculpture behind the statue includes an inscription of the poet's lines: "Moscow, Moscow, I love you as a son, as a Russian—strongly, fierily and tenderly."

He was indeed a son of Moscow: born in a house on this site in October 1814 and christened in a nearby church, neither of which remains today. Having spent much of his youth in the countryside, on his grandmother's estate, the young Lermontov returned to Moscow in 1827 and studied first at the Nobleman's Pension on Tverskaya ulitsa and later at Moscow University for two years before transferring to St. Petersburg. There is a small Lermontov museum on ulitsa Malaya Molchanovka, just off ulitsa Povarskaya near the Novyi Arbat, in one of the houses where Lermontov lived with his grandmother during his Moscow years.

Lermontov led an intrepid life: expelled from St. Petersburg by the Tsar for writing a subversive poem about Pushkin's death, he was exiled to the Caucasus region. It was here amid the warring tribes of the southern mountains that he wrote the first Russian novel, *A Hero of Our Time*, about a restless young Guards officer and his adventures in the Caucasus. His writings had a dark side to them, a preoccupation with evil and the emptiness of human existence. At the age of twenty-seven Lermontov was killed in a duel just like his hero, Pushkin, four years earlier.

Another writer born in Moscow but who spent little time here in adult life was Fyodor Dostoevsky. He was born in 1821 in a wing of the

Mariya hospital to the north of the Garden Ring on what is now ulitsa Dostoevskogo, not far from Novoslobodskaya metro station. His father worked as a doctor in the hospital and the building now accommodates a museum devoted to the writer's life. The young Fyodor was educated in Moscow until 1838 when he was sent away to Engineering College in St. Petersburg. Although his return visits to his native city were quite frequent—as we have seen, he visited in 1880 to make a speech at the unveiling of the Pushkin statue—they were rarely prolonged and it was his adopted city of St. Petersburg that provided the backdrop for much of his literary work. In 1997 the city of Moscow honoured him with a statue in a very prominent and central position outside the former Lenin Library just across the road from the Kremlin on the corner of Mokhovaya and Vozdvizhenka. The library itself was renamed the Dostoevsky Library in his honour at the same time, but few people ever refer to it as such.

Lev Tolstoy
Taking the metro to Park Kultury on the circle line and walking down Komsomolsky prospekt, the second right turn takes you onto ulitsa Lva Tolstogo or Lev Tolstoy Street. This is the Khamovniki district of the city, the weavers' district, and a silk factory still operates here. The attractive seventeenth-century white, red and green church on the corner with a tent roof tower and five gold onion domes is dedicated to St. Nicholas of the Weavers. Walking up the street, you soon find the Tolstoy museum on the left in the large, mustard-coloured wooden house with green shutters and window frames where Tolstoy lived during the 1880s and 1890s. One visitor during these years, the celebrated bass singer Fyodor Chaliapin, described it as a "very charming house, modest and intimate in character". The house is set in a large garden of which Tolstoy was particularly fond. "What a pleasant place the garden is," he wrote in a letter to his wife on one occasion. "You sit at the window overlooking it and all is pleasant and peaceful." A brewery still stands on the street just as it did over one hundred years ago. The interior of the house is a beautifully preserved example of nineteenth-century gentry living, with its dark walnut furniture and oak parquet floors and the upstairs salon for entertaining visitors. The stuffed bear cub standing on its hind legs near the entrance holds out a tray on which visitors were invited to leave their cards.

Tolstoy spent a few years living in Moscow during his childhood and spent some winters in the city in the early 1850s after leaving university, during which time he was a frequent visitor at brothels and gambling dens. Of this period he noted in his diary that he lived

in a very disorderly manner, without a job, without any occupations and without a purpose...I have lived like this, not because, as is often said and written, everyone in Moscow lives like this, but simply because I liked this sort of life. But it is partly the case too that the situation of a young man in Moscow society disposes him to idleness.

On leaving the army in 1856 after his return from fighting in the Crimean War, Tolstoy again spent some time living in Moscow and it was here, in September 1862, that he married Sofiya (Sonya) Behrs, the young daughter of the Kremlin doctor. Her father's position at court allowed them to hold their wedding in the Church of the Nativity of the Virgin in the Kremlin, situated within the Terem Palace. Although Tolstoy based himself in his country estate at Yasnaya Polyana for the following two decades while he attempted to adopt a simple farming life, he made regular visits to Moscow. These were particularly frequent during the 1860s while he was working on the manuscript of *War and Peace*.

He bought the estate in Khamovniki in 1882, persuaded by his wife that their children needed to be in Moscow for their education. For the next twenty years the family spent most of their winters here, but in 1901 Tolstoy returned to live in Yasnaya Polyana on a permanent basis. Sofiya Tolstaya was concerned at the impact that living in Moscow had on her husband. In one diary entry shortly after their move to the city she wrote that

our life in Moscow would be quite delightful if only it did not make Lyovochka so unhappy. He is too sensitive to survive the city, and his Christian disposition cannot reconcile all this idle luxury with people's struggling lives here.

During this period of his life Tolstoy became very interested in social issues and spent time researching the conditions of the poor in the most run-down districts of the city and campaigning for social reform. He also wrote much of his last novel, *Resurrection*, at the desk with the small balustrade around it, depicted in the famous painting of Tolstoy by the painter Nikolai Ge. Staff at the museum describe how, rather than take to wearing glasses to correct his failing eyesight in old age, Tolstoy preferred to saw off the legs of his desk chair in order to bring his head closer to the page.

Other new developments during this period include Tolstoy's decision to embrace vegetarianism and his hobby of boot making, adopted as part of his effort to live more like a peasant. He invited a boot maker to come to the house and teach him his craft, and Tolstoy's cobbling equipment is on display in the workroom in the house. Tolstoy's son Ilya recalled how his father sometimes used to go out to the Sparrow Hills to saw wood with the peasants he met there. He even walked the hundred miles to Yasnaya Polyana on more than one occasion. Tolstoy played host to a great many members of the Moscow cultural intelligentsia in this house—Chekhov, Diaghilev, Chaliapin, Rachmaninov—and made frequent visits to the theatre, both the Maly and the new Moscow Art Theatre.

A vast seated statue of the writer can be found at the eastern end of the wooded park of Maiden's Field, the triangular piece of open space that borders Bolshaya Pirogovskaya ulitsa at the top of ulitsa Lva Tolstogo. The area is said to derive its name from the fact that young girls used to be left here as tribute to the Tatars. It was here that Pierre Bezukhov was held by his French captors in *War and Peace* and that he was forced to watch his fellow prisoners being shot. Here, too, he gazed out one morning and felt a sense of renewal at the scene that met his eyes:

> *He got up early, and went out of the shed at dawn, and saw the cupolas and crosses of the New Convent of the Virgin still dark at first, the hoar frost on the dusty grass, the Sparrow Hills, and the wooded banks above the winding river vanishing in the purple distance, when he felt the contact of the fresh air, and heard the noise of the crows flying from Moscow across the field, and when afterwards light gleamed from the east and the sun's rim appeared solemnly from behind a cloud, and the cupolas and crosses, the hoar frost, and distance and the river, all began to sparkle in the glad*

light—Pierre felt a new joy and strength in life such as he had never before known.

Tolstoy was excommunicated in 1901 following his attacks on the church in *Resurrection*. He continued to act as a social and religious critic in the final years of his life, attacking the actions taken by the authorities during the 1905 Revolution. In 1910 he set out from his home in Yasnaya Polyana on a pilgrimage to a monastery that he had visited before. After contracting a fever, he was taken to the stationmaster's house in the small town of Astapovo where he died. The church refused him an Orthodox funeral and he was buried at Yasnaya Polyana, the home that he loved. After his death, his widow gave their Moscow house to the city council and after the Revolution it was converted into a museum. Another Tolstoy museum can be visited in Moscow although the building itself has no connection with his life: it is to be found on Prechistenka ulitsa on the western site of the Zemlyanoi gorod.

Andrei Belyi and Alexander Blok

Twentieth-century writers began to move away from the earlier tradition of realism in Russian literature and to explore new ways of writing. A statue of Alexander Blok can be found in a little park just off ulitsa Spiridonovka, standing with his hands in the pockets of his long coat. The spot is near the house where Blok stayed on his first visit to Moscow in January 1904; he had come here from St. Petersburg with his wife, Lyubov Mendeleeva, the daughter of the famous chemist Dmitry Mendeleev, and one of the main purposes of their trip was for him to meet his fellow Symbolist poet, Andrei Belyi, with whom he had been corresponding over recent months. Belyi was a Muscovite, the son of a professor of mathematics at Moscow University, born and brought up in the house on the Arbat which now contains a small museum in his memory. Belyi was originally called Boris Bugaev but changed his name in order not to embarrass his father with his literary activity.

Both of these poets were members of the Symbolist movement and were sometimes described as "Scythians" due to their interest in the myths of primeval Russian identity. Belyi's interest in music led him to attempt to develop the symphony as a literary form, and his most famous novel, *Petersburg*, contained visions of impending apocalypse engulfing that city. The relationship between the two men fluctuated wildly between passionate devotion and implacable hostility, the latter emotion fuelled by Belyi's declaration of love for Mendeleeva: over the years of their acquaintance each poet challenged the other to a duel, but nothing came of it and they were able to patch up their differences. Blok reacted to the Revolution by writing the marvelously ambiguous poem "The Twelve", which weaves Christian imagery with the onward march of the Red Guards of Bolshevism; his final years before his early death in St. Petersburg in 1921 were filled with bitter disappointment at the path that Russia had taken.

Belyi welcomed the Revolution with enthusiasm and declared himself a Marxist, but after a short period in Berlin in the early 1920s he found his work coming under attack from Trotsky. According to Trotsky, Belyi "has no hint of ideal revolutionism. In his core he is a realistic and spiritual conservative who has lost the ground under his feet and is in despair... Belyi is a corpse, and will not be resurrected in any spirit."

Belyi lived in Moscow between 1923 and his death eleven years later; among his later works was a novel entitled *Moscow*, which was intended to be the first in a cycle. The hero of the novel is a mathematics professor at Moscow University, clearly based on the author's father. Belyi died of a stroke in 1934: a story went around Moscow that it was brought on by his hurrying around all the bookshops in the city trying to buy up every single copy of his memoirs, *Between Two Revolutions*, in order to tear out an unflattering preface by Party leader Lev Kamenev. Osip Mandelstam, who attended the funeral, wrote a poem on the event:

> ...*fur coats heaved. And shoulders rubbed.*
> *Blood, sweat—vermillion of health was seething.*
> *A dream wrapped in a dream; inside it, you were dreaming*
> *Of moving forward, if for half an inch...*

Vladimir Mayakovsky

Enthusiasts of the futurist poet Vladimir Mayakovsky are spoiled for choice in the range of Moscow memorials dedicated to him. The most obvious public tribute is his statue in Triumfalnaya ploshchad (formerly Mayakovskaya ploshchad) at the point where Tverskaya intersects with the Garden Ring. Had Mayakovsky not killed himself in 1930 he would almost certainly have found himself falling from favour with the authorities; as it was, Stalin proclaimed him to be a great Soviet poet and his future as a cultural icon was sealed. His works were reprinted many times and taught in Soviet schools. The statue is a marvellous example of socialist realist sculpture and was erected in 1958. The metro station on the square, the main underground hall of which provides an attractive example of some of the virtues of 1930s Soviet design with its white marble and silver metallic arches, still bears the poet's name. It was in this hall, incidentally, that Stalin made his rousing speech on the eve of Revolution Day 1941 as the Wehrmacht stood at the gates of Moscow.

Mayakovsky was born in a village in Georgia in 1893 and moved to Moscow as a child. He became involved in the revolutionary movement from a young age and spent six months in the Butyrki prison in 1909 for his political activities. He later trained as an artist and was attracted to the avant-garde movement known as Futurism during his student years. Alexander Pasternak described his appearance at this time:

In 1911, Moscow was full of gossip about a gang of hooligan rebels strolling about the Kuznetsky Bridge with provocatively made-up faces and extravagant clothes... one... was particularly conspicuous—a tall good-looker with a monocle and top hat, in a garish yellow and black shirt and sporting an ivory cane. Apparently they used to recite as they walked, offending passers-by with their mocking remarks and generally impudent behaviour.

The tall good-looker was, of course, Mayakovsky, whom Pasternak had known slightly at school. He moved frequently within Moscow, living at different times in the Presnya district, around Chistye Prudy, near Taganka, in Sokolniki and most famously in 3 Lubyansky proezd, just around the corner from the Lubyanka, which is now the Mayakovsky museum. He had a room in a communal apartment here from 1919 and kept hold of it until his death even while he was living elsewhere. In a curious domestic arrangement he spent much of the 1920s, when he was not abroad, living in a series of different apartments together with his mistress, Lili Brik and her husband. In one of these flats, on Mayakovskogo pereulok, near Taganka, they had a bathroom which was the envy of all their friends. Lili said she had been deprived of a bathtub for so long that she loved it "as if it were a living creature."

The house at Lubyansky proezd has been entirely gutted on the inside so that visitors start at the top of the building and descend in a spiral, walking through a series of Futurist-style exhibitions devoted to the different phases in the poet's life and work. While the museum is hardly user-friendly for the non-Russian speaker it is still a fascinating example of a very different kind of memorial museum from the standard Moscow fare of rooms preserved exactly as they were in the subject's lifetime.

Futurism hit the Moscow artistic scene in the second decade of the twentieth century as a violent reaction against the realist art prevalent at the time. Mayakovsky's first volume of poetry summed up his entire approach in its title, *A Slap in the Face of Public Taste*, and he devoted his energies to insulting his bourgeois audiences and demanding that all previous culture be jettisoned in favour of remaking the world from its foundations. Inspired by the Revolution, he threw himself into working for the new regime, designing propaganda posters for the Telegraph Agency during the Civil War and reading his work at the Poets' Café on Tverskaya ulitsa opposite the Central Telegraph office. Civil War Moscow was full of literary night-spots of this kind where concerts, readings and debates took place and Mayakovsky became a star of this world. His talents were prodigious: as well as producing poetry and journalism he also wrote and acted in plays and designed advertising and propaganda posters.

Boris Pasternak summed up his impressions of Mayakovsky as a man of firm will and inner drive:

He was handsome, witty, talented—perhaps even superlatively talented, but you knew at once that these were not the most important things about him; the important thing was his iron mastery over himself, the rules or principles of honour, the sense of duty which prevented him from being any different, any less handsome, talented or witty than he was. His resolute expression and the mane of hair which stood on end as he ruffled it with all five fingers immediately reminded me of some young terrorist conspirator out of a Dostoevsky novel.

In April 1930 the poet shot himself in his flat at Lubyansky proezd. His motives, whether primarily political or personal, have long been debated. Certainly the prevailing atmosphere in Soviet literary circles was deeply hostile to those of an avant-garde persuasion, and his recent play *The Bathhouse*, a satirical critique of the Soviet bureaucracy, had been subject to very hostile reviews. Some friends speculated over whether he had met his end in a game of Russian roulette or whether he had been assassinated by a secret police agent, but Mayakovsky had often written about suicide in the past and he left a poetic suicide note behind.

After his official canonization by Stalin in 1935 as "the best, most talented poet of our Soviet epoch", Mayakovsky's work was reinterpreted by Soviet critics within the framework of the new artistic orthodoxy of Socialist Realism. Downplaying the innovatory and avant-garde qualities of his poetry, critics instead emphasized the simplicity and mass appeal of his work. The poet's legacy became a point of contention between different interested parties: in 1972 the museum devoted to his life and work and situated in the apartment where he lived near Taganka was closed down and the contents moved to the new State Mayakovsky Museum at Lubyansky proezd. Part of the reason was to detach the poet from his associations with the Briks, with whom he had shared the Taganka apartment. Mayakovsky's grave in Novodevichy cemetery is a place of regular pilgrimage: a celebration is held here on the poet's birthday, 19 July, organized by officials from the Mayakovsky Museum including poetry readings and eulogies to their hero.

Sergei Yesenin

Another poet of Mayakovsky's generation, but one who took a very different approach to literary activity, was Sergei Yesenin. His grave can be found in the Vagankovskoe cemetery in the Krasnaya Presnya district of the city, not far from Ulitsa 1905 Goda metro station. Yesenin was the son of a peasant and came to Moscow at the age of sixteen to work in a butcher's shop and then a printing works. He had received a secondary education at a church boarding school and followed this in

Moscow by enrolling for evening classes at the Shanyavsky People's University, which offered higher education to members of the working class. Yesenin did not stay long in Moscow; he already had ambitions of following a literary career and he abandoned his first wife and child in order to move to St. Petersburg—Petrograd, as it was then called—in 1915 in search of fame and fortune.

Fame and fortune were not long in coming, as Yesenin was a great hit in literary circles in the capital and he had little trouble getting his poems published. He had a short period of military service between 1916 and 1917, which he spent working on a military train used for transporting sick and wounded soldiers. In 1917 he was married to Zinaida Raikh, who at that time was working as a secretary in Petrograd but who would later go on to become a famous actress. They moved to Moscow in the spring of 1918 but the marriage lasted little more than a year, as Yesenin left her shortly after the birth of their daughter, Tatyana. Raikh herself later married the theatre director Vsevolod Meyerhold.

In Moscow, Yesenin fell in with a crowd of poets who defined themselves as the Imaginists: they laid great stress on the importance of the image that a poem created. His best friend from this period was Anatoly Mariengof and the two shared a flat together on Petrovsky pereulok, a lane that runs between Petrovka and Bolshaya Dmitrovka within the Boulevard Ring. The two became inseparable; they lived and worked in the same room and took great delight in outraging polite society. It was at around this time that Yesenin began drinking heavily and he eventually succumbed to alcoholism. He made regular appearances at the literary cafés of Civil War Moscow: on one occasion he caused a scandal by rising to address the audience and declaring:

> *Do you imagine I've come out to recite my poems to you? No, I came out to tell you all to fuck off! Speculators and charlatans!*

Yesenin was going through a rebellious phase at this time: shortly after this incident, he and his Imaginist friends were arrested for daubing their verses on the walls of the Strastnoi Convent (the Convent of the Passion), which once stood on the site now occupied by the Rossiya cinema on Pushkin Square. The convent, which was pulled down in 1937, gives its name to the boulevard on which it once stood.

Towards the end of 1921 Yesenin met the American dancer Isadora Duncan, who had come to Moscow to set up a school of dance on ulitsa Prechistenka. She had been thrilled by the Russian Revolution, writing in a newspaper article that:

> *I am convinced that here in Russia is the greatest miracle that has happened to humanity for two thousand years... Moscow is a miracle city and the martyrdom submitted by Russia will be for the future what the crucifixion was...*

For Duncan, it seems to have been love at first sight. She and Yesenin were married in May of the following year and immediately set off on travels across Europe and to the United States. They were rather an odd couple. Duncan was seventeen years older than Yesenin and spoke little Russian; he spoke no English. When Maxim Gorky met them in Berlin he came away describing Duncan as the "perfect embodiment of everything unsuited" to her husband. His drinking became a serious problem during their marriage and he was arrested on more than one occasion for his involvement in drunken brawls and smashing up hotel rooms. Their relationship swiftly broke down and they separated soon after their return to Russia a year later. Yesenin took a dim view of life in the West. He liked the New York skyline, but otherwise he described the West as "this most terrible realm of philistinism which borders on idiocy" and dreamed of returning to Moscow. "In my head there is Moscow, nothing but Moscow. I'm even ashamed at feeling so Chekhovian," he wrote in a letter to Mariengof. It was during his time abroad that Yesenin wrote his cycle entitled *Moscow of the Taverns*, an exploration of drunkenness and debauchery in poetic form.

In the last year of his life, Yesenin married Tolstoy's granddaughter, Sofiya Tolstaya. It is unclear whether he had ever actually gone through the formalities of divorcing Isadora Duncan. Mariengof rather rudely said of Sofiya that she looked "impossibly like her grandfather. All she lacked was a bald patch and a grey beard." Their relationship, like all of Yesenin's relationships with women, was a troubled one, made worse by the poet's ongoing love affair with the bottle. His alcoholism had already become the subject of press commentary and was starting to make him ill: he began to cough up blood after his drinking binges. Mariengof described how:

> *In the last months of his terrible existence Yesenin was a human being for no more than one hour in the day, and sometimes even less. His consciousness already began to darken after the first morning glassful. And yet after the first glass there inevitably followed—a second, then a third, fourth, fifth... And so on from day to day, from night to night...*

Yesenin had often talked of suicide and in December 1925 he went to Leningrad, locked himself in his room at the Hotel Angleterre, wrote his last poem "Goodbye, My Friend, Goodbye" in his own blood and hanged himself. His body was returned to Moscow on the train and he was buried amid heavy snow at Vagankovskoe. The gravesite includes a carving of the youthful poet in white stone, and lovers of his work come here to leave flowers. Yesenin's friend and sometime lover, Galina Benislavskaya, shot herself over his grave a year later and is buried nearby.

Maxim Gorky

In 1931, as part of an attempt to lure him back from exile, the writer Maxim Gorky was given a grand Art Nouveau mansion on Malaya Nikitskaya, the former home of the Old Believer merchant Ryabushinsky. Although there is some evidence that Gorky objected to such luxury, he did nonetheless decide to return to Russia and remained there until his death in 1936. Stalin had good reasons to want to tempt Gorky to return: he was a respected writer with an international reputation; he had been on close—although not always uncomplicated—terms with Lenin and his homecoming would be a valuable propaganda coup for the Soviet authorities. Gorky had left Russia in 1921, having become very critical of the anti-democratic approach taken by the Bolshevik Party leadership. In an early response to the October Revolution he had written that "Lenin and Trotsky and their followers already have been poisoned by the rotten venom of power."

Maxim Gorky was born Alexei Maximovich Peshkov in the Volga town of Nizhny Novgorod; both of his parents died while he was still young and he was brought up by his impoverished grandparents. He spent much of his young adulthood on the move, wandering between different towns and taking a whole series of jobs, in an icon shop, a bakery and as a construction foreman among others. It was during his time in Kazan that he first joined a left-wing reading group and developed an interest in revolutionary thought. He took up writing, adopted the pen-name Gorky (meaning "bitter") and by the turn of the century he had become a celebrity in literary circles through his short stories and plays that explored the degrading conditions of working-class life in contemporary Russia. His play The Lower Depths, set among the poorest of the urban poor, was first performed by the Moscow Art Theatre in 1902 to great acclaim.

Gorky was in Moscow during the uprising of December 1905; he helped to raise funds for the revolutionary cause and his apartment was used by activists as a meeting place, arms cache and bomb-making laboratory. He left Russia shortly after the failure of the revolution for an unsuccessful fund-raising tour to the United States on behalf of the Bolshevik Party and then spent the next seven years in Italy, on the island of Capri where he helped to establish a school for training Party activists. Gorky returned to Russia in 1913 and witnessed both the February and October Revolutions in Petrograd. He worked for a time on cultural and educational projects on behalf of the new Soviet government and became known among writers as a valuable patron. He abandoned his native land once again in 1921 and lived for several years in Sorrento before his first return visit to Russia in 1928. Like the composer Prokofiev, Gorky made a number of long stays in Moscow before making the final decision to return for good.

He was given a hero's welcome. On each of his trips, Gorky was publicly feted, taken to meet leading politicians and showered with material incentives to throw in his lot with the new regime. As well as the house on Malaya Nikitskaya he was given a dacha and a holiday villa, his collected works were reissued and his home town, as well as Tverskaya ulitsa in Moscow, were named after him. In October 1932 a notorious meeting took place in his Moscow home: about fifty Soviet writers were invited to meet with members of the Party leadership in order to hear Stalin's views on the future course of Soviet literature. Most of the greats of Soviet literature—Bulgakov, Pasternak, Mandelstam, Belyi, Akhmatova—were not present, but those who did attend were to witness Stalin's famous pronouncement on the task of the writer. They should be, he said, the "engineers of human souls". It was at this meeting that Socialist Realism was first discussed, the ideological aesthetic that required writers—and all other kinds of artists—to portray real life "not as it is, but as it is becoming," to depict the bright and optimistic future that awaited the fortunate citizens of the Soviet Union.

Gorky lent his public support to many state initiatives: never a fan of the peasantry, he approved of collectivization and participated in a writers' visit to the White Sea-Baltic Canal out of which a collective volume was published, praising the redemptive effect of forced labour on the Gulag inmates who had built the canal. He was also put up by Stalin to meet and greet visiting dignitaries, particularly foreign writers who visited the Soviet Union during the 1930s. One such meeting between him and the French writer Romain Rolland took place in 1935 and Rolland later described his host in the following terms:

> Gorky put his heart and soul in the Revolution, dedicated himself to the idea of Leninism-Stalinism, and with enthusiasm and optimism accepted the Five Year Plans... It seems, however, that the chorale is there to deafen a groan which comes from his inner self. I have felt a deep sorrow hidden in him... [he] is a weak, very weak man in spite of his looks of an old bear... Poor old bear! Surrounded by fame, and luxuries that he does not enjoy!

Gorky died in 1936; the question of whether he was poisoned by the authorities is one that has never been fully resolved. In the final Moscow show trial in 1938, two of the defendants were accused of his murder, but this hardly proves anything. His funeral was a grand state occasion on Red Square and he was buried in the Kremlin wall alongside fellow writer John Reed. Stalin's wish that Gorky should write his biography went unfulfilled. A trilogy of films based on Gorky's own autobiographical trilogy, *My Childhood, My Apprenticeship, My Universities* was directed by Mark Donskoi and produced in the late 1930s. Gorky's image for posterity has sadly been tarnished by the compromises that he made with the political authorities: the poor old bear is now no longer remembered for his radical early writings.

Boris Pasternak

A true devotee of the work of Boris Pasternak will want to visit his dacha in Peredelkino, outside the city but easily accessible in a day trip. There are, however, a number of places associated with the Nobel Prize-winning author in the city itself. The house where Pasternak was born in 1890 was situated on Oruzheiny pereulok, just north of the Garden Ring near the intersection with Karetnyi Ryad or Coachmakers' Row. The house was opposite the eighteenth-century Ostermann mansion, which now houses the Museum of Applied, Decorative and Folk Art. Pasternak's family soon moved and he spent his childhood living in an apartment in one wing of the Academy of Painting and Sculpture on Myasnitskaya ulitsa (the name derives from the butchers who used to work here) in the attractive district within the Boulevard Ring to the east of the city centre around Chistye Prudy (Clean Ponds) metro station. Pasternak's father, Leonid Pasternak, was an artist and taught at the Academy; his mother was a gifted pianist who gave up her performing career when she married. The Academy of Arts building, the former Yuzhkov House, can still be seen: it is the peach-coloured classical style building with a colonnaded semi-circular balcony just across the road from the main Post Office. Pasternak described the building in his *Essay in Autobiography*.

> *The building was old, beautiful and remarkable in many ways. The fire of 1812 had spared it. A century before our time under the Empress Catherine, it had been the secret refuge of a Masonic Lodge. One corner... had a pillared, semi-circular balcony... From it, you could have a clear view of the Myasnitskaya running into the distance towards the railway stations.*

It was from this spot that Pasternak remembered as a child being taken to watch the funeral procession for Tsar Alexander III in 1894 as well as the coronation procession for Nicholas II two years later. The apartment where the family lived was created as an afterthought out of a set of underused classrooms. Pasternak recalled how

The kitchen was oval and the dining-room had a semi-circle bitten out of it. There was always a muffled din coming from the passages and workrooms outside, and from the end room Professor Chaplygin could be heard lecturing on heating methods to the architecture class next door.

After the Revolution the Academy was taken over by Futurists and during the 1920s it became a centre for the artistic avant-garde.

His family background meant that the young Boris grew up surrounded by artists. Tolstoy and Scriabin were family friends and Pasternak initially intended to follow a musical career. In 1911 the family moved to a house on ulitsa Volkhonka near the Cathedral of Christ the Saviour, a house which has since been demolished. After studying at Moscow University and for a term at the University of Marburg in Germany, where the founder of Moscow University, Mikhail Lomonosov had also been a student, Pasternak was rejected for military service in the First World War because of a disability related to a childhood riding accident.

Like so many members of his social class, Pasternak welcomed the February Revolution but was more ambivalent in his attitude toward the Bolshevik takeover. He joined the great wave of emigration after the Revolution, moving to Berlin in 1922, but he did not remain there for long. Convinced that post-revolutionary Moscow was turning the corner and becoming, once again, a vibrant centre for the arts, he returned to live in one room of the family's former Volkhonka abode in 1923. His parents and his sisters Lydia and Josephine remained abroad. Pasternak had by this time decisively rejected the idea of a musical career and had published a number of volumes of poetry including the celebrated collection *My Sister, Life*.

As a leading figure in literary circles during the 1930s, Pasternak was able to gain access to housing provided by writers' organizations. In 1932 he was given a small flat in the Herzen House on Tverskoi Boulevard and in 1937 he acquired two rooms in a house built by the Union of Soviet Writers at 17 Lavrushinsky pereulok, south of the river on the same street as the Tretyakov Gallery. It was at around this time that he also acquired the dacha at Peredelkino in a writers' settlement to the west of the city and he spent increasing periods of time here, particularly in the post-war years.

Pasternak was fortunate that Stalin greatly admired his poetry: he was able to get away with much more than some of his more unfortunate contemporaries. Although Stalin never agreed to the personal meeting that Pasternak requested, it seems almost certain that the Soviet leader took a personal interest in his affairs because the writer was never seriously troubled by the authorities during the 1930s and 1940s. It is said that when the subject of arresting Pasternak was raised, Stalin said they should "leave that cloud-dweller in peace." Pasternak was involved in helping fellow poets and writers during the period of the Terror. He protested against Osip Mandelstam's arrest in 1934 (this was the incident that prompted Stalin's famous telephone call to Pasternak in which Stalin reassured him that Mandelstam's case was under review); he tried to help Marina Tsvetaeva find work when she returned to Russia in 1939, and he refused to sign his name to a letter calling for the execution of Terror victims (his name was included on the list of signatories anyway). He also failed to turn up for the Writers' Union meeting in 1946 when two of his Leningrad colleagues, the writers Anna Akhmatova and Mikhail Zoshchenko, were condemned. At the same time Pasternak became quite reclusive. He wrote very little poetry during the Stalin years; most of his work during this time involved translations of European classics including *Hamlet* and *Faust*. Nadezhda Mandelstam noted that when they met in the summer of 1937: "Pasternak was still obsessed by Stalin and complained that he could not write poetry any more because he had not been able to get a personal meeting with him…"

It was only in the last decade of his life that Pasternak, in Nadezhda Mandelstam's words, "put himself in open conflict with the Soviet literary world." His most famous work, *Doctor Zhivago*, took him ten years to write, during which time his lover and the woman who is said to have inspired the character of Lara in the novel, Olga Ivinskaya, was arrested and sent to the labour camps. Pasternak was convinced that her relationship with him was the cause of her arrest and he redoubled his creative efforts on his novel. As Yevgraf, Yury's younger brother in the novel said: "you must never, under any circumstances, despair. To hope and to act, these are our duties in misfortune. To do nothing and to despair is to neglect our duty."

Pasternak's attempt to get *Doctor Zhivago* published in the literary journal *Novyi Mir* was unsuccessful and he chose to take the ultimate "anti-Soviet" route of publishing it abroad, in Italy, in 1957. Widely celebrated in international circles, it was this novel with its story of how the events of the Revolution and Civil War affected the life of an intelligentsia family that prompted Pasternak's successful nomination for the Nobel Prize for literature in 1958. This tribute provoked a scandal. Pasternak was denounced in the Soviet media and his novel was condemned as "the life story of a malicious philistine, an enemy of the Revolution". Expelled from the Writers' Union, the pressure exerted on him caused him eventually to renounce the prize. He died not long after this affair, in 1960, and was buried at Peredelkino. *Doctor Zhivago* circulated in underground editions among dissident intellectuals during the late Soviet period but was not published in Russia until the *glasnost* era of the late 1980s. Pasternak's Nobel Prize was eventually accepted on his behalf some thirty years later by his son, Yevgeny.

Mikhail Bulgakov

Mikhail Bulgakov is probably best known for his extraordinary novel *Master and Margarita* about the devil's visit to Moscow. The story opens with two figures sitting on a bench at Patriarch's Ponds, an attractive open space inside the Garden Ring on Malaya Bronnaya ulitsa. The nearest metro stations are Pushkinskaya and Mayakovskaya, and the Garden Ring trolleybuses stop nearby. It is here, under the linden trees that line the square around the pond, that the poet Ivan Bezdomnyi and the literary agent Mikhail Berlioz meet the mysterious Professor Woland, who predicts Berlioz's imminent demise under the wheels of a tram. Trams are few and far between in central Moscow these days and they no longer run in this district. It was also here, sitting on a bench at Patriarch's Ponds, that Bulgakov courted both his second and his third wives, Lyubov Belozerskaya and Yelena Shilovskaya.

From here a short walk up the Garden Ring towards Triumfalnaya ploshchad takes you to the five-storey grey apartment building where Bulgakov lived during the early 1920s. Flat 50, at 10 Bolshaya Sadovaya was to become the model for Berlioz's flat which Woland and his associates take over in the novel, and Margarita acts as hostess here for Satan's ball. The building itself dates from around the turn of the century and became a communal house shortly after the Revolution, with residents expected to provide services for one another on a mutual exchange basis. Bulgakov and his first wife, Tasya, managed to acquire a room in a communal apartment and he wrote to his sister describing how "the room is terrible, the neighbours too... I don't feel secure there, and it was an awful lot of bother to get it."

Master and Margarita was Bulgakov's last novel, written in the late 1930s, but it was not published in full until 1973 when it became a literary sensation. In the late 1970s it was performed at the Taganka Theatre under Yury Lyubimov's directorship, and staged versions of the novel are often produced in Moscow theatres today. In the mid-1980s during the *glasnost* period graffiti artists began work in the stairwell at 10 Bolshaya Sadovaya, and pictures of key characters from the novel as well as famous quotations—"Don't talk to strangers," "Manuscripts don't burn"—began to appear on the walls leading up to apartment 50.

Bulgakov was born in Kiev in 1891 and trained as a doctor there; he moved to Moscow in 1921, having decided to devote his life to writing. He later wrote of his impressions on arriving in Moscow at what is now the Kiev station to the west of the city just over the bridge from the Garden Ring that September night:

> *Till the day I die, I will remember the dazzling lights at the Bryansk station and the two street lights of Dorogomilovsky Bridge which showed the way to my native capital. For no matter what they say, Moscow is the mother, Moscow is the native city: and that was the first panorama.*

The 1920s witnessed the publication of several works including *The White Guard*, set in Kiev during the Civil War, *The Heart of a Dog*, a comic novel set in the Prechistenka area of Moscow, an old district inhabited by gentry and intelligentsia around Kropotkinskaya metro, and a number of plays. His works for the stage included a theatrical reworking of *The White Guard* entitled *The Days of the Turbins*; a play set in the Moscow underworld of the 1920s and peopled with prostitutes, drug dealers and thieves, *Zoyka's Apartment*; and Flight, another depiction of life among members of the White opposition in the Civil War. Although Stalin enjoyed The Days of the Turbins so much that he saw it fifteen times, by the end of the 1920s it was nevertheless clear that Bulgakov had fallen from official favour. His plays were withdrawn from the theatre and he was subjected to a campaign of press vilification. Stalin himself criticized Flight, describing it as "one manifestation of an endeavour to stimulate pity, if not sympathy, for certain sections amongst the most contemptible anti-Soviet émigrés… (it is) an anti-Soviet phenomenon."

By 1930 Bulgakov had come to the end of his tether. Having written one letter complaining about his treatment to the Soviet government a year earlier, he now followed this with a second letter in which he attacked the lack of press freedom in the USSR and asked that he and his wife be given permission to leave the country or, if that was not granted, to be given a job as an assistant director in the Moscow Art Theatre. Less than a month after writing this letter Bulgakov was at home in his apartment on Bolshaya Pirogovskaya, the continuation of ulitsa Prechistenka that runs alongside Maidens' Field leading down to the Novodevichy convent, when he received a telephone call from Stalin himself. Having ascertained that Bulgakov did not really want to leave Russia, Stalin advised him to apply for work at the Moscow Art Theatre. Evidently the dictator had put in a good word for him because the application was successful and Bulgakov began work at the theatre soon after.

Bulgakov's work during the 1930s consisted in a number of adaptations and translations of works for the theatre as well as his writing and rewriting of several versions of *Master and Margarita*. The novel is about more than simply the devil's decision to come and conduct a series of entertaining experiments on Muscovites: it weaves together a series of stories, including that of the Master, the writer of a novel about Pontius Pilate which is rejected by publishers and the woman he loves. Chapters from the Pontius Pilate novel are interspersed throughout the book, offering an uncommon example of a serious treatment of a Christian theme by a Soviet writer. When the Master tells the mysterious Woland what his novel is about, the response is explosive:

> Woland burst into thunderous laughter… "About what? About what? About whom?" said Woland, ceasing to laugh. "And that—now? It's stupendous! Couldn't you have found some other subject? Let me see it." Woland held out his hand, palm up. "Unfortunately, I cannot do that", replied the master, "because I burned it in the stove."

"Forgive me, but I don't believe you," Woland replied, "that cannot be: manuscripts don't burn."

This line would come to seem almost prophetic when the novel was finally published, thirty years after it was written. At the end of the novel Woland and his companions, together with the Master and Margarita, all leave the city, riding through the air on magical steeds in the midst of a thunderstorm. Before they abandon Moscow for good, Woland takes one last look at the city from the roof of the classical Pashkov Mansion overlooking the Borovitsky gate of the Kremlin:

…resting his sharp chin on his fist, hunched on the stool with one leg drawn under him, Woland stared fixedly at the endless collection of palaces, gigantic buildings and little hovels destined to be pulled down…

Woland began to speak: "Such an interesting city, is it not?"

Bulgakov's last years were fraught with professional difficulties. In 1936, amid a storm of high-profile attacks on artistic figures, Bulgakov's play about Molière was described in *Pravda* as having "superficial glitter and false content" and pulled from the repertoire of the Art Theatre. Several attempts to gain permission to travel abroad during the 1930s were refused, even though Bulgakov repeatedly assured the authorities that he had no intention of emigrating. He was invited to write a play about Stalin to celebrate the Soviet leader's sixtieth birthday, but this work, *Batum*, was pulled from production and remained unpublished for fifty years. Bulgakov's sight began failing him in 1939 and he died of a kidney disease in March 1940. Unlike many of his contemporaries and those he had worked with—Mandelstam, Meyerhold and others— he died of a natural, if premature, cause in his bed. He is buried, like so many other Soviet writers and artists, in Novodevichy cemetery in the same plot as Chekhov, Gogol, Stanislavsky and Shostakovich.

Marina Tsvetaeva

Not far from Patriarch's Ponds, Trekhprudnyi pereulok, the Lane of Three Ponds, is a street parallel with and in between Malaya Bronnaya ulitsa and Tverskaya. This was the birthplace of the poet, Marina Tsvetaeva, although the house where she spent her early childhood no longer exists: it was pulled down after the Revolution so that its timbers could be used for firewood. By all accounts it was a large and imposing house, set in a garden in which a neighbouring family kept their cow. (This practice, incidentally, was not at all unusual in wealthy Moscow houses at the end of the nineteenth century. According to one visitor who enquired into the presence of cows wandering the streets of the city apparently unattended, they were let out each morning and were taken by a local cowherd to Petrovsky Park. At the end of the day they were brought back to the city gates and left to find their own way home: "each cow knows her way home, and finds it unmolested up to the very heart of the city.")

Marina Tsvetaeva was born in 1892 into an intellectual family, a very similar background, in fact, to Boris Pasternak's. Her father was Ivan Tsvetaev, an academic who taught art history and worked as a curator in the Rumyantsev Museum, housed in the Pashkov House on Mokhovaya ulitsa overlooking the Kremlin. Her mother, a talented pianist, died of tuberculosis in 1906. It is perhaps not surprising, given the tragedies that afflicted her adult life, that Tsvetaeva looked back on her childhood as an idyllic time. After a period spent at boarding schools in Switzerland and Germany she returned to Russia and in 1911 she met and fell in love with Sergei Efron, the son of a pair of active revolutionaries. They married the following year in a quiet ceremony at the Church of the Nativity of Christ, which used to stand on Bolshoi Palashevsky pereulok, just around the corner from Tsvetaeva's childhood home.

After a short period living on ulitsa Sivtsev-Vrazhek, the same street near the Arbat where Alexander Herzen had made his home and where Tolstoy also lived for a short time, Tsvetaeva and Efron moved to Borisoglebovsky pereulok, a lane that today runs between Povarskaya ulitsa and Novyi Arbat. Her apartment is now preserved as a museum and the rest of the building houses a literary centre. By this time, Tsvetaeva's father had died, having finally achieved his aim of founding a fine arts museum in Moscow: the Alexander III Museum, later renamed the Pushkin Museum, with its impressive collection of European painting and sculpture, which was opened in 1912. She had also begun to publish her poetry and had given birth to her first child, a daughter named Alya (short for Ariadna).

During the years of the war and the later Civil War, Tsvetaeva remained in Moscow as living conditions steadily worsened. With

Efron away at the front she had an affair with a fellow poet, Sofiya Parnok, and an intimate relationship with Osip Mandelstam. Tsvetaeva and Mandelstam wrote verses dedicated to one another about their walks around Moscow. In one of Tsvetaeva's poems of this period she wrote of how:

...slowly puffing out smoke, we
walk like solemn foreigners
throughout my native city.

After the Revolution and with food supplies dwindling, she became increasingly dependent on the generosity of her Muscovite friends to keep going. She rented out rooms in the apartment and sold off her possessions in a desperate attempt to get money to buy food. With two daughters to look after, she took a clerical job at the Commissariat of Nationalities but left after less than six months and took to spending her days walking all over the city trying to find food for sale. In one of her diary entries, she wrote that "we have no flour and no bread." Convinced that her children would be better off, she sent them to an orphanage and it was here that her younger daughter, Irina, starved to death in February 1920.

The Mandelstams visited Tsvetaeva in her Moscow flat towards the end of the Civil War, and Nadezhda Mandelstam left this description of what they found:

Like all former upper-class apartments, it was now given over to
dust, dirt and decay... I thought of all the giant spiders that might
be lurking unseen in the darkness, the mice frisking about, the Lord
knows what other vermin beside.

Having learnt that Efron, who fought against the Bolsheviks in the Civil War, had made his way to Prague, Tsvetaeva and Alya left Moscow in May 1922. She would not return to her homeland for seventeen long years.

Tsvetaeva's émigré years were spent in a village near Prague and later among the large Russian community in Paris. Her relationship with Sergei Efron deteriorated as she had a series of love affairs and he moved across the political spectrum to abandon his former opposition to Soviet communism. Anxious to return to Russia, he began working for the secret police, known at this time as the NKVD. In 1937 both Efron and Alya returned to Moscow, and Tsvetaeva found herself isolated in émigré circles. Her feelings were confused: she was desperately homesick and yet unsure of what she would find on her return. Boris Pasternak, with whom she conducted an extensive correspondence throughout her time in exile, felt a deep sense of guilt that he had failed to warn her against the notion of coming back to Russia. Many years later, he wrote of how

> *I did not know what to advise her, and was too much afraid that she and her remarkable family would find life hard and unsettling in Russia. The tragedy that befell the whole family was infinitely greater than even I had feared.*

In 1939 she made the decision to apply for a visa and left Paris, together with her fourteen-year-old son Georgy, nicknamed Mur, in the summer of that year. For a couple of months the family was reunited but disaster soon struck when first Alya and then Efron were arrested on charges of espionage. Alya was sentenced to fifteen years in the labour camps and Efron was shot in the Lubyanka. Tsvetaeva and her son moved between temporary apartments within and outside Moscow while Pasternak tried to help her find work as a translator. "Moscow has no room for me... with these changes of abode, I gradually lose my sense of reality. I am slowly being whittled away..." she wrote. After the German invasion, they were evacuated from Moscow to Yelabuga in Tatarstan. Pasternak saw them off at the river port. They lived with a peasant family and she tried to find work, without success. At the end of August 1941 Tsvetaeva hanged herself. Her son refused to attend the funeral and she was buried in an unmarked grave. He himself died in combat in 1944.

Osip and Nadezhda Mandelstam

Tsvetaeva's close friend, Osip Mandelstam, was not a Muscovite, but it was in Moscow that he was first arrested in May 1934 and it was here that his wife Nadezhda, an author in her own right, made her home for the last twenty-five years of her life. At the time of his arrest, Mandelstam and his wife were living in an apartment block designated for writers on Nashchekinsky pereulok near to Gogolevsky Boulevard. Mandelstam wrote about the apartment in his poem "The flat is silent, like a sheet of paper". From these verses, written in 1933, it seems that the writer was fully expecting the secret police to come for him any day. The poem ends:

... and instead of the stream of Hippocrene
A stream of home-grown fear
Will break through the cardboard walls
Of this wretched Moscow home.

Mandelstam's relationship with the Soviet authorities was initially an ambiguous one. He started out by viewing the new regime with contempt: shortly after the Revolution he published a poem describing Lenin as "Red October's opportunist", with his "yoke of violence and hate"; but Mandelstam nevertheless worked for the People's Commissariat of Enlightenment for a short time during the Civil War. His loathing of Stalin was virulent and unremitting, however, and in 1933 he wrote a poem about the Soviet leader that was nothing if not unflattering:

All we hear is the Kremlin mountaineer
The murderer and peasant-slayer...

... His fingers are greasy as worms
And his words hit home like twenty pound weights.
His cockroach moustaches laugh
And bright shine his jackboots.

Having spent a few years in Moscow between 1922-4 living in the Herzen House, the literary centre founded in the house where Herzen was born on Tverskoi Boulevard, Mandelstam and his wife returned to the city in the early 1930s, eventually settling in the small apartment on Nashchekinsky pereulok (later renamed Furmanov pereulok, now returned to its original name). It was during this time that he wrote his two collections of poems, the *Moscow Notebooks*, both of which were published posthumously.

His arrest in 1934 shocked literary circles in Moscow. Friends appealed on his behalf to the authorities and word of these developments reached Stalin, prompting him to make a personal intervention with his famous telephone call to Boris Pasternak. The sentence of exile to Cherdyn in the Urals, where the poet made a bungled suicide attempt by jumping from a hospital window, was commuted to a ban on living in any of the twelve main cities in the Soviet Union. Mandelstam and his wife, who accompanied him into exile, chose to continue their sentence in the town of Voronezh, south of Moscow. Released from exile in 1937 they were not permitted to return to Moscow and spent a year moving between towns on the outskirts of the capital. Nadezhda Mandelstam wrote of this time that:

Moscow drew us like a magnet all the time—we went there for gossip, news, money… Each time, remembering where we were, we raced for the last train back to Kalinin, fearful of getting stranded for an extra night in the forbidden city.

Rearrested in May 1938 Mandelstam was sentenced to five years' hard labour. In very poor health by this stage, he wrote to his brother that he felt exhausted, emaciated and very cold. He died in a transit camp in the Far East of Russia in December 1938. Nadezhda Mandelstam had lost her Moscow residence permit and was only permitted to return in 1964 when she acquired a small flat in a cooperative housing development in the new suburb of Novye Cheryomushki in the south of the city. She wrote two volumes of autobiography about her life with Mandelstam, *Hope Against Hope* and *Hope Abandoned.* She died here in 1980.

Chapter Six
CITY OF THEATRES AND MUSIC

Theatre in Moscow began long before the laying out of Teatralnaya ploshchad. Tsar Alexei Mikhailovich enjoyed theatrical performances at the Poteshnyi Palace in the Kremlin in the seventeenth century and Count Pyotr Sheremetyev had hundreds of his serfs trained in drama and music so that they could put on performances for himself and his guests. He had two theatres, indoor and outdoor, built at the family estate at Kuskovo to the south of Moscow, but these were soon eclipsed by the theatre that was constructed at Ostankino, the Sheremetyev palace situated to the north of the Garden Ring, by his son Nikolai. The Ostankino theatre could seat more than 250 people and considerable technical mastery went into the design of the movable stage and the facilities for creating sound and light effects. It was at Kuskovo that Nikolai Sheremetyev met his future wife, the serf girl Praskovya Zhemchugova, who was trained as a singer and became the star of his opera company. He caused scandal in high society by taking her to live with him and in 1801 they married in secret; she died a year later of tuberculosis in St. Petersburg. A lovely portrait of her hangs on a wall of the palace at Ostankino.

The Bolshoi Theatre
The original theatre on the site of what is now the Bolshoi was the Petrovsky Theatre, built in 1780 by an English entrepreneur named Michael Maddox. A mechanic by training, he came to Moscow and helped to set up a theatre company which became known for the high standards of its theatrical productions and the wide variety of its repertoire; operas and ballets were staged at the Petrovsky as well as plays, both Russian and European. The theatre burned down in one of Moscow's periodic fires in 1805 and was replaced in the 1820s by a new building designed by Bove. It was at this time, in the aftermath of the great fire of 1812, that the Neglinnaya river was channeled underground and Theatre Square was created on the site. The second

building met an equally unfortunate end: it too was destroyed by fire. The pink and white building with its great portico topped by a statue of Apollo's chariot that we know today was built in the 1850s by the architect Albert Cavos. The Bolshoi is an extraordinary place to visit even if only to catch a glimpse of the curtain, a rich red velvet, embroidered with a lavish golden hammer and sickle design. Sadly this curtain is destined for removal in the theatre's ongoing refurbishment programme.

Contemporary descriptions of Cavos' building complimented the architect on his mastery of acoustics, and the theatre rapidly gained an international reputation for opera and ballet. Tchaikovsky's ballets and operas were performed here and Rachmaninov worked as a conductor for a time during the early years of the twentieth century. After the Revolution, the Soviet censors took considerable interest in the repertoire offered by the Bolshoi. Attempts were made to revolutionize the operatic repertoire by rewriting the libretti of established works: thus, Puccini's *Tosca* became *The Struggle for the Commune* and Meyerbeer's *The Huguenots* became *The Decembrists*, taking as its theme the uprising against Nicholas I in 1825. These operas did not remain long in the repertoire. Politically inspired works that were written by Soviet composers and staged at the Bolshoi included Reinhold Glière's ballet *The Red Poppy*, which explores themes of colonial oppression and workers' uprisings through a love story about a Chinese dancer and a Soviet sea captain, and the opera *Quiet Flows the Don*, based on the famous Soviet novel about the collectivization of agriculture by Mikhail Sholokhov. This last opera, by Ivan Dzerzhinsky, was one that Stalin particularly enjoyed when he went to see it in 1936.

Among some of the most noteworthy productions at the Bolshoi one should mention the staging of Shostakovich's opera *Lady Macbeth of Mtsensk* at the Bolshoi's second stage, which Stalin went to see in January 1936 and which provoked a tirade of criticism directed at the unfortunate composer. In 1940 the film director Sergei Eisenstein was commissioned to mount a production of Wagner's *Die Walküre* to mark the new era of Russo-German friendship sealed with the signing of the Nazi-Soviet non-aggression pact a year earlier: it was swiftly dropped from the repertoire after the German invasion in 1941. The Bolshoi Theatre was also used as the venue for political congresses and important state occasions during the Soviet period.

One innovation that the new authorities were anxious to apply to all Moscow theatres was to open them up to new audiences. Arthur Ransome, who spent significant periods in Russia during the Civil War, described one trip to the Bolshoi in 1919.

It had certainly changed greatly since the pre-revolutionary period. The Moscow plutocracy of bald merchants and bejewelled fat wives had gone. Gone with them were evening dresses and white shirt fronts. The whole audience was in the monotone of everyday clothes. The only contrast was given by a small group of Tartar women in the dress circle, who were shawled in white over head and shoulders, in the Tartar fashion. There were many soldiers, and numbers of men who had obviously come straight from their work. There were a good many grey and brown woollen jerseys about, and people were sitting in overcoats of all kinds and ages, for the theatre was very cold.

Twentieth-century stars of the Bolshoi included Fyodor Chaliapin, Antonina Nezhdanova, Sergei Lemeshev, Ivan Kozlovsky, Leonid Sobinov and the ballerina Galina Ulanova, who transferred to the Bolshoi from the Kirov Theatre in Leningrad in 1944. Galina Vishnevskaya, the operatic soprano and wife of the cellist Mstislav

Rostropovich, made her name at the Bolshoi during the 1950s. The couple became involved in dissident activity during the Brezhnev era when they allowed the writer Alexander Solzhenitsyn to stay at their dacha outside Moscow. Solzhenitsyn, author of a number of books about the Soviet Gulag including *One Day in the Life of Ivan Denisovich*, had recently been expelled from the Soviet Writers' Union and in 1970 he became even more unpopular with the authorities when he was awarded the Nobel Prize for Literature. Rostropovich wrote an open letter to the press on his friend's behalf and, as a result, both he and Vishnevskaya began to face persecution: concert engagements were cancelled without warning. After Solzhenitsyn's arrest and expulsion from the USSR, the two musicians themselves received permission to leave the country in order to work in the United States for a temporary period. In her memoirs, Vishnevskaya recalled her last visit to the Bolshoi before their departure:

> *I put on one of my best dresses as if I was having a date with someone I knew and loved a long, long time... All the operas that I had ever sung in, nearly a thousand in all, were floating one by one in my mind... "No, I can't just leave! I want to tell you, Bolshoi, my best-kept secret for I came to curse you and now that I'm here, I cannot do it! I feel neither hatred nor anger—all I feel is pain, unbearable pain... I gave you all I had—my youth, my beauty, my energy. And you took it all, insatiable you... No, I have no hard feelings about it because, in exchange for my being so madly in love with you, you made me famous, you gave me a career one can only dream of, you made me a celebrity admired everywhere... And now... goodbye..."*

Four years later they learned from the television that their Soviet citizenship had been revoked. Rostropovich played a musical role in the events surrounding the collapse of communism: he played his cello at the Berlin Wall as crowds worked to demolish it in November 1989; two years later he flew into Moscow from Paris, borrowed a Kalashnikov and joined Boris Yeltsin in his stand against the coup plotters outside the White House. More recently, Vishnevskaya has sponsored the founding of a school for opera singers on ulitsa Ostozhenka in Moscow.

The Bolshoi Theatre has been no stranger to scandal and intrigue in the post-Soviet era. Critics complained throughout the 1990s of declining artistic standards in Bolshoi productions as the best home-grown stars left Russia altogether or chose to spend most of their time on tour where they could earn a decent wage. Matters came to a head early in the Putin era when the artistic director, Vladimir Vasilev, was dismissed following a series of flops, and the government took over responsibility for running the theatre. Control was transferred to the Ministry of Culture and the government also promised a fresh injection of capital in order to help restore Russia's reputation for artistic achievements on the world stage. Change did not come about immediately, however. In the spring of 2001 the internationally renowned conductor Gennady Rozhdestvensky resigned from his post as artistic director after less than a year in office, complaining of shambolic management, performers who missed rehearsals with impunity, claiming that their wages were so small as to make it not worth their while to turn up, and a lack of support from the Ministry of Culture. His successors have taken on a massive and hugely expensive reconstruction project to modernize the stage equipment and backstage facilities, to improve the acoustics and to restore the grand public spaces to their former glory. Controversy over the funding of this project means that it is at present unclear how long the renovations will take.

The Maly Theatre

The low yellow building that you can see to your right as you stand in Teatralnaya ploshchad with your back to Karl Marx and facing the Bolshoi is the Maly or small Theatre. Built as a private house in the 1820s, it was soon converted and the Imperial Theatre Company moved here in 1824 from its original home on Mokhovaya ulitsa. After damage by fire in 1841 the theatre was restored by Konstantin Ton. From the mid-nineteenth century onwards the Maly became closely associated with the name of Alexander Ostrovsky, Russia's most prolific playwright of that era. Ostrovsky was born in 1823 in the Zamoskvorechie district to the south of the river and began his career as a legal clerk. He became interested in the theatre and began writing plays in the late 1840s, drawing on his personal experience of mixing with merchant society in his youth and his professional experience of seeing disputes fought out in the courts. In 1849 he was disinherited

by his father after refusing to abandon his common-law wife and he turned to full-time writing as a means of earning a living: by the end of his life he had written almost fifty plays. His dramas were usually set in the world of Moscow's merchants and although they painted an uncompromising portrait of this milieu, with its social conservatism, financial disputes and family tensions, merchants nonetheless flocked to see them produced at the Maly Theatre. Ostrovsky's most famous play is probably *The Storm*, a tragedy in which a young woman, trapped in an unhappy marriage to an alcoholic from a merchant family, falls in love with an idealistic student and ends up killing herself. Ostrovsky plays are still regularly staged at the Maly and a seated statue of the writer wearing a dressing gown and waving a pencil, apparently lost in thought, can be seen outside the entrance to the theatre.

Another playwright whose works are often produced at the Maly is Alexander Griboedov, who was born and brought up in Moscow and studied at the university but then spent much of the rest of his life either in St. Petersburg or travelling in Central Asia and the Caucasus. His most famous play, *Woe from Wit*, a satire on contemporary Moscow life, was produced—in expurgated form—at the Maly in 1831. A statue of Griboedov can be found on Chistoprudny Boulevard not far from the house on Myasnitskaya where he wrote much of *Woe from Wit* over the winter of 1823-4. Griboedov, whose name means "mushroom eater" in Russian, went to Tehran in 1828 as a diplomat and met a violent end in the storming of the Russian embassy there a year later. His mutilated body was taken to Georgia for burial, and the Shah of

Persia sent an 89-carat diamond to the Tsar as an apology: the stone can be seen in the State Diamond Fund in the Kremlin.

Famous actors in the Maly Theatre company included Mikhail Shchepkin, often described as Russia's greatest ever character actor. Born to a serf family in Kursk province, he came to Moscow in 1822 and won fame and great popularity for his novel technique of attempting to play his roles in a realistic manner and getting away from the traditional approach to acting that emphasized declamation and melodramatic gestures. Alexander Herzen, who knew Shchepkin in Moscow, wrote of how he "created truth on the Russian stage. He was the first to become non-theatrical in the theatre, his presentations were without any affectation or exaggeration."

Shchepkin also taught acting at the Maly's drama school which today bears his name. Another well-loved Maly actor of the 1820s and 1830s was Pavel Mochalov who created many of the great Shakespearian roles for the Russian stage. His private life was often as dramatic as those of the characters he portrayed on the stage as he was a notorious philanderer and alcoholic. His fans adored him and merchants closed their shops on the day of his funeral so as to be able to attend. Towards the end of the nineteenth century one of the best-known members of the Maly troupe was Maria Yermolova, a great tragic actress famous for her portrayals of strong women. Of her acting skill, Vladimir Nemirovich-Danchenko wrote that:

We were even embarrassed sometimes when Yermolova appeared in our plays. Her talent was so much richer than the parts we could offer her, that at times it seemed as if the roles split at the seams when Yermolova filled them with her genius.

Yermolova's flat on Tverskoi Boulevard is now a museum dedicated to her life and career and the Yermolova Theatre on Tverskaya is named after her.

Konstantin Stanislavsky had an association with the Maly Theatre early in his professional life: he founded an amateur company called the Society of Art and Literature where he worked to develop some of his ideas about acting. Writing later, he declared that "the Maly Theatre defined our spiritual life... I can safely say that I have received my education not in a grammar school but in the Maly Theatre."

Private Theatres

The Moscow theatre world was changed forever in 1882 when the Imperial monopoly on theatres was lifted. Private theatres suddenly began to spring up all over the city: one of the earliest of these was the Korsh Theatre, set up on Petrovsky pereulok by a businessman who fancied himself as an impresario. His theatre generally offered the same kind of repertoire as the Maly but he also put on crowd-pulling popular farces and experimental modern plays on Friday nights. In the late 1880s the premieres of Chekhov's first plays, *Ivanov* and *The Bear*, could be seen here. Korsh offered cheap seats to attract younger audiences and his was the first theatre in Moscow to introduce electric lighting. The Korsh Theatre moved into a new building on Kamergersky pereulok in 1885, which later became the home of the Moscow Art Theatre.

Another independent commercial theatre set up during the 1880s was Mikhail Lentovsky's extraordinary enterprise at the Hermitage Gardens just off Karetnyi Ryad in the northern part of the Zemlyanoi gorod. Lentovsky had studied with Shchepkin at the Maly and in his productions at the Hermitage he specialized in crowd-pleasing special effects. The Fantastic Theatre, as it became known, was the scene of a series of elaborate spectacles depicting travels in Africa or trips to the moon, accompanied by fireworks, acrobatics, tightrope walking and performing animals. The theatre eventually went bankrupt and Lentovsky died a pauper. The Hermitage Gardens were subsequently taken over by Yakov Shchukin, who invited the Lumière brothers to showcase their new invention of cinema here in 1896. In 1898 the newly created Moscow Art Theatre performed its first season at the Hermitage Theatre before moving into the old Korsh Theatre building in 1902.

The Private Opera

The Moscow Operetta Theatre is situated just off Theatre Square on Bolshaya Dmitrovka ulitsa. This building was once known as the Solodovnikov Theatre and was hired as the home of the Private Opera Company, founded in 1885 by the wealthy businessman and patron of the arts Savva Mamontov. Mamontov's name is inextricably linked with the artists' colony at Abramtsevo, an estate outside Moscow on the road to the great monastery at Sergeev Posad. Here he gathered around him many of the great artists of the time to explore together their shared interest in Russian folk traditions, making wooden furniture, painting icons and ceramic tiles and rediscovering traditional Russian church design. Many of the most famous paintings of the period that hang in the Tretyakov Gallery by artists such as Mikhail Nesterov, Viktor Vasnetsov and Valentin Serov were painted at Abramtsevo: the subject of Serov's beautiful painting, *Girl with Peaches*, was Mamontov's daughter Vera. Productions of Russian operas and plays were staged in Mamontov's Moscow residence at 6 Sadovaya-Spasskaya, as well as at Abramtsevo, and it was from these roots that his professional venture, the Private Opera, sprang.

The Private Opera was distinctive in a number of ways. First of all, it displayed a marked preference for works from the Russian, rather than the Italian, repertoire, at a time when Russian operas were often ignored by the Imperial Theatres. The company demonstrated its commitment by staging Rimsky-Korsakov's *The Snow Maiden* and Dargomyzhsky's *Rusalka* during its first season. In the second place, it gave a new prominence to the art of set and costume design. Leading artists of the day were brought in to work on Private Opera productions and the resulting, folk-inspired designs by artists such as Mikhail Vrubel and Viktor Vasnetsov were unlike anything that had ever been seen before on the Russian stage. Some critics went away more impressed by the sets than by any other aspect of the productions. Rimsky-Korsakov became a great enthusiast for the theatre's work and several of his operas were performed there.

It was not at all unusual in late nineteenth-century Moscow for rich merchants to act as patrons of the arts. The most famous of these, perhaps, was the great art collector Pavel Tretyakov, but other entrepreneurs who played a part in supporting artistic ventures included Nikolai Ryabushinsky, who supported the Symbolist movement, and Savva Morozov, patron of the Moscow Art Theatre. They tended, on the whole, to concentrate on spheres of the arts that were ignored by aristocratic patrons, taking an interest instead in modern artistic movements. Mamontov had an artistic background himself, having studied acting, sculpture and singing and he also tried his hand at writing and directing plays. The theatre director Konstantin Stanislavsky, a cousin of Mamontov's wife, described him as "a striking figure with his shining eyes, passionate way of speaking and eloquent mimicry", and a portrait of the businessman by Vrubel can be seen in the Tretyakov gallery. In 1899 Mamontov's world collapsed around him. Accused of fraudulent financial dealings, he was imprisoned and put on trial in the following year. Although he was acquitted by the court, the case had brought about his financial ruin and his opera company folded soon after.

During its short existence, the Private Opera had not only offered a showcase to talented designers, but had also launched the careers of a number of musicians. Sergei Rachmaninov was hired by Mamontov to work as a conductor at the Opera, and it was Mamontov who first brought the name of Fyodor Chaliapin to public prominence in Russia. Chaliapin was a phenomenally talented bass singer, born in the city of Kazan on the Volga into a peasant family, who sang in a church choir and later began working in provincial opera theatres, first in the chorus and later graduating to solo roles. It was Mamontov—anxious to find singers who possessed dramatic talents as well as musical ability—who gave him his first major break onto the Moscow stage in 1896. Chaliapin had huge success in the role of Ivan the Terrible in Rimsky-Korsakov's *Maid of Pskov* during his first season with the company. In 1898 he created what was probably his most famous role, that of Boris Godunov in the Musorgsky opera of that name, with the Private Opera. Mamontov wrote to Rimsky-Korsakov that Chaliapin was "simply in love with the role of Boris". Later in life, in voluntary exile, Chaliapin looked back on this time with great fondness: "I am still filled with joy at the wonderful period I spent working in Moscow. The atmosphere of trust and friendship seemed to increase my normal strength tenfold."

Konstantin Stanislavsky later said that he based his famous "system" of training actors on the work of Chaliapin. Chaliapin emigrated in 1922, but the authorities never gave up hope of persuading him to return to his native land. Maxim Gorky, a returned émigré himself, was used as an intermediary and he set out the privileges that the Soviet government would afford Chaliapin if he chose to return. In 1936 Stalin himself asked Chaliapin's American agent why the singer persisted in living abroad. "We'll give him money, if it is money he needs... We'll give him a house in Moscow. We'll give him a house in the country too. Just tell him to come home." On hearing of this offer, Chaliapin is said to have muttered: "You'll give me a house? You'll give me a country cottage? And what about my soul? Can you give me back my soul?"

The singer died of leukemia in Paris in April 1938. A Russian choir sang at his funeral and he was buried amid great ceremony at the Batignolles cemetery. Nearly half a century later, the Soviet government succeeded in getting his remains transferred back to his homeland and he was reburied in Novodevichy cemetery in 1984. A statue of the singer lounges back in a characteristically louche pose above the grave.

The Private Opera may have had a short existence but its influence lived on, as several other artistic enterprises took up the work that it had begun. Sergei Diaghilev, the great ballet impresario, continued the principle of taking great care over set and costume design in his productions for the Ballets Russes, his touring company that took the West by storm in the early years of the twentieth century. The designs by Alexander Golovine for *The Firebird* used Russian fairy tale motifs that echoed Stravinsky's music with its folk influences. Lev Bakst, Alexander Benois and Nikolai Roerich were some of the other talented designers who worked with Diaghilev on making his ballets the extraordinary spectacles that they were. The Moscow Art Theatre can similarly be counted as a direct descendent of the Private Opera as Stanislavsky developed many of his ideas about acting from his involvement with Mamontov's productions.

Anton Chekhov and the Moscow Art Theatre

Anton Chekhov's statue can be seen on Kamergersky pereulok, one of the first lanes leading off Tverskaya on the right hand side as you walk up the street from Manezhnaya ploshchad. It stands opposite the theatre that is forever associated with his name: the Moscow Art Theatre. The Moscow Art Theatre building was converted for the company's use by the Art Nouveau architect Fyodor Shekhtel in 1902 and its signature motif, the seagull taken from Chekhov's play of that name, is depicted on the façade as well as on the theatre's curtain. *The Seagull* was one of the Moscow Art Theatre's earliest productions and the company succeeded in transforming the play from the flop it had been when first produced in St. Petersburg into a colossal theatrical triumph.

Chekhov moved to Moscow in 1879 from Taganrog, a port town in the south of Russia on the Sea of Azov, to join the rest of his family who had moved there three years earlier. He had done well at school and had been awarded a bursary to study medicine at Moscow University. His family lived at first in cramped conditions in a damp basement flat on Trubnaya ulitsa, the continuation of ulitsa Rozhdestvenka as it runs north between the Boulevard and the Garden Ring. Trubnaya ulitsa was at that time home to a Sunday pet market where Muscovites went to buy birds, rabbits, guinea pigs and fish for their aquariums. Chekhov combined his medical studies with literary activity, earning money on the side by writing short stories for popular journals. The family moved house frequently during the 1880s, settling in 1886 on the western side of the Garden Ring at 6 Sadovaya Kudrinskaya, where the Chekhov Museum can now be found.

A brass nameplate can still be found on the door announcing the home of Doctor A. P. Chekhov, and he based his medical practice here in one of the ground-floor rooms. It was during the period when he lived at this address that Chekhov's career as a writer really began to take off as his short stories, often depicting eclectic aspects of Moscow life, became increasingly popular with the public and were published in leading literary journals. He also began to turn his hand to writing plays. Chekhov's early works, *Ivanov* and *The Bear*, were both commissioned by the Korsh Theatre and premiered in Moscow in 1887 and 1888.

Chekhov's attitude towards his adopted city varied according to the seasons and his mood. Shortly after his first arrival in the city, he had been converted to its charms: "I love Moscow tremendously. Once you get used to Moscow, you'll never leave it. I'm a Muscovite forever." Yet by 1888 he was desperate to avoid spending another winter in the city, writing that "Moscow with its cold, its rotten plays, bars and Russian thoughts makes my flesh creep… I'd gladly spend the winter as far away from Moscow as possible." In the early 1890s he took an apartment on Malaya Dmitrovka ulitsa, a street that has so many associations with the writer that it was briefly renamed ulitsa Chekhova in the post-war Soviet period. His name still adorns the nearby metro station.

While living in Malaya Dmitrovka, Chekhov introduced a pair of mongooses as family pets. He had acquired them during a short trip to Colombo in what is now Sri Lanka on his way back from the island of Sakhalin in the Far East, where he had been to investigate conditions at the penal colony there. Either Chekhov had a strange idea of what a mongoose looked like, or his pets were an odd-looking couple, as he described them in a letter to a friend as "a cross between a rat and a crocodile, a tiger and a monkey". He was evidently fond of them, writing in another letter:

If only you knew what lovely animals I brought from India! They are mongooses, the size of half-grown kittens, very cheerful lively beasts. Their qualities are daring, curiosity and affection for man...

His family were less enamoured of the new pets. Chekhov's father became exasperated at the way in which they dug up the potted plants, climbed up his beard and at how the female—which turned out in fact to be a palm civet and not a mongoose at all—would jump out from behind the furniture and bite guests. In a letter to Chekhov's younger brother Vanya he complained "the mongoose gives us no peace, it bit off a piece of mama's nose in the night." In the end, after one had died, Chekhov donated the remaining animal to Moscow's zoo.

Already in the late 1880s Chekhov had diagnosed in himself the early stages of the tuberculosis that would eventually kill him, and from 1892 he began to spend most of his time in Melikhovo, his newly acquired estate in the countryside, a short distance from Moscow. In 1897 he had a haemorrhage of the lungs and was admitted to hospital; from then on until his death in 1904 he spent his winters seeking out warmer weather, usually in Yalta on the Crimean peninsula and his summers either in Melikhovo or in Moscow.

It was only during these final years of his life that Chekhov gained his lasting fame as a playwright, thanks in no small part to the efforts of the Moscow Art Theatre company. The Theatre was founded in 1898 by Konstantin Stanislavsky and Vladimir Nemirovich-Danchenko, born out of their epic all-night meeting in June 1897 at the Slavyansky Bazar restaurant on Nikolskaya ulitsa, one of the streets that run into Red Square. The two found much common ground in their dislike of established theatres such as the Maly and their fervent desire to transform the theatrical world of Russia. Their aim was to produce contemporary as well as classical plays and for their theatre to have a social mission, reaching out to wider audiences by putting on special free performances for members of the working class. They also sought to move away from the traditional practice of having designated members of the company to play certain roles such as the leading lady or comic turn, and instead aimed to build up a versatile company of actors so that casting decisions could be made according to the demands of the particular role and the individual talents of the actor.

Other than Stanislavsky, the only big investor in the new enterprise was Savva Morozov, another of the great merchant-patrons of late nineteenth-century Moscow. The company rehearsed through the summer of 1898 and opened that autumn in the Hermitage Theatre on Karetny Ryad (Coachmakers' Row) with a mixed repertoire programme including works by Shakespeare, Sophocles and Alexei Tolstoy together with Chekhov's *The Seagull*. It had taken some persuading on Nemirovich-Dancheko's part for Chekhov to give his permission for them to stage the play: after a disastrous production in St. Petersburg he was not particularly anxious to see the work revived. In a letter to the author, written in April 1898, Nemirovich-Danchenko assured him that:

> *a real production with fresh talents, free of routine, will be a triumph of art... I guarantee you will never find greater reverence in a director or worshippers in the cast... Our theatre is beginning to arouse the strong indignation of the Imperial theatres. They understand we are making war on routine, clichés, recognized geniuses and so on.*

Although the Moscow Art Theatre's opening night performance of Alexei Tolstoy's play *Tsar Fyodor* was a success, subsequent productions were less well received and the company was pinning all its hopes on *The Seagull*. At the end of the first night, Nemirovich-Danchenko sent a telegram to Chekhov:

> *Just finished playing The Seagull: colossal success. After the first act such applause that a series of triumphs followed. At my statement after the third act that the author was not present the audience demanded a telegram be sent to you on their behalf. We are delirious with joy.*

Chekhov was committed to offer the Maly Theatre the first option on *Uncle Vanya*, but disagreements with the management meant that he ended up giving it to the Moscow Art Theatre and his next play, *Three Sisters*, was written specially for the company. Another playwright who was closely associated with the theatre in its early days was Maxim Gorky, who praised the intelligence and artistic sense of the productions. "How sorry I am I don't live in Moscow," he wrote in a letter to Chekhov in 1900, "I would be at this wonderful theatre all the time." His play *The Lower Depths*, set in the slums among people at the very lowest point on the social spectrum, was performed at the Moscow Art Theatre in 1902. Relations with Gorky broke down a few years later, however, after he received an extremely tactless letter from Nemirovich-Danchenko subjecting his play *Summer Folk* to scathing criticism.

By the turn of the century, Chekhov was a very sick man, but he was still writing plays and had fallen in love with a member of the Moscow Art Theatre company, Olga Knipper; he married her in 1901 in a quiet ceremony in Moscow and wrote the part of Masha in *Three Sisters* with her in mind. His last play, *The Cherry Orchard*, received its premiere in the new building of the Art Theatre on Kamergersky pereulok in January 1904, six months before his death. He died in Badenweiler, a German spa town, after being ordered to go abroad by his doctors. His body was brought back to Moscow by train for burial in the cemetery at Novodevichy. Maxim Gorky, who attended the funeral, found the whole thing depressing and particularly disliked the behaviour of the crowds who processed through Moscow accompanying the coffin from the station to the cemetery:

> *Anton who squirmed at anything vile and vulgar was brought in a car "for transporting fresh oysters" and buried next to the grave of a Cossack widow... People climbed trees and laughed, broke crosses and swore as they fought for a place...*

Although the Moscow Art Theatre had enjoyed a number of successful productions following the move to new premises in 1902, the relationship between its two directors, Stanislavsky and Nemirovich-Danchenko, steadily worsened. Nemirovich-Danchenko had never been happy about the dominant position that Savva Morozov had acquired as the theatre's main financer, and Stanislavsky began to develop interests in other spheres: he set up a short-lived Studio Theatre in 1905 with the involvement of Vsevolod Meyerhold, a former member of the Art Theatre company. Morozov shot himself in Nice in 1905, in despair over the failure of the 1905 revolution and affairs at the Art Theatre continued to go badly. By 1908 Stanislavsky had taken the drastic decision of resigning from the board and devoting more and more of his time to developing his famous "system" of method acting.

Having started life as a revolutionary force in the Moscow theatre world, after the 1917 Revolution the Moscow Art Theatre found itself under attack as a conservative and bourgeois institution. In a letter written in 1923, Stanislavsky described how:

> In Moscow they are slinging mud at us because we are preserving the tradition of bourgeois theatre and because plays by Chekhov and other authors of the "intelligentsia" are successful with Russian émigrés and American capitalists; they think we are rolling in dollars while in fact we are up to our ears in debt.

In 1926 a new alliance began between the theatre and the writer Mikhail Bulgakov. His play, *Days of the Turbins*, received its premiere at the Moscow Art Theatre, and in 1930 Bulgakov was employed as a member of staff. Stanislavsky lived long enough to see the Soviet theatrical world beginning to embrace his method as an official orthodoxy; after a heart attack and a long period of illness, he died in 1938.

The Moscow Art Theatre remained an important force in the Soviet theatre world, particularly in the training of young actors, but it lost its earlier cutting-edge reputation in theatrical circles and it was not until the 1970s that any attempt was made to breathe new life into the institution. This was spearheaded by the actor-director Oleg Yefremov, who had been responsible for setting up the Sovremennik (Contemporary) Theatre in the later 1950s where he had developed his ideas about psychological realism on the stage. He sought to modernize the Art Theatre's repertoire and brought in new writers and actors to work with him. In 1987 divisions within the company over the running of the theatre led to a split, and two entirely separate organizations emerged: the Chekhov Art Theatre, led by Yefremov, which remained in the old theatre on Kamergersky pereulok, and the Gorky Art Theatre, which made its home on Tverskoi Boulevard. Yefremov died in 2000 at the age of 72; both Vladimir Putin and Mikhail Gorbachev were present at his funeral.

Malaya Bronnaia Theatre

The theatre on Malaya Bronnaya ulitsa may be a relatively minor venue today, but in the early Soviet period it housed the Moscow State Yiddish Theatre. Established at a time when official policy stated that non-Russian cultures and languages should be fostered and promoted, it celebrated Jewish culture in the Soviet Union. Marc Chagall worked for the theatre in the early 1920s, designing sets and painting murals for the foyer. Productions staged in the 1930s concentrated on plays by Soviet Jewish playwrights such as David Bergelson and Shmuel Halkin. Director of the theatre from 1928, Solomon Mikhoels was a highly talented actor, famous for his portrayal of King Lear, who fell foul of the political authorities in the years following the Second World War. He had been the leader of the Jewish Anti-Fascist Committee during the war, an organization set up primarily in order to raise funds from America to help the Soviet war effort. These activities made him a useful asset to the regime, but after the war his continued calls for the setting up of a Jewish homeland in Crimea made him an object of suspicion. Stalin's anti-Semitism became increasingly apparent in the late 1940s, and in 1948 he ordered the murder of Mikhoels while he was on a trip to Minsk, the assassins arranging the body of their victim to make it look as though he had been involved in a car accident. The Yiddish Theatre was closed in 1949 and subsequently reopened as an ordinary drama theatre.

Vsevolod Meyerhold

Immediately on the left as one turns off Tverskaya through the archway onto Briusov pereulok is the apartment block where the theatre director Vsevolod Meyerhold once lived; there is a plaque outside to mark the building and a small museum with erratic opening hours within his old flat. A leading figure in the avant-garde theatre of the 1920s, his fame is due chiefly to his role in pioneering the technique of "biomechanics", a form of actors' training that was supposedly based on scientific principles, and for his conflict-ridden relationship with the Soviet authorities in the 1930s that resulted ultimately in his arrest, torture and execution.

Meyerhold was the youngest son of a German businessman from the provincial town of Penza. He went to Moscow University in 1895 where he developed his early love of the theatre and took a course in drama at the Moscow Philharmonic Society. It was there that he met some of the people who would soon become colleagues in the Moscow Art Theatre. Meyerhold was involved with the Theatre from its origins until 1902 and played the part of Konstantin Treplev in the famous 1898 production of *The Seagull*, a part that contained the prophetic lines: "What we need is a new kind of theatre. We need new forms, and if we can't get them, we'd be better off with nothing at all." Having fallen out with the Art Theatre management when they failed to invite him to become a shareholder in the company, Meyerhold left Moscow altogether and worked for several years in theatres in Kherson in Ukraine and later in St. Petersburg. He supported the Bolshevik Revolution and worked for a short time as the director of the government theatre department on his return to Moscow in 1920.

During the 1920s Meyerhold worked for a number of different institutions, both as theatre director and as a teacher of drama. Famous productions that he worked on included Gogol's *The Government Inspector* and a series of plays by Vladimir Mayakovsky: *Mystery-Bouffe*, *The Bedbug* and *The Bathhouse*. In his work for the State Higher Theatre Studios his students included Sergei Eisenstein and Zinaida Raikh, the ex-wife of the poet Sergei Yesenin, who became Meyerhold's second wife. Students who were trained in biomechanics had to learn physical skills such as gymnastics, acrobatics, boxing and fencing as a route to gaining greater mastery over their physical self-expression. "The art of the actor consists in organizing his material," Meyerhold announced in a lecture on the subject delivered in 1922, "that is, in his capacity to utilize correctly his body's means of expression." A wonderful portrait of the director lying on his side with a pipe in his mouth and a dog hanging over his legs by Pyotr Konchalovsky hangs in the New Tretyakov Gallery.

During the later 1930s Meyerhold's fortune turned. The attack on modernism in the arts that was sparked off by official criticism of the composer Shostakovich prompted attacks on Meyerhold's work, culminating in a damning *Pravda* article entitled "An Alien Theatre", in which the author, the head of the state Arts Committee, condemned Meyerhold for failing to mark the anniversary of the October

Revolution with a special production and accused him of "systematic deviation from Soviet reality, political distortion of that reality, and hostile slanders against our way of life". Colleagues—some out of vindictiveness, others simply out of terror—rushed to join in the chorus of condemnation and in 1938 his theatre was closed. The new theatre that was being built for Meyerhold's company on the corner of Tverskaya and the Garden Ring at Mayakovskaya ploshchad was converted into a concert hall and is now the Tchaikovsky Concert Hall.

Konstantin Stanislavsky, who retained a lasting respect for Meyerhold's work despite their artistic and personal differences, stepped in at this point to invite Meyerhold to come and work at his Opera Theatre on Bolshaya Dmitrovka ulitsa. Two months after Stanislavsky's death in August 1938, Meyerhold succeeded him as artistic director. Yet the authorities had not lost interest in him, and despite some indications of a change in the official policy on the arts Meyerhold was arrested in June 1939 while on a trip to Leningrad and charged with working as a foreign agent. Secret police officials visited his Moscow flat and removed a collection of papers. A month later, Zinadia Raikh had another set of visitors to the flat on Briusov pereulok: two men broke in during the small hours of the morning and murdered her, stabbing her repeatedly. It all seemed very well organized, and witnesses reported seeing the men escape to a waiting car. She was buried in the Vagankovskoe cemetery and her children were swiftly evicted from the flat. Meyerhold never learned of her death.

Meyerhold was taken to the Lubyanka where, under torture, he wrote a confession in which he incriminated other writers including Ilya Ehrenburg and Boris Pasternak. In a letter to Molotov written just before his trial, Meyerhold described the tortures to which he had been subjected and retracted his earlier admission of guilt:

> I repudiate the confessions that were beaten out of me in this way, and I beg you as Head of Government to save me and return me my freedom. I love my motherland and I will serve it with all my strength in the remaining years of my life.

The appeal fell on deaf ears. Meyerhold was tried at the beginning of February 1940; he denied all charges but was sentenced to death, the execution carried out the very next day. He is buried in the cemetery of the Donskoi Monastery, in Common Grave Number One, one of a series of common graves of the victims of political violence during the Stalin era. There are two stones over the grave, the inscription on one simply reads: "Common Grave Number One: Unclaimed Ashes from 1930-42". The other stone is more forthcoming: "Here lie the remains of the innocent victims of political repressions in 1930-42 who were tortured and shot. To their eternal memory." Orange lilies bloom here in the summer and around the plot people have added little plaques with names and dates of some of the victims.

The Taganka Theatre

Although the Brezhnev era is normally remembered as a time of stagnation, exciting work was taking place in one corner of the Moscow theatre world, at the Taganka Theatre on Taganskaya ploshchad just across the Yauza river to the southeast of the Kremlin. A theatre had been set up here just after the Second World War, but it was only after 1964 and the appointment of Yury Lyubimov as artistic director that the Taganka really began to make waves. He opened his first season with a play by Brecht, *The Good Person of Szechwan*, and followed this with a series of productions, many of which explored social and political themes. In 1972 he staged a production of *Hamlet* using an adapted version of Pasternak's translation of the play with a guitar-playing Vladimir Vysotsky cast in the lead role. It was the Taganka Theatre that created the very successful stage version of Bulgakov's masterpiece, *Master and Margarita*, in 1977, only a few years after the novel was first published in the Soviet Union. This production sealed Lyubimov's position as the most politically adventurous and daring director working in contemporary Soviet theatre and the theatrical censors took a great deal of interest in his work.

In 1983, Lyubimov went on tour to Britain. Two of his most recent productions had just been banned in Moscow: a play devised as a tribute to Vysotsky, who had died only recently, and a version of Pushkin's *Boris Godunov*. Lyubimov took the opportunity while in London to complain to the western press about his treatment at the hands of the Soviet authorities. In response, he was stripped of his Soviet citizenship, removed from his position at the Taganka and replaced by fellow director Anatoly Efros, who had a difficult time managing a company that remained loyal to their former leader. After

Efros' death in 1987, and with *glasnost* already under way in the Soviet Union, the Taganka revived Lyubimov's productions of *Vladimir Vysotsky* and *Boris Godunov*, and members of the company began lobbying for his return. Lyubimov's passport was returned to him in 1989 and he was reinstated to his former position as director.

The post-communist period has witnessed considerable instability at the Taganka. Internal divisions within the company brought about a split in the early 1990s and a long-running dispute between the two warring factions over the use of the main theatre building. Lyubimov himself lived mainly in Israel and continued to do much work abroad; Moscow critics began to suggest that he had lost touch with the Russian audience and that his theatre was failing to adapt to changing conditions and to carve out a new role for itself in the post-socialist society. They may have written the theatre's obituaries too soon, as more recent productions by Lyubimov, who is now in his eighties, have drawn much more favourable reviews. The Taganka remains an important venue for contemporary drama and retains a loyal following among theatre-going Muscovites.

MUSICAL MOSCOW

One non-Russian musician who made Moscow his home was John Field, the Irish pianist and composer who first came to Russia in 1802 with his teacher, Muzio Clementi, to open a piano showroom. He stayed on in Russia, giving concerts and taking pupils, including Mikhail Glinka and Alexander Griboedov. His compositions included several works for solo piano and the Nocturne, a musical genre that would come to be associated with the name of Chopin, was first created by Field. He died in 1837 and is buried in the Vvedenskoe cemetery near the Lefortovo Park to the north-east of the city centre. This cemetery was founded in the late eighteenth century for non-Orthodox interments and many foreigners are buried here. Famous names include Franz Lefort and Patrick Gordon, brought in by Peter the Great to help reform the Russian army; the common grave of French soldiers who died in Moscow in 1812 can also be found in Vvedenskoe.

Pyotr Tchaikovsky and Moscow Conservatoire

The Moscow Conservatoire, one of my favourite places in Moscow, can be found on Bolshaya Nikitskaya ulitsa. The yellow building is fronted by a statue of Pyotr Tchaikovsky who worked here in the 1860s and 1870s. (In the original plan for the monument, a shepherd boy was to have appeared under Tchaikovsky's arm as he raises his hands to conduct an orchestra, but this blatant reference to the composer's sexuality was sadly omitted from the final design.) The statue was executed by Vera Mukhina, the sculptor who also created the massive statue of the *Worker and Collective Farm Girl*. If you are able to attend a concert here, the Great Hall is worth a visit to see the medallions of famous composers adorning the walls. One story has it that a western visitor who was taken to see these portraits expressed surprise that Arnold Bax had been included in the ranks of Mozart, Beethoven and so on: he had, quite understandably, been confused by the Cyrillic spelling of Bach. Although the café next door to the Conservatoire has changed hands frequently over the last ten years, it has always been a pleasant spot for a drink.

Tchaikovsky arrived in Moscow in 1866 to join the staff of the new Conservatoire that had been set up by Nikolai Rubenstein, brother of the more famous Anton who had founded the first Russian Conservatoire in St. Petersburg a few years earlier. Tchaikovsky, who had originally trained as a lawyer, was among the first students to graduate from the St. Petersburg Conservatoire and he transferred to Moscow to take up the position of professor of harmony at the new institution. He was not exactly a natural teacher. One of his early students left this description of his appearance and approach:

> *My youthful impressions of his first lessons in harmony are so vivid! How well I remember his appearance at that time: young, with fair, almost handsome features, a deep, soulful gaze in his handsome dark eyes, bushy, carelessly combed hair and a marvelous auburn beard, dressed rather poorly and carelessly, most often in a threadbare gray jacket, Tchaikovsky would enter his classroom in a rush, always somewhat embarrassed and irritable, as if annoyed at the tedium to come.*

It was while he was working at Moscow Conservatoire that he wrote two of his most famous works, the opera *Eugene Onegin*, based on the Pushkin poem of that name, and the ballet *Swan Lake*.

In 1877 Tchaikovsky's life was turned upside down by an error that was entirely of his own making: his decision to marry. A former student, Antonina Milyukova, had recently begun to pursue him, writing letters declaring her love and threatening to kill herself if he rejected her. Tchaikovsky, who may well have been attracted by the idea of acquiring the social respectability that marriage could bring, agreed to make her his wife but said that he could offer her only brotherly love. Friends of the composer were astonished; one friend and colleague commented that "the news was so unexpected and strange that at first I simply refused to believe it, for it was not unusual for the most ridiculous rumours to spread through Moscow." The couple were married in July 1877 at the Church of St. George, which once stood on Malaya Nikitskaya ulitsa: as with the marriage of Pushkin and Natalya Goncharova the ceremony was fraught with ill omens, as the rose-coloured satin cloth on which the happy couple was supposed to stand had been forgotten.

Tchaikovsky soon realized that he had made a dreadful mistake. In a letter addressed to his brother only two months after the wedding he wrote "Ah! How little I love Antonina Ivanovna Tchaikovskaya! What profound indifference this lady instills in me!" He left her a month later, fleeing to Geneva in an emotional state close to nervous breakdown. "Had I stayed but one more day in Moscow I should have lost my mind or drowned myself in the foul-smelling waves of the nonetheless dear Moskva River," he declared in a letter to a friend. It was this letter that fuelled the rumours that Tchaikovsky had indeed tried to kill himself by jumping in the river in the hope that he might contract pneumonia. His *Fourth Symphony* was written at the time of this crisis in his personal life, and some critics have sought to read the work as an expression of his tortured state of mind during this period.

The composer later tried to explain his actions by making a comparison between himself and the character of Eugene Onegin, a man who also received a passionate letter from a young girl. Tchaikovsky claimed that, immersed in the story as he was at the time, he did not feel that he could behave towards Antonina in the heartless way that Onegin had treated Tatyana. It seems that this was little more than a romantic excuse as he took up his work on *Onegin* only after beginning the relationship. Antonina moved in with another man a few years after her unfortunate marriage but she continued her pursuit of

Tchaikovsky for many years. Considered to be mentally unbalanced, she was confined to an institution in 1896.

Tchaikovsky's relationship with another Muscovite lady was a much more successful affair. In 1876 he began his correspondence with Nadezhda von Meck, the wealthy widow of a businessman, who lived at 12 Rozhdestvensky Boulevard. Although the two never met, they exchanged many hundreds of letters over the next fourteen years as von Meck became his patron, enabling Tchaikovsky to give up his teaching post at the Conservatoire and to devote himself entirely to composition. She took a dim view of the Conservatoire in any case, writing on one occasion that she would "never send even a son there, much less a daughter" on account of the appalling reports she had heard about moral laxity among the student body. After spending a number of years moving between Europe and Russia, Tchaikovsky settled in the small town of Klin to the north-west of Moscow, renting a series of houses in the area and spending most of his time there. He died of cholera in 1893 in St. Petersburg and was buried in the Alexander Nevsky cemetery after a massive state funeral.

There is another building in Moscow that bears Tchaikovsky's name: the Tchaikovsky Concert Hall just outside Mayakovskaya metro station on Triumfalnaya Square but it has no connection whatsoever with the composer. A stretch of the Garden Ring near to the United States Embassy used to be named in his honour (ulitsa Chaikovskogo) to mark the fact that he lived in that area for a short period, but since the end of communism it has reverted to its original name of Novinsky Boulevard.

Sergei Rachmaninov

Next door to the main Conservatoire building stands the Rachmaninov Hall, named after the illustrious former student Sergei Rachmaninov. He moved to Moscow in 1885 at the age of twelve to live at the house of the celebrated piano teacher Nikolai Zverev and to study music with him. This was a very intensive period of training as Zverev insisted on very strict discipline and hours of daily practice from his pupils, but he also offered them unparalleled opportunities to go to concerts and to meet with luminaries of the Moscow musical world—Rubinstein, Tchaikovsky, Taneev—who were regular guests for Sunday lunch. His pupils became known, colloquially, as the *zveryata,* "cubs", a play on his own name *Zverev* meaning "wild beast".

Rachmaninov entered the Moscow Conservatoire in 1888 and Tchaikovsky himself was present at his examination for entrance to the Composers' Division of the school. At this time, the Conservatoire was dominated by Sergei Taneev, who took over as Director from Nikolai Rubinstein. In an obituary written for his former teacher Rachmaninov described him as "the most scholarly musician of his time, a man of rare originality, of rare spiritual quality, Moscow's musical leader, maintaining this high position with unwavering authority until the end of his days."

After an argument with Zverev, Rachmaninov moved out of his house and went to stay with his relations, the Satin family. He ended up marrying his first cousin, Natalya Satina, in 1902. As a composer, Rachmaninov was very much shaped by the strong influence that Tchaikovsky's work had in Moscow at that time. Although Tchaikovsky had ceased working at the Conservatoire by the time Rachmaninov entered it, the older man clearly had a high opinion of Rachmaninov's skill as a composer. He made a great show of publicly applauding the one-act opera, *Aleko*, a piece based on a Pushkin poem that Rachmaninov wrote for his final examinations at the Conservatoire.

Without a rich patron to take care of him, Rachmaninov made a living by conducting, teaching music at a girls' school and by making concert tours both at home and abroad as a virtuoso pianist. A statue to the composer has recently been erected on Strastnoi Boulevard at the top of ulitsa Petrovka near the school where he once worked. In 1897, Savva Mamontov approached him to become a conductor with his Private Opera and it was in this capacity that he first became acquainted with the singer, Fyodor Chaliapin, who was to become a lifelong friend. When not abroad, Rachmaninov divided his time between Moscow and Ivanovka, his country estate.

Much of the music that Rachmaninov wrote during these years was inspired by the Russian Orthodox Church. Of his choral symphony, *The Bells*, he wrote that "if I have been at all successful in making bells vibrate with human emotion in my works, it is largely due to the fact that most of my life was lived amid vibrations of the bells of Moscow." His *Vespers*, written in 1915 for unaccompanied choir, used traditional Russian plainchant as its inspiration. Many critics both at the time and since commented on the romantic nature of his compositions and his failure to engage with modernist influences: one described him as "the last of the musical Mohicans of the past century, stubbornly ignoring new trends in music." Rachmaninov himself was aware of his isolation in the modern world of music, remarking to an interviewer in 1939 that "I cannot cast out the old way of writing, and I cannot acquire the new."

Rachmaninov avoided being enlisted in the First World War because, as a teacher, he worked in a reserved profession. October 1917 found the composer in Moscow, working hard on revising his *First Piano Concerto*. In his memoirs he described how he barely noticed the commotion going on in the city as the Bolsheviks seized power:

> *I was so engrossed with my work that I did not notice what went on around me. Consequently, life during the anarchist upheaval, which turned the existence of a non-proletarian into hell on earth, was comparatively easy for me. I sat at the writing-table or the piano all day without troubling about the rattle of machine-guns and rifle-shots.*

Despite this preoccupation, Rachmaninov clearly understood the implications of the recent developments and, having been invited to give a concert tour of Scandinavia, he applied for exit visas for his whole family. They left Russia in November 1917 and Rachmaninov spent much of the rest of his life on the road, giving concert tours in Europe and the United States. This unsettled lifestyle meant that he was able to devote less time to composition and his creative output suffered as a result. Rachmaninov never returned to his homeland and his music was blacklisted for a long time as the work of a decadent bourgeois émigré.

Alexander Scriabin

One year after the untimely death of Alexander Scriabin, as the memorial plaque was being erected outside the house where the composer spent his last years before his untimely death in 1915, the poet Vyacheslav Ivanov wrote the following lines:

> *Stop, passerby! Within these walls*
> *Scriabin lived and found his resting place.*
> *Stern stone in letters few has told you all.*

The seed is sown. In our primeval depths
A star is lit. Now go your way.

The best way to visit the Scriabin Museum is to attend a concert there. Recitals are given regularly in the house at 11 Bolshoi Nikolopeskovsky perulok, a two-storey yellow building situated in a small turning off the Arbat. As well as hearing music here, one can also see the special coloured bulb device that was designed to order for use in the performance of Scriabin's *Prometheus* symphony. The contraption was intended to flood the concert hall with different coloured lights that would change as the music was performed. Scriabin was very interested in Wagnerian ideas about achieving a synthesis of the arts, and his experimentation with sound and light was merely one aspect of this lifelong project.

Born in Moscow in 1871, Scriabin had an unusual upbringing in the care of his grandmother, aunt and great-aunt. Some biographers have argued that his overweening self-confidence in his own greatness may derive from being spoiled as a child by his doting female relatives; it is said that they were so over-protective that he was not allowed out of the house on his own until he was fourteen. He studied music with Taneev and with Nikolai Zverev, the leading music teachers of the day at Moscow Conservatoire, and began by composing works in the style of Chopin before moving on to develop his own distinctive musical style. He was fortunate in gaining the support of two of Moscow's wealthy merchant patrons, Mitrofan Belyaev and Margarita Morozova, who helped to finance his career as a composer.

Scriabin's work was strongly influenced by the Symbolist movement, itself inspired by the writings of the philosopher Vladimir Soloviev who exhorted artists to search for a higher realm of truth and beauty beyond the banality of the everyday world. The composer took philosophy very seriously and believed that he had been called to change the world and to bring the human race through to a higher state of being through his music. His final work was to have brought about a fusion of the arts into a ritual, the *Mysterium* in which there would be no separation between audience and performer, and changing lights and columns of incense would work together to elevate mankind to a higher plane of existence. This great project, which dominated his final years, was never to be realized: Scriabin developed a spot on his upper lip which turned gangrenous, plunging him into the fever that killed him in April 1915.

The funeral was a grand affair. Rachmaninov, who attended it, recalled the event in his memoirs:

> *I am still conscious of the deep and soul-stirring impression I received at Scriabin's funeral. All the literary, musical and artistic celebrities of Moscow were assembled there, and filled not only the little church situated opposite to Scriabin's flat, but the whole vast square in front of it.*

He was buried initially at the Dorogomilov cemetery and later his remains were transferred to Novodevichy.

Contemporaries were divided in their assessment of Scriabin's work. The young Boris Pasternak, who heard him composing music at the piano in his dacha, fell in love with the music, worshipped its composer and vowed to follow in his footsteps and pursue a musical career himself. In his view, Scriabin's work was "wholly contemporary, it had an inner correspondence, in musical terms, to the surrounding world, to the way people thought, felt, lived, dressed and travelled in those days." Others were much less enthusiastic; some listeners came to the conclusion that he must have been insane, while Scriabin's former teacher at Moscow Conservatoire, Sergei Taneev, said that hearing the *Poem of Ecstasy* made him feel as if he was being beaten with sticks. Scriabin's fellow Symbolist, Valery Briusov, left a more poetic assessment of his work:

> *He dared to melt the metal of melodies*
> *and to cast it in new forms.*
> *He aspired to lofty aims:*
> *to praise God and to illuminate*
> *the spirit by means of sound.*

Sergei Prokofiev

Sergei Prokofiev and Dmitry Shostakovich are probably the two best-known composers of the Soviet period. Although neither was a Muscovite by birth, both lived for significant periods of their lives in Moscow and both are buried there, in Novodevichy cemetery. Prokofiev was born in Ukraine and studied at St. Petersburg Conservatoire; he left Russia shortly after the Revolution and lived in Europe and the United States for over a decade. From 1927 onwards, the Soviet authorities began a concerted campaign to lure him back to Russia. On a concert tour to the Soviet Union in 1927 he was treated to the best of everything with a room at the Metropol hotel and meals in fine restaurants. Prokofiev was not entirely naïve: he commented in his diary that "we feel completely stunned by Moscow, but I am at all times solidly conscious of the fact that the Bolsheviks are adept at showing off in order to impress foreigners."

He gave a series of eight concerts in Moscow, including two performances with the Persimfans, an innovatory Moscow orchestra of the 1920s that chose to dispense with the bourgeois tyranny of a conductor. Another visit followed in late 1929, and from 1932 Prokofiev began to spend ever longer periods living in the USSR. He eventually took out Soviet citizenship. His reasons for returning from emigration were probably largely economic: he had been having difficulty arranging concert engagements in the depression-hit United States, whereas the economic position for artists in the Soviet Union looked bright and the authorities were prepared to offer him substantial privileges if he was willing to return.

From 1936, Prokofiev and his Spanish wife Lina lived in a luxury apartment located in a large block on Zemlyanoi Val, the eastern side of the Garden Ring not far from the Kursk station. The whole building was given over to elite members of the intelligentsia: neighbours included the pianist Genrikh Neigauz and the violinist David Oistrakh. The Prokofiev family was given a four-room apartment including a study and dining room and a piano was specially imported from Czechoslovakia for the composer's use. Prokofiev's privileged position was underlined by the fact that the authorities continued to permit him to travel; his last trip abroad was taken in 1938. It was during this period before the war that Prokofiev wrote two of his best-known works: the ballet *Romeo and Juliet*, commissioned for the Bolshoi, which provided ballerina Galina Ulanova with her greatest role; and *Peter and the Wolf*, written for the Moscow Children's Musical Theatre. Prokofiev's collaboration with the film director Sergei Eisenstein began in 1938 when he wrote the music for the film of *Alexander Nevsky*; he wrote another film score for Eisenstein's *Ivan the Terrible* in the 1940s.

By the time of the German invasion in 1941, Prokofiev had left his wife and moved in with his young lover, Mira Mendelson, and her parents. They were evacuated from Moscow during the war, traveling to Tbilisi and later to Alma Ata in Kazakhstan. In October 1943 they returned to Moscow and after the war they lived first on Kutuzovsky prospekt and later on Kamergersky pereulok near the Moscow Art Theatre, where a small museum to the composer has been established. In 1948 Prokofiev came under fire from the authorities when the cultural commissar, Andrei Zhdanov, included him by name in his general attack on "formalism" in Soviet music. A month later, Lina Prokofieva was arrested on charges of spying for foreign powers and sent to the Gulag for twenty years; their sons, who had witnessed the ransacking of their apartment by the secret police, had to walk much of the way to Prokofiev's dacha outside Moscow to find their father and give him the news.

Prokofiev died on exactly the same day as Stalin, 5 March 1953. Members of the Borodin Quartet, who came to play at his coffin found they had to fight their way through the crowds as they hurried from this engagement to their next one, at the Hall of Columns for Stalin's lying-in-state. Prokofiev's funeral was small and low-key; every flower in Moscow had been taken for Stalin. David Oistrakh played two movements from the composer's *First Violin Sonata* and then his body was taken for burial to Novodevichy cemetery.

Dmitry Shostakovich

Dmitry Shostakovich moved to Moscow with his family in 1943 and lived here until his death thirty-two years later. He is, nevertheless, rightly considered a Leningrader: born and brought up in the city, he identified himself as a Leningrader and continued to support the Zenith football team even after he had moved cities. He had considered moving earlier: even as early as 1924 the talented seventeen-year-old composer had completed an application and been accepted by the professors of Moscow Conservatoire to study composition, but the move never took place. In 1928 he spent a few months working as a pianist at Meyerhold's theatre in Moscow and during this time he lived with the Meyerhold family. In a description of his time there, the young composer wrote:

I am living here in an environment of geniuses (a genius director, a "genius actress," "Akh, Zinka! How well you acted yesterday. It was genius"), a "genius" composer and a "genius" poetess. The last two are the offspring of the "genius" poet Yesenin and the "genius" actress.

His first opera, *The Nose*, based on the short story by Gogol about a bureaucrat whose nose runs off and has a series of adventures, owed a great deal to Meyerhold's influence. Shostakovich had recently seen Meyerhold's production of Gogol's *The Government Inspector*, and his early work on the opera was undertaken while living in Meyerhold's Moscow apartment. He worked with the director again in 1929 when he wrote the music for Mayakovsky's play *The Bedbug*. Both *The Bedbug* and *The Nose* were the subjects of considerable controversy and were criticized by self-styled "proletarian" critics: *The Nose*, in particular, was attacked as being too complex and inaccessible and lacking social relevance.

As we have already seen with regard to some of the writers of the early Soviet period, the 1920s had been a time when artists were given considerable leeway to explore different approaches and ideas. This would all change at the end of the decade: as more liberal economic policies were abandoned in favour of the Five Year Plans, so too, artists were coerced into abandoning their experimental ideas in favour of producing works that could, in some way, provide service to the state. Initially the pressures for this kind of revolution in the arts came from below, from the groups who disliked anything that smacked of modernism, but from the early 1930s onwards the political authorities took increasing control.

Shostakovich's career was buffeted by these changes in the political environment. The composer came under more serious fire in 1936 when an unsigned article appeared in *Pravda* attacking his second opera, *Lady Macbeth of Mtsensk*, which Stalin had recently seen performed at the Bolshoi in Moscow. The article derided the work as "chaos instead of music", an example of "leftist art" which left its listeners "stunned by the deliberately dissonant, confused stream of sounds". The attack, together with later criticism of Shostakovich's ballet, *The Sparkling Stream*, about life on the collective farm, caused uproar in Soviet musical life. Meetings were held to discuss the articles and colleagues heaped further criticism on the head of the unfortunate

Shostakovich. In the following year he was questioned by the secret police about the extent of his connections with Marshal Tukhachevsky, a high standing army officer and musical patron who was executed on charges of spying for Nazi Germany in June 1937. His official rehabilitation came only in November 1937 when his *Fifth Symphony*, later subtitled "A Soviet artist's creative response to just criticism", was premiered to acclaim.

Shostakovich, together with his wife Nina and two young children, were evacuated from Leningrad in October 1941: the Wehrmacht had by this time already encircled the city and the nine hundred day siege had begun. They went to Moscow and from there were able to get tickets to travel eastwards as part of the evacuation of the Bolshoi Theatre: they settled in the city of Kuibyshev where he wrote his seventh symphony, the *Leningrad Symphony*. By 1943, with the Germans defeated at Stalingrad, Shostakovich returned to Moscow where he was persuaded by his friend Vissarion Shebalin to take up a teaching position at Moscow Conservatoire. The family lived initially at the Hotel Moskva, but soon moved into an apartment on Myasnitskaya ulitsa, at that time called ulitsa Kirova. Flora Litvinov, a friend of the family, described their living quarters as "a dark apartment on Kirov Street that looked out on the courtyard. But they were delighted with it, as it meant that at last they could establish a normal family life in their own home."

They lived here until 1947 when they were awarded a larger apartment, in fact two apartments knocked together to house two grand pianos in the composer's study, on Kutuzovsky prospekt, the grand avenue west of Kievskaya metro where much elite housing was constructed in the post-war period. It is rumoured that Stalin took a personal hand in arranging the composer's accommodation, and Shostakovich's position as a privileged member of the elite was further confirmed when he was granted a dacha outside Moscow. It was clear that he had abandoned his earlier plan to move back to Leningrad and by November his mother, who still lived there, was writing to a friend that "I still can't get accustomed to the idea that Mitya has abandoned his city. But in all probability it was necessary."

Privileged or not, Shostakovich was by no means exempt from criticism and in 1948 his name was included, along with Prokofiev's, in the attack on "formalism" in Soviet music. He made the required gestures of public repentance at composers' meetings during the following months but to no avail: in September of that year he was dismissed from his position at Moscow Conservatoire. In an attempt to rehabilitate himself in the eyes of the authorities, he turned his hand to writing music for a series of films about the Second World War as well as a pair of works composed according to strict socialist realist guidelines: the *Song of the Forests* dedicated to Stalin's reforestation campaign, and a cantata entitled *The Sun Shines Over Our Motherland*. He also wrote his song cycle *From Jewish Folk Poetry*, which may have been an attempt to take seriously the injunction that he should try to base his compositions on folk music in order to make it more accessible to ordinary people; this backfired when a campaign of official anti-Semitism took off during Stalin's declining years and the piece remained unperformed until after the dictator's death.

His wife, Nina, died of cancer in 1954 and the opera singer Galina Vishnevskaya who visited Shostakovich at home not long after described how his domestic affairs had gone to pieces: "When I first entered the apartment I was amazed by the disorder that reigned within—the lack of comfort, despite the fact that two women lived there: the maid Mariya Dmitriyevna and the old nanny Fenya. Everything bore the stamp of neglect."

In 1962 he moved again, having been allocated a large apartment in the Composers' Union block on Briusov pereulok just off Tverskaya. That same year he married Irina Supinskaya, a music publishing assistant who was only a few years older than his daughter Galina. It was also in 1962 that Shostakovich's *Thirteenth Symphony* was given its premiere. This work was a setting of the well-known Soviet poet Yevgeny Yevtushenko's *Babiy Yar*: a poem that summoned up memories of a massacre of Jews in Ukraine during the war. It was a controversial choice as the Soviet authorities had never acknowledged the Holocaust, and Yevtushenko had been accused of trying to make it seem as though Jews had suffered more greatly than Russians. The resulting work was premiered on 18 December 1962 to a massive ovation from the Moscow audience, although the newspapers chose to downplay the event and critics largely ignored it. Yevtushenko was hugely impressed by the work, recalling that:

what astonished me first of all in the Thirteenth Symphony was that if I (a total musical ignoramus) had suddenly developed an ear, that would be the music I would have written. Moreover, Shostakovich's reading of my poetry was so exact in intonation and sense that it felt as if he had been inside me when I was writing the poem and he had composed the music as the lines were born.

Shostakovich was troubled by failing health during the late 1960s and 1970s: heart trouble compounded by a rare form of polio and finally lung cancer. He died in August 1975. It was a bad time of year for a funeral: all the Moscow orchestras were on tour, so taped music predominated at his lying-in-state in the Great Hall of the Moscow Conservatoire. Mark Lubotsky, a violinist who attended, remembered how the dead composer had been given too much make-up and looked almost unrecognizable and how, in the official orations, all the speakers took pains to emphasize how "first and foremost, he was a communist." He described the burial in his diary:

A notice on the gate of the Novodevichy cemetery said "It is forbidden to visit the cemetery on Thursdays." It was cold. A military band was butchering its way through Chopin's Funeral March. We stood around a platform listening to more speeches...Hammers banged. They were nailing down the lid of the coffin. Then they moved. Then they stopped. The Soviet anthem was played. It was cold and it started to drizzle.

Bulat Okudzhava

A very different kind of music was written and sung by the post-war Soviet guitar poets, musicians whose songs often explored themes of identity, social problems and melancholy. Bulat Okudzhava was a Muscovite born and bred whose songs betray his deep love of his native city. His parents were both Communist Party members who came from the Caucasus, his father from Georgia and his mother from Armenia. Both fell victim to Stalin's purges in 1937: his father was accused of spying and shot, and his mother was sent to the labour camps; he did not see her again until her release in 1955. In 1995 Okudzhava won the Russian Booker Prize for a novel, *The Show is Over*, which told the story of his parents and their tragic fate.

In 1942 the seventeen-year-old Okudzhava volunteered for the army; he survived the war and later studied at Tbilisi University. After the rehabilitation of his parents in 1955 he and his mother returned to live in Moscow and Okudzhava joined the Party and the Soviet Writers' Union. A prolific writer, he chose to sing his poems rather than recite them, accompanying their melancholy tunes on the guitar. His verses, which often took a philosophical approach to life, touched on themes of love, hope, war and his beloved Moscow. One famous song is devoted to the Arbat, the old gentry and intelligentsia district that has now become a centre for vulgar souvenir stalls.

Flowing on like a river, with your odd name
Your asphalt transparent like river water;
Arbat, my Arbat, you are my vocation
You're my joy and my disaster too

In other songs he sang about the Moscow metro, about nostalgia for how Moscow must have been in Pushkin's day and about traveling home on the last trolleybus of the night:

...the last one, a chance one.

Midnight trolleybus, sweep through the streets
Make your circuits round the boulevards
Picking up everyone who in the night has suffered
Disaster, disaster...

His work could not have been more different from the officially sanctioned music of the time with its upbeat rhythms, and for the most part it was circulated secretly, with tapes passed from hand to hand between groups of likeminded enthusiasts. During the 1960s Okudzhava joined the dissident movement, signing letters of protest against the arrest of the writers Andrei Sinyavsky and Yury Daniel in 1966 and against Alexander Solzhenitsyn's expulsion from the Writers' Union in 1969. In 1972 these activities brought about his expulsion from the Communist Party. It was not until the *glasnost* era of the late 1980s that official recordings began to appear and today it is relatively easy to acquire them from the CD kiosks at metro stations.

Okudzhava died in 1997 in Paris. His body was brought back to Moscow where leading politicians of the day, including Anatoly Chubais and Boris Nemtsov, attended his lying-in-state and thousands of people lined the Arbat to pay their respects. The guitar poet whom fellow poet Bella Akhmadulina described as "the conscience of the epoch" was buried in Vagankovskoe cemetery. A statue of him standing beneath an archway, slouched, with his hands in his pockets, has recently been erected on the Arbat near the corner with Plotnikov pereulok.

Vladimir Vysotsky

Okudzhava's gentle melodies contrast sharply with the harsh and angry tones of some of the later guitar poets, yet it was he who provided the inspiration for their work. The best- known and best loved of his successors was Vladimir Vysotsky whose funeral in 1980 overshadowed the city's excitement at hosting the Olympic Games and brought huge crowds of people out onto the streets. Vysotsky was born in Moscow in 1938, trained as an actor at the Moscow Art Theatre school and entered the Taganka theatre company in 1964 when Yury Lyubimov took it over. His charisma made him a popular performer and his 1972 interpretation of the role of Hamlet received considerable acclaim. He also appeared in films and lived a glamorous lifestyle, marrying the French film star Marina Vlady in 1975, enabling him to travel abroad during the final years of his life.

Vysotsky's singing voice was that of a hardened smoker and heavy drinker, deep and rasping, but his songs had a directness and an intensity that connected with audiences. Many of his earlier songs were about underworld themes: drunkenness, violence, criminality, but later works explored the Second World War and the legacy that it had left.

His songs, like those of Okudzhava, were circulated illicitly and won him widespread popularity across the Soviet Union. His death, from heart failure accelerated by alcohol abuse, at the age of forty-two came as a shock. Despite the lack of any official announcement, the news spread quickly and thousands of Muscovites came to the Taganka Theatre to view his coffin. Police were brought in to prevent his burial in Vagankovskoe cemetery from turning into a political demonstration. Lyubimov famously commented that "after Vysotsky's funeral… I began to respect the people of Moscow."

Many of Vysotsky's friends sought to honour him after his death. Lyubimov created a play at the Taganka, *Vladimir Vysotsky*, which used his songs and poems together with excerpts from *Hamlet* to create a memorable production. The authorities thought otherwise, with one official stating starkly that "the play is anti-Soviet and cannot be staged." The official view of Vysotsky had always been negative: very few of his works were ever published or recorded officially during his lifetime and the themes explored in the play—alcoholism and death among others—were not likely to endear it to the censors. One special performance of the play to a selected audience was permitted on the anniversary of his death, but otherwise the production was banned and it was in part over this issue that Lyubimov confronted the regime and lost his Soviet citizenship.

A characteristically philosophical tribute to the poet was written by Bulat Okudzhava:

> *I wanted to make up a song about Volodya Vysotsky*
> *But my hand trembled, and the tune didn't fit the line*
> *A white Moscow stork has flown up into the white sky*
> *A black Moscow stork has come down to the black earth.*

In 1995, in an indication of how much things had changed with post-communism, a rather unattractive statue of the singer, with his arms outstretched, was erected along the stretch of the boulevard between Pushkinskaya ploshchad and the Petrovka. Vysotksy himself had written a song containing the lines:

> *And although I believed in the radiant everything,*
> *For example in our Soviet People.*

Even so, don't build me a statue
Anywhere near the Petrovsky gates.

They ignored him, but in any case fans of Vysotsky had already made his grave in Vagankovskoe their place of pilgrimage: flowers are routinely placed around the plot with its golden statue of the singer, his guitar strapped to his back, creating a halo effect behind his head.

Chapter Seven
CITY OF RICH AND POOR

The Pashkov Mansion
The Pashkov Mansion, "one of the most beautiful buildings in Moscow" in Bulgakov's view, was built in the 1780s by Vasily Bazhenov for a nobleman named Pyotr Pashkov. It stands on the slope of ulitsa Mokhovaya, overlooking the Kremlin and is notable for its columned exterior, the decorated balustrade around the roof and the circular belvedere at the very top of the building offering panoramic views across the city. The grounds of the house, which originally swept down to the banks of the Neglinnaya river, were a favourite spot for lavish parties: an orchestra would be hired to play as guests strolled around the garden admiring the fountains and statues as well as the swans, cranes and peacocks.

Such were the leisure pursuits of wealthy Muscovites in pre-revolutionary times. It was not like this for everybody. In a description dating from the early nineteenth century,

> ...here, luxury and indigence, abundance and utter poverty, piety and unbelief, old-time steadfastness and extraordinary frivolity are, like hostile elements, in perpetual discord and compromise, this wondrous, shapeless, colossal whole that we know by the general name of Moscow.

One would be forgiven for surveying Moscow now and reaching the conclusion that not that much has changed: extravagant wealth and grinding poverty coexist side by side today, much as they did in earlier times. This chapter will explore the contrasting lives of Muscovites from different social backgrounds in the pre-revolutionary period.

Sadly, the gardens of the Pashkov Mansion have now been replaced by busy roads with endless traffic. Badly affected by the 1812 fire, the building was renovated by Bove using money donated by the King of Prussia. In the nineteenth century the house became a boys' school and in the early 1860s it was home to the Rumyantsev Museum, founded in St. Petersburg in the 1820s on the basis of the personal collections amassed by Count Nikolai Rumyantsev and later moved to Moscow. Rumyantsev, the son of a famous military commander, was a well-educated Russian nobleman who helped to fund geographical expeditions and archaeological excavations and put together an unrivalled collection of manuscripts, books, paintings and sculptures.

The museum housed a library that was said to be one of the best in Europe; the collection expanded over time as other aristocratic book collectors donated their libraries to the Rumyantsev. Tolstoy worked in the library when he was doing historical research for *War and Peace*, and Ivan Tsvetaev, father of the poet Marina Tsvetaeva, was the curator for many years before he achieved his lifelong ambition of setting up a museum of the fine arts—the Pushkin Museum—in 1912. After the Revolution, the museum's collections were broken up, with the art works, including the enormous canvas by Alexander Ivanov, *The Appearance of Christ to the People*, distributed between the Tretyakov Gallery and the Pushkin Museum. The book collection remained in place, however, and the Pashkov Mansion was used to house the manuscripts division of the nearby Lenin Library. It was from the roof of this building that the devil and his accomplice, Azazello, gaze down on the city as they bid farewell to Moscow in Bulgakov's *Master and Margarita*. The house fell into disrepair during the later Soviet period and only in the post-Soviet era has funding finally been made available for renovations, both to the Pashkov Mansion and to the nearby Lenin Library.

The Nobles' Club

The House of Unions on Okhotny Ryad next to the State Duma or parliament building, is another grand building in central Moscow with aristocratic associations. Originally built in the 1780s by Matvei Kazakov as a private mansion for Prince Dolgoruky, it later became the Nobles' Club and underwent several reconstructions, most drastically in the aftermath of the 1812 fire. Concerts and balls were held in the chandeliered gold and white Columned Hall, so named for its twenty-eight columns, and this venue became the centre of the Moscow marriage market in the winter months, when members of the aristocracy were in residence in their town houses. As Pushkin famously put it:

> *Moscow was the assembling place for all the Russian nobility who gathered here in the winter from all the provinces... In the hall of the Club of the Nobility five thousand people would meet twice a week. Young people would meet each other here; marriages were arranged. Moscow was as famous for its brides as Vyazma for its honey cakes.*

The British traveller John Parkinson visited the Club in 1793 and described how it operated at that time:

> *The members of this Club are about 2,500, a thousand men and 1,500 ladies. The subscription for the men is 20 roubles, for the ladies 10. But the supper and other refreshments are not included... The Club opens, I think, in the month of September and shuts in the month of May. They meet once a week. The company assembles at seven and sometimes don't break up till four in the morning.*

The French composer, Hector Berlioz, gave a concert in the Columned Hall in 1847 although he faced difficulty when an official demanded that Berlioz confirm his ability to play an instrument (something the composer was unable to do) before allowing him to conduct his own music. This was also the venue for the first performance of Rachmaninov's *Vespers* and concerts are still held in the hall from time to time.

The Nobles' Club was the scene of several important political events: Tsar Alexander II is said to have announced his intention to emancipate the Russian serfs to members of the aristocracy gathered here in 1856, just after the ending of the Crimean War. This was also the place where the celebrations to mark the unveiling of the Pushkin statue were held in 1880, when Dostoevsky made a famous speech in which he described the poet as a prophet. After the Revolution, the Bolshevik authorities turned the mansion over to the state-run trade union organization and it became the House of Unions. It was still used for political purposes: the Moscow show trials of 1936-8 were held in the building, and it remained an important venue for ceremonial events, in particular, the lying-in-state of dead leaders: both Lenin and Stalin lay here while thousands of mourners passed by their coffins.

The Moscow English Club

A member of the Moscow English club! O, that is a creature of a completely special kind, which has not its like either in Russia, or any other land. The chief distinguishing trait of its character is confidence in its own omniscience.

Filip Wiegel (a friend of Pushkin)

Muscovite noblemen were prepared to wait for years to win election to membership of the English Club, an aristocratic institution designed along the lines of an English gentlemen's club. Initially housed in the Gagarin mansion on the corner of Petrovka and Strastnoi Boulevard, a building that is now a hospital, the club was moved in the early 1830s to the grand mansion of the former Razumovsky Palace on Tverskaya, which later became the home of the Museum of Modern History (until recently known as the Museum of the Revolution). The museum is situated on the stretch of Tverskaya between the Boulevard and the Garden Rings and is easily identifiable by the lions on the gateposts, seemingly sculpted by someone who had never actually seen a lion in his life. One room of the museum reproduces the interior of the club with its marble columns, richly decorated ceilings and chandeliers, and displays in this room trace the club's history through documents and pictures.

Enthusiastic members of the English Club wrote in glowing terms about the attractions offered by the library, with its peaceful atmosphere, comfortable seating and ready supply of periodicals. Women were only permitted to enter the building on the day of a Tsar's coronation, otherwise it was an entirely male establishment where friends could meet up and play cards or have dinner together. Captain Colville Frankland cast an Englishman's expert eye over the club during his visit to Russia in 1830-1 when he was taken there by Pushkin, who had only recently gained membership himself. Frankland claimed it derived its name, perversely, from the fact that it did not have any English members and described the club:

It is a splendid establishment, upon a very large scale, and is clean and cool, and comfortable… I never sat so short a time at dinner anywhere… No English newspapers are taken in the English Club; nor any of our Reviews… the library consists of almost exclusively old French works. There is a very spacious and agreeable garden in the rear of the club-house, where the gentlemen amused themselves in bowling at nine-pins…

The most famous literary depiction of the club appears in *War and Peace*, in Tolstoy's description of the dinner held for General Bagration in 1806 in the old club building on the Petrovka. The dinner, for 300 people, is organized by Natasha's father, Count Rostov, who "had been a member and on the committee of the club from the day it was founded." A grand banquet is planned with asparagus, strawberries, veal and turtle soup with cocks' combs in it and the Count brings his own orchestra to provide entertainment for the guests. On the evening of the dinner:

all the rooms in the English Club were filled with a hum of conversation, like the hum of bees swarming in spring-time. The members and guests of the club wandered hither and thither, sat, stood, met and separated, some in uniform and some in evening dress and a few here and there with powdered hair and in Russian kaftans. Powdered footmen in livery with buckled shoes and smart stockings stood at every door anxiously noting visitors' every movement in order to offer their services…

The Old Equerries Quarter

Catherine the Great took a dim view of Moscow. She disliked what she saw as the city's medieval backwardness and felt that the noblemen who lived there were a bunch of lay-abouts. "Moscow is the seat of sloth," she wrote, "partly due to its immensity: one wastes a whole day trying to visit someone or getting a message across to them. The nobles who live there are excessively fond of the place and no wonder: they live in idleness and luxury, and become effeminate." She was not alone in holding such opinions. The poet Konstantin Batyushkov felt that in Moscow:

indolence is something all can share, an attribute exclusive to this town, and which can be observed primarily in a kind of restless curiosity which possesses its inhabitants, driving them towards a continual search for new distractions.

Muscovite noblemen were generous in their hospitality and many issued an open invitation to guests wishing to dine or take tea with them. The anarchist Prince Kropotkin recalled how, during his childhood, his father used to like having plenty of guests and how their house was open to anyone who wished to join them at the samovar after dinner. Batyushkov believed that this liberal approach to hospitality was the product of the Muscovite "search for new distractions"—curiosity led them to open their doors to all comers in the hope of meeting new and interesting people. In contrast with other towns, where complete strangers were not likely to be showered with invitations to dinner, "in Moscow they invite you first, and get to know you later."

Noble mansions in Moscow tended to be clustered in a number of fashionable districts. The Old Equerries quarter (*Staraya Konyushennaya*) is the name given to the area between the Old Arbat and Prechistenka ulitsa, the road leading out towards Novodevichy where members of the old Muscovite upper classes had their homes. Kropotkin was brought up in this district, in the street that now bears his name, Kropotkinsky pereulok. The house, no. 26, is now the Palestinian Embassy. Kropotkin left a memorable description of the area in the mid-nineteenth century:

In these quiet streets, far away from the noise and bustle of commercial Moscow, all the houses had much the same appearance. They were mostly built of wood, with bright green sheet-iron roofs, the exteriors stuccoed and decorated with columns and porticoes; all were painted in gay colours... A second story was admitted only in the back part of the house, which looked upon a spacious yard, surrounded by numbers of small buildings, used as kitchens, stables, cellars, coach-houses, and as dwellings for the retainers and servants... Life went on quietly and peacefully—at least for the outsider—in this Moscow Faubourg Saint-Germain.

The district is now home to several foreign embassies. Ulitsa Prechistenka contains a wealth of post-1812 classical "empire style" mansions in pastel colours with colonnades, arches and pediments. The street climbs uphill, giving a good view of the Kremlin towers below. Museums devoted to Tolstoy and Pushkin can be found along Prechistenka although neither building has any connection with the writer. In the Soviet period it was renamed Kropotkinskaya ulitsa, but it later reverted to the old name although the nearby metro station continues to bear the name of Kropotkin. The Brezhnev-era statue at the traffic intersection just outside the metro station is not of Kropotkin, as might have been supposed, but of Friedrich Engels. The intention was that he would stand at one end of prospekt Marksa (Marx Prospect) facing towards the Karl Marx statue in Teatralnaya ploshchad at the other. Today, Engels' gaze is met instead by the towering edifice of the newly rebuilt Cathedral of Christ the Saviour: the opium of the people proved more potent than he could ever have supposed.

Moscow *Style Moderne*

Other houses in this area offer good examples of early twentieth-century *style moderne*, a Russian variant of the European Art Nouveau movement. One of the most prominent architects of the short-lived *moderne* movement was Lev Kekushev, who was born in Poland (at that time a part of the Russian empire) in the 1860s and moved to Moscow in 1890. The turn of the century in Moscow witnessed a boom in the construction of medium sized family houses and of large apartment buildings, and Kekushev has left examples of both types of design. One of his earliest buildings in the *moderne* style was the List House, named after a later owner of the building, on Glazovsky pereulok, a lane that runs between Denezhny pereulok and Smolensky Boulevard just south of the Ministry of Foreign Affairs wedding cake building. Kekushev worked on this building during 1898-9 and its most distinctive features include the use of mosaics, ceramic tiles and elaborate window designs. The house was later sold to the family of the conductor Serge Koussevitzky, who emigrated after the Revolution and made his career in the United States.

Other Kekushev buildings include the Prague Restaurant on the Arbat, the Metropol Hotel and the beautiful Art Nouveau mansion on 44 Povarskaya ulitsa, which incorporates stained glass and rich

sculptural decoration into the design, a building that today houses the New Zealand Embassy. He also designed the six-storey apartment building at 28 Prechistenka ulitsa, known as the Isakov House after the merchant who commissioned it, and the house with a tower at 21 ulitsa Ostozhenka, the parallel street to Prechistenka, which was originally commissioned by the businessman Savva Mamontov, of Moscow Private Opera fame, but which the architect ended up living in himself.

Fyodor Shekhtel was the other great exponent of *style moderne*, and his buildings include, most famously, the Ryabushinsky mansion on Malaya Nikitskaya, which was later given to the writer Maxim Gorky. Australasian ambassadors to Moscow are fortunate in their residences, as another lovely example of Shekhtel's work in the *moderne* style is the Derozhinskaya house on 13 Kropotkinsky pereulok, now the Australian Embassy. The *style moderne* movement in Russian architecture was short lived: it barely lasted a decade as the 1910s saw increasing attention given to neo-classicism in architecture. Shekhtel himself was successful in adapting his designs to fit the prevailing trends—he continued to do this into the Soviet era—but Kekushev proved less flexible and he stopped building houses in Moscow after about 1912.

The Metropol Hotel, on Okhotny Ryad, is one *style moderne* building that deserves a closer look. Designed by William Walcott, an architect and draughtsman who was born in the city of Odessa to a Russian mother and English father and studied architecture in St. Petersburg and in Paris, the hotel was built by Kekushev in the early years of the twentieth century to provide luxury accommodation for visitors to the city. It is particularly notable for the large mosaics on the façade designed by Mikhail Vrubel as well as the sculpted plaster frieze and ornate balconies. The hotel was taken over by the new government after the Revolution and was renamed the Second House of Soviets. Trotsky's Commissariat of Foreign Affairs had its headquarters here for a time, but in the 1930s the building was reconverted into a hotel. Famous guests have included George Bernard Shaw, Bertolt Brecht, Sergei Prokofiev and John F. Kennedy.

Another large hotel not far from the Metropol is the National Hotel on the corner of Tverskaya and ulitsa Mokhovaya, built during the same period at the turn of the twentieth century by Alexander Ivanov. It combines elements of the *moderne* with neo-classical design and, like the Metropol, was used as government accommodation in the period just after the Revolution. Lenin himself lived here for just over a week, in room 107, and a plaque on the wall outside the hotel commemorates his stay. Both hotels underwent refurbishment programmes during the 1990s and today they offer luxury accommodation for those who can afford it.

The Good Life

Kuznetsky Most, the blacksmiths' bridge, takes its name from a community of smiths who lived in this area in medieval times and from the fact that this street once served as a bridge over the Neglinnaya river. Neglinnaya ulitsa or the Neglinka, as it is popularly known, follows the route of the river which, since the early nineteenth century, has been channelled underground. In the eighteenth century, Kuznetsky Most became a fashionable shopping street, with a number of foreign owned, particularly French owned, shops selling luxury goods—clothes, perfumes, books, jewellery and confectionary. A guide to Moscow dating from the 1860s remarked that "Everything is three times more expensive than elsewhere; but our dandies do not care: the word that it was purchased on Kuznetsky Most gives a special charm to every little thing."

Old pictures of the street show shops with signs outside written in French as well as Russian. The upper part of the street between Rozhdestvenka and Neglinnaya ulitsa became home to a number of the major pre-revolutionary Moscow banks. Kuznetsky Most was also the location of the Yar restaurant, at the junction with Neglinnaya ulitsa, which was set up in the 1820s and specialized in French cuisine. It was famously visited by Pushkin and his friends in 1831 to commemorate the death of the poet Anton Delvig. In 1848 the restaurant moved to the Hermitage Gardens on Petrovka and soon after moved even further north, to Petrovsky Park along what is now Leningradsky prospekt, the road leading out of the city to Sheremetyevo airport. Gypsy singers were a noted attraction for diners at the Yar.

In the 1880s the restaurant was taken over by new management and refurbished: mirrors were brought in to line the walls of the dining room. The singer Fyodor Chaliapin recalled spending New Year's Eve here on one occasion: "amidst truly exotic splendour—mountains of fruit everywhere, tables groaning with salmon and caviare, and every brand of champagne." It was also known that the infamous Grigory Rasputin enjoyed eating in private rooms at the Yar on his trips to Moscow; on one occasion Rasputin had apparently caused a public scandal in the restaurant when he drunkenly announced that he held the Tsarina in the palm of his hand and could do anything he liked with her. He then swore and dropped his trousers. Robert Bruce Lockhart, who was working as a British diplomat in Moscow at the time, was dining in the restaurant on the same evening and recalled the event in his memoirs:

> *Wild shrieks of women, a man's curses, broken glass and the banging of doors raised a discordant pandemonium. Head waiters rushed upstairs… The cause of the disturbance was Rasputin—drunk and lecherous, and neither police nor management dared evict him.*

He was eventually led away.

The restaurant was closed after the Revolution but reopened in 1952 as part of the Sovietsky Hotel built on the same site. Both hotel and restaurant have undergone refurbishment in the late 1990s and the restaurant in particular makes much of its pre-revolutionary heritage. In nostalgic mood, and thinking of the original Yar restaurant on Kuznetsky Most, the late Soviet era guitar poet, Bulat Okudzhava, sang of how:

> *You never can bring back the past, it's pointless to rue it*
> *Every age will grow its own forest.*

But all the same it's a pity that one can't have dinner with Pushkin
Even drop into the Yar for fifteen minutes.

Another famous pre-revolutionary Moscow restaurant was the Slavyansky Bazar on Nikolskaya ulitsa, a stone's throw from Red Square. It offered hotel accommodation as well, and the Lady with the Dog in Chekhov's short story of that title stayed here when she came to Moscow to meet her lover. It was also at the Slavyansky Bazar that Konstantin Stanislavsky and Vladimir Nemirovich-Danchenko held their epic meeting when they agreed to collaborate together in setting up the Moscow Art Theatre.

Yeliseev's and the Sandunovsky Baths

The Yeliseev delicatessen on Tverskaya, near Pushkinskaya ploshchad, is a long-standing Moscow institution. Its building is a Kazakov design from the 1790s that survived the 1812 fire; in 1898 the Yeliseev opened. The grand interior, with its chandeliers, stained glass and mirrors soon became home to Russia's best-known food emporium, offering such exotic produce as bananas and pineapples. After the Revolution the Yeliseevsky family emigrated and their shop acquired the typically Soviet name of Grocery Shop Number One but it continued to operate as a place where those with money—principally foreigners and members of the Party elite—could buy luxury foods. Restoration was undertaken in 2003, and the old Soviet system of forcing customers to queue up three times in order to undertake a single transaction (once to select their goods, once to pay and then again to collect their purchases) has been done away with. Sales assistants wearing uniforms based on pre-revolutionary designs add a kitsch dimension to the whole shopping experience.

The Sandunovsky Baths, the most luxurious public baths in Moscow, are situated on Neglinnaya ulitsa, the street that leads up from the back of the Maly Theatre and TsUM following the old course of the Neglinnaya river. The baths date back to 1808 when they were founded by the Georgian businessman and comic actor Sila Sandunov. Sandunov started out as a businessman but became hooked on the theatre and entered Michael Maddox's company at the Petrovsky Theatre on the site of the present-day Bolshoi. He met his future wife, the opera singer Elizaveta Uranova, in St. Petersburg and legend has it that because she was being pursued by an important nobleman at court, Uranova and Sandunov were forced to marry in secret, with the cooperation of the Tsarina who acted as Uranova's patron. They moved to Moscow together, and Sandunov eventually decided to go into the public baths business. He built a bath house and pitched his establishment at the very top end of the market.

The Sandunovsky Baths offered separate facilities for men and women and soon became very popular with the upper classes: noblewomen even brought their lapdogs with them to the baths. Sandunov and Uranova eventually split up, and Uranova received the baths as part of her settlement, but by then the name had already stuck. In the later nineteenth century they were bought by Alexander Gonetsky, who decided to raze the building to the ground and construct a new bathhouse, designed in Beaux Arts style by Boris Freidenberg with a grand central arch and statues lining the roof top. The interior is lavishly decorated with marble swimming pools, stained glass windows and rococo decorations. Famous bathers included Pushkin, Tolstoy, Chekhov and Chaliapin; Bulgakov described one visit in 1938 as "sheer delight". Still functioning to this day, they continue to provide luxurious facilities for visitors.

Higher Education

The first institute of higher education to be founded in Moscow was the Slavonic-Greek-Latin Academy, opened in 1687 within the Zaikonospassky Monastery on Nikolskaya ulitsa, a short distance from Red Square. The monastery itself is recognizable for its red and white octagonal tower. Its founder was the scholar and poet, monk Simeon Polotsky. Many of the first teachers at the Academy came from Kiev, where an earlier school had been established, and the Moscow institution's students included Mikhail Lomonosov, who went on to found Moscow University. One former student, recalling his experiences there at the end of the eighteenth century, noted the dominant impression of "darkness, heat, dampness, noise, cries and whistling in class". He was similarly underwhelmed by the food provided for students at the Academy: damp cabbage, onions and kvas.

It was Peter the Great who was responsible for setting up Moscow's first western-style, secular academy, the School of Mathematics and Navigation, in 1701. The establishment of this school helped to meet two of Peter's key objectives for his country: to make it more western and to create a set of formidable and well trained armed forces that included a navy. The academy was housed in the Sukharev Tower, a massive structure which once stood on Sukharevskaya ploshchad on the north side of the Garden Ring. A pair of anchors and a commemorative stone were placed on the site in 1996 to mark the 300th anniversary of the foundation of the Russian navy: the stone has a carving of a picture of the tower and an inscription explaining brief details of its history. The tower was erected in the 1690s and named after one of the units of *streltsy* which had its quarters in this area. Most of the initial members of staff at the school were foreign experts, among them two Englishmen, Richard Grice and Stephen Gwyn, and a Scot, Henry Farquharson, and it offered training in mathematics, trigonometry, geometry, geography, astronomy and navigation to members of the armed forces. An observatory was subsequently created in the top floor of the building by a Muscovite of Scottish descent, James Bruce. Bruce fought in the Great Northern War against Sweden and rose to the rank of field marshal; a scholar, he built up an impressive library and is said to have introduced the ideas of Isaac Newton to Russia. Briusov pereulok, a turning off Tverskaya, was named in his honour.

The ground floor of the Sukharev Tower contained an arched gateway serving as one of the entrance points into the Zemlyanoi gorod: in *War and Peace*, when the Rostovs join the mass exodus from Moscow as the French troops advance on the city, Natasha spots Pierre walking through the archway of the tower. Tolstoy describes the building as the Sukharev water-tower, although this seems to have been an anachronism: the building was not in fact converted into a water tower until after the Napoleonic wars were over. The Academy had been closed by this time and the tower contained a massive cistern that supplied the city with water for its fountains and public taps. After the Revolution restoration work was undertaken on the tower, which became a museum, but in 1934 it was torn down, like so many other city monuments, to make more space for traffic. Objections from architects and conservationists, who proposed either adapting the building to allow trams to pass underneath the arches or moving the entire tower to a different location, were brushed aside and the entire square was cleared. The Sukharevka market had already been closed down and its stalls destroyed in the Soviet war against private trade. Even the name of the square was changed to Kolkhoznaya ploshchad or Collective Farm Square. Proposals to rebuild the tower were discussed during the Brezhnev and Gorbachev years, but the funding for such a project has never thus far been available.

Mikhail Lomonosov, the founder of Moscow University, was an extraordinary eighteenth-century polymath. The son of a peasant from Arkhangelsk on the White Sea, he had a quite remarkable career encompassing both the arts and the sciences. He studied at both the Slavonic-Greek-Latin Academy and the Mathematics and Navigation School as well as at the Universities of Marburg and Freiburg in Germany. He was a scientist who worked in the fields of physics and chemistry, he wrote poetry and history, he made mosaics of coloured glass and he played a key role in codifying the modern Russian literary language. The University of Moscow, which opened in 1755 with three faculties—Philosophy, Law and Medicine—was initially located opposite St. Basil's on Red Square, where the Historical Museum now stands, but was soon moved to the yellow classical style buildings on Mokhovaya ulitsa designed by Matvei Kazakov and restored after the 1812 fire by the Italian architect Domenico Gilliardi. The statue of Lomonosov outside the main university building dates from the Khrushchev period. These buildings now house the faculties of Journalism and Psychology and the Institute of African and Asian countries (the rest of the university moved to its new campus in the Sparrow Hills shortly after the Second World War).

Mikhail Lermontov wrote about the university in one of his poems as "a sacred place. I remember like a dream your departments, auditoriums, corridors, your sons' arrogant debates..." Alexander Herzen, another former student whose statue stands outside the old university building, described how, after 1812, the institution grew in importance for Russia: "The conditions for its development were a combination of historical significance, geographical position and the absence of the Tsar." Herzen was particularly impressed by the lectures given by the historian Timofei Granovsky which were regularly greeted by applause from his audience. Other alumni were less enthusiastic about their experiences. In *On the Eve*, one of Ivan Turgenev's characters describes his student days: "to tell you the truth, there was not a single remarkable man among us... There was, they say, a good time once in the Moscow University! But not now. Now it's a school, not a university. I was not happy with my comrades…"

Turgenev himself only studied in Moscow for a year, but Chekhov, who completed his medical training at the university, was equally impolite about his alma mater. He suggested that the dismal state of the buildings might have had a psychological impact on its students: "the dilapidated university buildings, the gloomy corridors, grimy walls, bad light and the cheerless stairs, coat racks and benches have undoubtedly played a key role in shaping the history of Russian pessimism."

In the early twentieth century, a new type of higher educational institution was established in Moscow, sponsored by a local merchant. The Shanyavsky People's University was opened in 1908 and occupied the buildings now occupied by the Russian State University for the Humanities on Miusskaya ploshchad near Novoslobodskaya metro station just north of the Garden Ring. This university, which offered evening classes and public lectures that anyone could attend, was set up by Alfons Shanyavsky, a gold trader who originally came from Poland. Although he died in 1905, he left a considerable fortune to the municipal authorities on condition that they used the money to set up a higher education institution to offer workers a chance to gain advanced qualifications. The university opened in 1908 and moved into its new buildings in 1912. The poet Sergei Yesenin was one of the workers who benefited from the evening courses, and many important academics of the time gave lectures. One observer described the mixture of students that the institution attracted:

What a variegated picture, what a mixture of ages, types, clothing. I saw there sitting next to one another an officer of the general staff and a conductor of a city tram, a university assistant professor and a shop clerk, a noblewoman with a feather boa around her neck and a monk in his everyday cassock.

After the Revolution, the Party opened a Higher Party School on this site, and in 1991 it became a university once again.

Merchants' Moscow

The story of nineteenth-century Moscow is in many ways the story of the rise of the Muscovite merchant class. Industrialization brought a new class of citizens to the fore, some of whom built up huge fortunes and played a dominant role in the economic, political and cultural life of the city. The earliest merchant district of the city was the Kitai gorod within the medieval walled settlement to the east of the Kremlin, but frequent fires in this area forced them to move out and colonize other parts. The main area where merchant families clustered in mid-nineteenth century Moscow was the Zamoskvorechie, the district across the Moskva river to the south of the Kremlin. Pyotr Kropotkin, who grew up in Moscow, described the neighbourhood at this time:

> with its broad, sleepy streets and its monotonous gray-painted, low-roofed houses, of which the entrance-gates remain securely bolted day and night, [which] has always been the secluded abode of the merchant class, and the stronghold of the outwardly austere, formalistic and despotic Nonconformists of the "Old Faith".

According to the playwright Ostrovsky, the Zamoskvorechie had the loudest church bells and the most delicious smelling pies to be found anywhere in the whole city. It remains a lovely area to wander around, with a much more intimate feel than other central districts. The classical buildings, painted in pastel colours, have only two or three storeys, giving the area a much more human scale. As Kropotkin pointed out, many of the merchant families of Moscow were Old Believers, descendants of those nonconformists who had split from the Orthodox Church during the schism of the seventeenth century.

Old Believers saw themselves as upholding the ancient traditions of pre-Petrine Muscovy and they tended to live in close-knit communities, often distinguished by their old fashioned dress with long kaftans and bushy beards. Apart from the Zamoskvorechie, Old Believers also congregated in the area across the Yauza river in the east of the city: Preobrazhenskoe and Rogozhskoe were both home to Old Believer communes, and the churches where they worshipped in these districts can be visited today. Restrictions on Old Believers had been gradually lifted by a series of acts of toleration passed from the late eighteenth century onwards, culminating in 1905 with a law that granted them full religious rights. Old Believers encouraged literacy within their communities. They tended to adhere to an ascetic lifestyle, abstaining from alcohol and tobacco and cultivating an image of hard working self-discipline. Members of the Old Believer community often intermarried, and many families built successful businesses that were passed down from father to son.

A significant proportion of merchant families started in the textiles business, which played a key role in Moscow's industrial development: the city was sometimes described as "Calico Moscow" because of the dominance of the cotton business. By the late eighteenth century Moscow and the villages that surrounded the city had several weavers' mills producing linen, silk and cotton: one estimate puts the number of textile workers in 1770 at around 9,000. Conservative in their religious beliefs, members of the merchant class displayed considerable enterprise in their business affairs and often came to play a leading role in civic life.

A majority of Moscow's mayors in the later nineteenth and early twentieth centuries came from merchant families, including Sergei Tretyakov, brother of the art collector Pavel Tretyakov, and Nikolai Alekseev, with whom Yury Luzhkov has compared himself. Alekseev came from a family that worked in textiles, specializing in silk and gold threads. He was a cousin of the theatre director Konstantin Stanislavsky and was elected mayor in 1885 by the City Duma. He was responsible for a whole series of large-scale municipal improvements that included extending the water supply and sewerage systems, paving the streets, setting up municipal slaughterhouses and a lunatic asylum and overseeing the construction of new buildings such as the Upper Trading Rows on Red Square and the Municipal Duma building. It was also during his time in office, in 1891, that Jews were expelled from the city and sent to live in the Pale of Settlement in the western borderlands of the Russian empire. After 1899 rules were relaxed somewhat and they were permitted to return. In 1893 Alekseev fell victim to an assassin's bullet inside the Duma building.

Members of the nobility tended to take a rather condescending view of merchants, despite their increasing importance in the life of the city. A city guidebook dating from the early twentieth century described the merchant district of Zamoskvorechie as a "dreadful, provincial, godforsaken place", and merchants tended to be stereotyped as greedy, stupid, uncultivated and conservative people with whom it was better not to associate. In Tolstoy's *Anna Karenina*, Levin and his university friend Professor Katavasov make the acquaintance of a young merchant on a train journey:

He was unmistakably tipsy... Katavasov learned that he was a wealthy Moscow merchant who had run through a large fortune before he was two-and-twenty. Katavasov did not like him, because he was unmanly and effeminate and sickly. He was obviously convinced, especially now after drinking, that he was performing a heroic action, and he bragged of it in the most unpleasant way.

As Moscow's merchants grew in wealth and power, many families moved across the river to live in traditional gentry areas around Malaya Bronnaya or Prechistenka, and abandoned their kaftans in favour of business suits. Portraits of Pavel Tretyakov and Savva Mamontov in the Tretyakov Gallery depict both men wearing western dress. Another painting of merchants in the Tretyakov is the humorous *Jokers: Gostiny Dvor in Moscow* by Illarion Pryanishnikov, who depicts a clerk making bunny ears with his fingers behind the head of a man who appears to be drunk for the amusement of a group of corpulent, top-hatted Moscow merchants.

Merchants were to play an influential role in helping to change architectural trends in the city as they patronized new styles of building design for their houses. When Pavel Milyukov, the liberal politician, returned to Moscow after years abroad, he remarked on the architectural changes that had taken place as a result of merchant involvement:

I could hardly recognize parts of the city. Thanks to the merchant class, a striking new trend was introduced in Moscow architecture. Amidst the old aristocratic mansions in the Empire style, there arose along the boulevards and side streets the most fastidious imitations of European architectural achievements.

The House of Europe, formerly the House of the Friendship of the Peoples, opposite Arbatskaya metro station on ulitsa Vozdvizhenka, offers a bizarre example of merchant tastes. Built for the merchant Arseny Morozov in 1894, its lavish external decorations were inspired by the Casa de las Conchas in Salamanca, which he had visited during a tour of Spain. The Perlov Tea House on Myasnitskaya ulitsa, another building commissioned by a merchant family in the same period, draws its inspiration from China, with dragons adorning the façade. Nikolai Alekseev preferred the Russian Style used by the architects designing the Upper Trading Rows and the City Duma. Other merchant families of this period preferred Art Nouveau: the Ryabushinsky Mansion at Nikitskie vorota is a good example, built in the early twentieth century with mosaics, curving window frames, stained glass windows and wave-like designs in the interior. The carved limestone staircase is a particularly spectacular feature of the house as a whole and, as befits a house that was built for a family of Old Believers, a little chapel was hidden away at the very top of the house for private worship. Given to the writer Maxim Gorky after his return from exile in 1931, the house is now a museum dedicated to Gorky's life and times.

Komsomolskaya ploshchad offers further examples of the eclectic architectural styles sponsored by nineteenth-century entrepreneurs in the three railway buildings surrounding the square. The first major railway line, between St. Petersburg and Moscow, was opened in 1851, terminating at the Nikolaevsky (now the Leningrad) Station. The station was built in the neoclassical style by Konstantin Ton, the architect who was also responsible for the Cathedral of Christ the Saviour, and has a square clock tower rising from its centre. Russia experienced a railway boom in the 1860s, and the new lines helped to connect Moscow to far-flung reaches of the empire. The famous Trans-Siberian railway was built between 1891 and 1904; trains left Moscow from the Yaroslavl Station, designed by Fyodor Shekhtel, the *style moderne* architect of the Ryabushinsky Mansion. The last station to be built on the square was the Kazan Station, to a design in the Russian Style by Shchusev complete with extravagant decorative features and a tiered clock tower topped by a spire.

As well as supporting new trends in building design, many Moscow merchants also sought to raise their public profiles through charitable work and through patronage of the arts. Old Belief fostered a concern for public welfare, but merchants also had a business interest in creating a skilled and able-bodied workforce and hence they were active in helping to fund hospitals, schools and charitable organizations. The Ryabushinsky family funded a shelter for widows and orphans in the Zamoskvorechie district and made donations to welfare organizations providing free meals for the poor and maintaining Rogozhskoe cemetery.

In the artistic sphere, merchants mostly tended to support movements that aristocratic patrons ignored: either new developments such as Art Nouveau and the Moscow Art Theatre (which Morozov helped to fund), or revivalist movements such as the traditional folk crafts sponsored by Savva Mamontov. Pavel Tretyakov collected art works by Russian realist painters, and Nikolai Ryabushinsky backed modernist artists including Vasily Kandinsky and Kazimir Malevich. Konstantin Stanislavsky, from a merchant family himself, remarked in his memoirs on how:

Fate has been kind to me all through my life. It has surrounded me with people and society. To begin with, I began my life at a time when there was considerable animation in the spheres of art, science and aesthetics. In Moscow, this was due to a great degree to young merchants who were interested not only in their businesses but also in art.

Appropriately given its origins as the collection put together by an Old Believer merchant, the Tretyakov Gallery, the largest collection of Russian art, is located in the Zamoskvorechie district on Lavrushinsky pereulok. Pavel Tretyakov, a man described by Stanislavsky as having a "bashful, timid, tall and thin figure with [a] bearded, priest-like face", collected an enormous number of paintings and was the main patron of the *peredvizhniki* or Wanderers, an artistic movement dating from the second half of the nineteenth century whose members had turned their backs on the Academy of Arts and sought to create a new Russian style of painting instead of simply copying Italian artists. They focused on Russian themes—landscapes, ordinary people, historical scenes—and worked to create a private market for their art by exhibiting in provincial towns and cities.

Members of this association included Ivan Kramskoi, whose portrait of a *Nameless Lady* is often taken for Anna Karenina, and Ilya Repin, whose painting of a revolutionary returned from exile, *They Did Not Expect Him*, and portrait of Tolstoy—dressed in peasant costume and pushing a plough—can be seen in the gallery. He also produced a portrait of Tretyakov himself sitting in the gallery that bears his name. Famous canvases by Vasily Surikov include the depiction of the *streltsy* being led out to execution on Red Square and his painting of the

Boyarina Morozova, an Old Believer noblewoman being dragged away, two fingers of her right hand upraised to indicate her refusal to abandon her beliefs, to begin her sentence in exile. Other members of the *peredvizhniki* included Viktor Vasnetsov and Vasily Vereshchagin, who specialized in painting historical scenes, Vereshchagin concentrating on depicting episodes from the recent wars in Central Asia, and Nikolai Ge, who explored religious themes in his work. The quintessentially Russian painting, *The Rooks Have Returned* by Alexei Savrasov, which shows the coming of the thaw to a Russian village settlement, was said to be Tretyakov's favourite picture of all. Tretyakov gave his entire collection to the city of Moscow in 1892. The gallery itself was designed by Viktor Vasnetsov in the Russian Style with elaborate gables and a decorative frieze around the outside of the building.

Sergei Shchukin and Ivan Morozov were two other wealthy Moscow merchants who amassed significant art collections, but rather than patronizing their fellow countrymen they preferred to purchase works by contemporary French artists. Shchukin developed a fondness for post-impressionist painting and built up a large collection of works by Matisse and Picasso. He opened up his Moscow house at weekends to young painters who wished to come and view his vast collection and study the new techniques and ideas being pioneered by their French contemporaries. Matisse even travelled to Moscow in 1911 in order to oversee the installation of some of his larger canvases in Shchukin's home. Morozov's collection included works by Matisse, Cézanne, Monet, Gaugin and Renoir. The Morozov and Shchukin collections were confiscated after the Revolution and were eventually divided up between the State Hermitage in St. Petersburg and the Pushkin Fine Art Museum in Moscow, where they are on public display.

Among the artists who came to see works from the Shchukin and Morozov collections were members of the Russian avant-garde, including Natalya Goncharova, Mikhail Larionov, Vasily Kandinsky, Vladimir Tatlin and Kazimir Malevich. These artists were strongly influenced by what they saw and rejected the realist approach adopted by the Wanderers. In 1910, with financial help from Nikolai Ryabushinsky, they mounted the first of the famous Jack of Diamonds exhibitions, which brought together all of the most recent trends in modern Russian art including neo-Primitivism, Cubo-Futurism and Constructivism. In the years immediately prior to the outbreak of the

First World War, Moscow became known throughout Europe as a centre for revolutionary movements in the arts.

Foreigners in Moscow

Not all of Moscow's merchant families were bearded Old Believers. Some of them were foreign entrepreneurs, and by the end of the nineteenth century Moscow had built up quite a substantial foreign business community. One of the earliest examples of international trading links is the white, wooden-roofed English Merchants' House in Kitai gorod next to the row of little churches on ulitsa Varvarka. The English Muscovy Company was founded in the mid-sixteenth century by Richard Chancellor to coordinate the English arms trade in return for Russian furs, honey and caviar, and was given this house to serve as an embassy. The merchants used this house for the next hundred years until they were expelled in 1649 by Tsar Alexei Mikhailovich, who was appalled by the execution of his fellow-monarch Charles I. Dutch and German traders were also involved with trading links to Moscow: in 1625 a Dutch church was established in Moscow which continued to serve the merchant community until it was moved to St. Petersburg in the eighteenth century. There were also the "Moscow Germans", who were not necessarily German, but northern Europeans who had chosen to settle in Moscow. Many of these people were foreign-born merchants, and from the mid-seventeenth century they inhabited what became known as the *Nemetskaya sloboda*, the German suburb in what is now the Zayauze district of north-eastern Moscow. In 1652 Tsar Alexei Mikhailovich ordered all foreigners to move here from the area of the Kitai gorod. (The word *nemets* in modern Russian means "German", but originally it meant "dumb" or "mute", and was used to refer to anyone who was unable to speak Russian.)

By the end of the nineteenth century a significant community of foreign businessmen was present in Moscow. The great majority were of German origin, but a significant number of French merchants opened up in the area of Kuznetsky Most, and traces of British business interests can still be found in the city today. One such site in central Moscow is the grey Gothic department store on the corner of Teatralnaya ploshchad, between the Bolshoi and Maly Theatres. Now the Central Universal Store, more commonly known as TsUM, it was originally built in the early twentieth century for Muir and Mirrielees, a department store specializing in luxury goods set up by a partnership of Scottish merchants. The firm had begun work in St. Petersburg but transferred its operations to Moscow in the 1880s as Archibald Mirrielees was most impressed by the expatriate community in the city: "a more hospitable set I never met with." After their original shop on this site burned down in 1900 a new building was commissioned from the architect Roman Klein, using reinforced concrete and glass to create a very modern impression despite the Gothic towers that adorn the exterior. Marina Tvetaeva's younger sister Anastasia was impressed by what she saw as the building went up: "Long before the shop opened, Muscovites kept going to see the building as it rose higher and higher into the sky, to be crowned eventually by its little pointed towers, and as its windows began to sparkle."

Muir and Mirrielees, or M and Ms as they became popularly known, gained a reputation as good employers and the new store stunned visiting Muscovites with its modern conveniences, including lifts, lavatories and a restaurant. Chekhov was a keen patron of the store: many of his letters and diary entries touch on his dealings with the shop where he bought his pens, writing paper, furniture and hats. He even called two of his pet dogs Muir and Mirrielees after the owners of the store, prompting the curious comment in one of his letters that "Bromide has fallen in love with Mlle Mirrielees." (Bromide and Quinine were the names of Chekhov's pedigree dachshunds.)

By the immediate pre-revolutionary period M and Ms had branched into many more businesses than just the luxury goods trade. They offered gas appliances and helped to build the water supply and sewerage system. Should you walk past the old Moscow University buildings along Mokhovaya ulitsa near the Alexander Gardens, as you get to the corner of Bolshaya Nikitskaya outside St. Tatyana's chapel, look down at the old manhole cover in the pavement and you will see the names of Muir and Mirrielees imprinted on it. The store was nationalized after the Revolution, and the bulk of the British left the country as quickly as they could.

As the British business community in Moscow grew larger during the nineteenth century it created its own social circle. This, for some people, revolved around the Church, most notably the Anglican Church of St. Andrew on Voznesensky Pereulok, a red brick church with a square tower, utterly unlike any Russian church building. It was built in the 1880s by an architect from Manchester to serve the British community and was maintained by business leaders. The wrought-iron gates onto the street have the emblems of the rose, thistle and shamrock built into them, and the crosses of St. Andrew and St. George adorn the gateposts. The church was seized by the new regime after the Revolution and was given over to the state record company, Melodiya, as a recording studio. Returned to the Church in 1991, the building is gradually being restored. It now has a resident chaplain and English services are held on Sundays. The building next door to the church was once St. Andrew's House, built by a rich Scottish woman who wished to provide accommodation for English and American governesses who either did not have live-in positions or who were in between jobs and needed a temporary place to stay.

Jewish Moscow

Unlike many other East European cities, Moscow has no obviously discernible Jewish district. Jews in the Russian empire were largely confined to the Pale of Settlement, a large area of what is present-day Poland, Belarus, Ukraine and Moldova in the western borderlands. From the early nineteenth century, Jewish merchants visiting Moscow were required to stay in a designated inn, the Glebovskoe podvore, in the Zaryade district just to the south-east of Red Square. Under Alexander II from the mid-nineteenth century onwards, residence restrictions on Jews were relaxed somewhat and it became easier for Jews with professional qualifications or personal wealth to move beyond the Pale and settle in other cities including Moscow. Estimates vary, but a figure of around 35,000 is commonly cited as the Jewish population of Moscow in the late 1880s. After the assassination of Alexander II, official anti-semitism became the order of the day and a wave of pogroms swept the towns and villages of the Pale. Legislation was passed placing limits on the number of Jewish students in secondary schools and universities, and in 1891 the decision was taken to expel all but a handful of the most privileged and long-established Jewish families from Moscow. The city authorities, who included the mayor, Nikolai Alekseev, and the governor-general, Grand Duke Sergei Alexandrovich, announced their decision on the first day of Passover in 1891. Areas of the city known to have a high concentration of poor Jewish inhabitants, such as the Zaryade and the Marina Roshcha district to the north of the Garden Ring around Savelovskaya metro, were surrounded by the police and their inhabitants rounded up and sent back to resettle in the Pale. Many emigrated from Russia, often ending up in New York.

The great Choral Synagogue on Bolshoi Spasoglinishchevsky pereulok, near Kitai gorod metro station, had only just been built when the expulsion took place. The city authorities had already demanded that the dome be removed so as not to confuse Orthodox believers into thinking that it was a church, and after the expulsion they ordered that the building be used as a charitable institution rather than as a place of worship. Jews began returning to Moscow from the very end of the nineteenth century and by the time of the 1917 Revolution they made up around three per cent of the city's population.

POOR MOSCOW

A huge gulf both of experience and of understanding separated the Muscovite nobility and wealthy merchant families from the life of the great mass of the people. Lev Tolstoy was unusual in being an aristocrat who took an interest in the living conditions of the poor; his awareness sparked pangs of personal guilt:

> ...at the sight of this hunger, cold, and degradation of thousands of persons, I understood not with my mind, but with my heart and my whole being, that the existence of tens of thousands of such people in Moscow, while I and other thousands dined on fillets and sturgeon, and covered my horses and my floors with cloth and rugs... was a crime, not perpetrated a single time, but one which was incessantly being perpetrated over and over again, and that I, in my luxury, was not only an accessory, but a direct accomplice in the matter.

The Imperial Foundling Home

On the banks of the Moskva, a short distance to the east of the Kremlin, stands an enormous classical building designed and built in the 1760s during the reign of Catherine the Great as the Imperial Foundling Home. It was the first secular and non-governmental public building in the city to be built of brick. Now a military academy, it is not open to visitors but its history is interesting. The Foundling Home was established to offer a home and an education to children who were abandoned, illegitimate, orphaned or whose parents were too poor to raise them. The aim was to provide a disincentive to infanticide and to create a pool of respectable urban citizens trained in skills useful to society. It had the space to offer refuge to thousands of babies and young children each year and it also organized a system of foster care whereby peasant families would be paid an allowance to raise the children in their own homes. Funding came in the form of charitable donations both from the imperial family and from wealthy noblemen and merchants.

By the end of the nineteenth century the Foundling Home had become Moscow's largest and best known welfare organization. Tours were offered to foreign visitors who could come and look around the institution and admire Russian methods of dealing with the serious social problem of child abandonment. Many of those who went on such tours came away impressed. In one account dating from 1868, a visitor remarked that:

> It is impossible to go through the Foundling Hospital without being struck with the admirable order and completeness of detail, brilliant cleanliness and attention to health which reign through all departments of this magnificent establishment. There is nothing superior to it in any country in all its substantial richness of material employed and in the intelligent knowledge displayed in carrying out the object in view.

He might have been less impressed had he been able to see the mortality rates: a very high number of children died shortly after admission to the Imperial Foundling Home, and those who were sent to foster homes were often poorly looked after.

The hospital was—remarkably—saved from the plague in 1771 by Charles de Mertens, a foreign doctor who worked there during

Catherine's reign and who left a detailed account of life in Moscow during the plague year. He placed the building under a strict quarantine: no one entered the building except himself and anyone who showed signs of developing sickness was isolated within the institution. In 1812, after the Russian defeat at Borodino, the older children were evacuated from the home but the youngest remained under the care of its director, General Ivan Tutolmin, one of the few Russians of any significant status to remain in the city when the French arrived. Napoleon, in fact, donated some money to the institution during his short time in Moscow.

Questions began to be asked about the Foundling Home's admissions policies towards the end of the nineteenth century. From its inception, mothers had been able to leave their children anonymously simply by putting them in a basket outside the door and ringing a bell. A nurse would then come to take charge of the baby and the mother could slink away into the darkness, safe in the knowledge that her child would be well cared for. The trouble was that some critics felt this system encouraged unscrupulous mothers to leave their babies, then apply for work as wet nurses and thereby receive money from the institution to bring up their own children. In the 1890s the admissions procedures were changed to require a certain level of paperwork to be completed for each child.

Children brought up by the Foundling Home could not be enserfed and they were trained for a variety of professions. Boys often entered the army or took up a trade, and girls were educated to the level where they could go out and work as teachers or governesses. Many of the girls who did not go into teaching or become seamstresses returned to work in the Foundling Home itself. It also provided girls with a small dowry when they were married.

The Labouring Poor

Russia industrialized late. It was not until the second half of the nineteenth century that factories began to spring up in the outlying districts of Moscow and the population soared with the influx of new peasant migrants seeking work. Industrialization changed the face—and the skyline—of Moscow forever. Instead of the old houses of one or two storeys, developers started to build upwards, and massive apartment blocks began to line the streets of parts of the city. The old wooden houses were dwarfed by new constructions, dispensing with the old-fashioned practice of having gardens or yards around the buildings. Boris Pasternak later recalled how:

> *It seemed to me as a child that the advent of the new century changed everything as at the stroke of a magic wand. The city was gripped by the same financial frenzy as were the leading capitals of the world. Tall blocks of offices and flats sprang up overnight in an epidemic of speculative deals. All at once, brick giants reached into the sky from every street.*

In a document dating from 1913 the municipal authorities noted how "Moscow has notably changed in appearance. New, multistoried buildings are going up... These properties have plumbing and sewer lines, buildings have electricity and telephones, indoor toilets and gas stoves." But it noted wryly that all of these new luxuries came at a price. "The mass of the propertyless population of course lives as it always has."

The mass of the propertyless population was growing rapidly. By the 1890s the population of Moscow had reached one million people, and rapid expansion continued apace. Most of these new inhabitants were peasant migrants, often entering the city's workforce on a seasonal basis and retaining links with their villages, returning home at the end of the summer to help bring in the harvest. These new migrants used networks of friends and family from their home regions to help them find jobs and places to stay. Most ended up living near the factories where they worked, in the working-class suburbs of the city beyond the Garden Ring. Factories specializing in textiles or metal working were mainly clustered to the south and east of the city centre, near the main railway stations, along the Yauza river and in what is now the Proletarskaya district. The Baedeker guide to Moscow, published in 1914, recognized this and remarked that "a visit to the Eastern quarter of the city offers little interest."

Living conditions for those who inhabited these districts were overcrowded and unsanitary. Epidemics of cholera, diphtheria and tuberculosis were common in fin-de-siècle Moscow. A report by the municipal authorities into working-class housing in 1899 described one place where:

*In a closet where there are three cots altogether, thirteen people
live...Upon entering the apartment it seems that one has gone into
an outhouse, the stench is so strong... all the children are sick... The
ceiling is covered with mould, the apartment is cold, there is a stench
from the slop pit.*

Boris Pasternak provided vivid descriptions of some of the poorer
districts of Moscow before the Revolution in *Doctor Zhivago*. The area
where Lara and her mother lived around the Belorusskaya station was
in "the most sordid part of Moscow—slums, shady dives... whole
streets given up to vice". For a more vivid description of Moscow vice
we must turn to Chekhov: in his short story, *A Nervous Breakdown*, he
depicts the violent reaction of a young student, Vasilyev, on his first visit
to a brothel on Bolshoi Golovin pereulok, one of the set of parallel lanes
running between Trubnaya ulitsa and Sretenka just to the north of
Rozhdestvensky Boulevard. Initially unimpressed by the cheap
fripperies and lack of taste on display in the house that he and his
friends enter—"what's worth sinning for here?" he muses to himself—
he ends up in a state of near-collapse, oppressed by the sense that the
women he met had no sense of their own degradation.

*"There is vice," he thought, "but neither consciousness of sin nor
hope of salvation. They are sold and bought, steeped in wine and
abominations, while they, like sheep, are stupid, indifferent, and
don't understand. My God! My God!"*

Figures from the 1890s showed that more than half of the women
working in the cheaper brothels of Moscow had syphilis, and in the
early years of the twentieth century some residents of the area that
Chekhov's students visited lobbied successfully for the brothels to be
closed down and moved out of the city centre.

Chekhov was very clear in his own mind that it was incumbent
upon the rich to donate money to help alleviate the situation of the
poor. In one of his letters he expressed the opinion that:

*it is essential that respectable Muscovites should provide for these
[charitable] societies by the regular and obligatory participation of
each and every one... The wealthy Muscovite spends hundreds and*

thousands of roubles to turn his lesser brethren into all manner of prostitutes, slaves, syphilitics and alcoholics—so let him give at least a few copecks for the treatment and relief of the sometimes unbearable sufferings of those brethren whom he has fleeced and corrupted.

Beggars were a common sight in pre-revolutionary Moscow: the eighteenth-century German visitor Friedrich Christian Weber noted that in Moscow there were "such Numbers of Beggars and Rogues and… so many Excesses and Disorders, that after Sun-set no body ventures abroad without sufficient Company." Beggars are an equally common sight today, their numbers having mushroomed since the end of communism and the removal of the social security safety net.

Begging continued long after the Revolution: the crowds of homeless children who slept rough in Moscow during the Civil War and the 1920s kept body and soul together by begging or thieving, and Walter Benjamin, who visited Moscow in the mid-1920s, noted many beggars in the streets. In one instance, he described the position adopted by one destitute man "in exactly the same pose as the miserable creature for whom St. Martin cut his cloak in two with a sword, on his knees, his arm outstretched."

The Khitrov Market

Just off the Boulevard Ring on the eastern edge of the Belyi gorod (on the corner with Podkolokolny pereulok) lies the district formerly known as the Khitrov market. Notorious for its flophouses, its dens of thieves, gambling houses and brothels, it was home to the poorest of Moscow's poor in the nineteenth and early twentieth century. The site was bought in the 1820s by Major General Khitrovo, who intended to build a food market, but he died not long after acquiring the land and the area gained its real notoriety only from around the 1860s as industrialization brought mass seasonal migration into the city. The Khitrov district became a labour market: contractors came looking to hire the casual workers who gathered early each morning. Cheap private lodging houses opened all around the square to accommodate these workers, and taverns and brothels sprang up to meet expanding local demand.

The journalist Vladimir Giliarovsky described the atmosphere of the Khitrov market in its heyday. It was, he said:

*a big square in the centre of the capital, near the Yauza river,
surrounded by peeling stone houses. It lies in a low place into which
lead several side streets, like streams into a swamp. It's always
bursting, especially towards evening. When it's a little foggy or just
after a rain, standing at the top of one of the side streets, you can
barely make out the figures below you descending into a crawling,
putrid pit.*

It was not just beggars, thieves and prostitutes who could be found in
the Khitrov market. This was where newcomers to the city came
looking for work and a place to stay, and artisans—tailors, cobblers,
cigarette makers—plied their trades from private rooms on the
square. Honest workers lived side by side with criminal elements,
skilled craftsmen with manual labourers.

Overcrowding was rife in the lodging houses on the square, giving
rise to fears that poor sanitation would spread contagious disease
throughout the city. Moscow had very high rates of tuberculosis in the
late nineteenth century, and cholera and typhus were also recurrent
problems. There were fears of moral contagion: a city commission
report in 1898 described the Khitrov market as "the most horrible ulcer
of the whole city", painting a picture of almost ubiquitous drunkenness,
crime and sexual immorality. In a later report from 1913 the authorities
warned of how "tens of thousands of workers pass yearly through
Khitrov Market, becoming infected there physically and morally and
carrying this infection with them. Many honourable workers fall into
the ready snares of the exploiting part of Khitrov Market, becoming
drunkards and parasites."

Lev Tolstoy went to visit this area in the early 1880s as part of his
work helping with the Moscow city census. His essay *What Then Must
We Do?* was inspired by his visits here and to another poor district
around Smolenskaya ploshchad on the western side of the Garden
Ring. He wrote in vivid terms about the overcrowding that he saw, and
his son, who accompanied him on one such visit, recalled the evening
in his memoirs:

*We spent the evening going into wretched little rooms where the filth
and stench were appalling and Father questioned each of the lodgers
as to what he lived on, what had brought him there, how much he*

*paid and what he ate. In the general room, where they were allowed
to sleep at no cost, it was still worse. There it was not even necessary
to make inquiries; it was obvious that they were all utterly degraded,
and that mass of destitute degenerated humanity aroused only
horror and disgust.*

The theatre director Konstantin Stanislavsky brought members of
the Moscow Art Theatre company to visit the Khitrov market when
they were working on a production of Gorky's play *The Lower Depths*,
in order to listen to ordinary people's stories and gain a sense of what
their lives were like. Municipal reformers also took an interest in the
area, sending in sanitary inspectors and producing reports. Although
some attempts at improving conditions were undertaken in the early
years of the twentieth century, it took the Soviet authorities to finally
raze the whole district to the ground. The houses were bulldozed after
the Revolution, and nowadays the site of the Khitrov market is
occupied by a large yellow apartment building, the entranceway flanked
by two white stone statues, one a traditional depiction of an armed
worker, the other a rather incongruous statue of a peasant woman with
one arm leaning on a wheatsheaf and the other brandishing a rifle.

Chapter Eight
CITY OF UTOPIAS AND SLUMS

Just off the Garden Ring, a short way south of Barrikadnaya metro and before you get to the United States Embassy, stands a curious building. Literally crumbling from years of neglect, this six-storey Constructivist edifice made of reinforced concrete with its long, horizontal windows on each floor was once a show-piece for the new Soviet way of life. Designed by Moisei Ginzburg and built in the late 1920s, it provided apartments for staff working at the People's Commissariat of Finance (Narkomfin). The building not only offered a place to live: the idea behind the new apartment block was that it would help to foster a new collective spirit among its residents, all of whom had access to the communal facilities—dining room, nursery, laundry and the like—which were provided for their use.

In combining private living space with communal facilities, the Narkomfin building was considerably less radical than some of the other experimental projects that were floated during the 1920s and 1930s. In its most utopian form, the ideal communal house was supposed to offer an architectural means by which the old habits of bourgeois individualism could be overcome and women could be truly liberated. Residents might or might not have their own separate rooms to sleep in, but all other facilities would be collectivized, freeing women from the daily domestic routines of laundry, food preparation and childcare (in the most extreme versions of such schemes, children would be brought up separately from their parents by professional carers) and offering their residents spaces for leisure activity such as clubs or reading-rooms. Cafeterias and communal dining rooms would take care of meal-times. Several hundred such house-communes were set up in Moscow in the 1920s, some of which took their enthusiasm for the new way of life further than others. One group of young collectivists set up their own political system with committees to decide on all aspects of house policy and slapped a ban on sex between members of the commune; another group collectivized their clothing as well as all other domestic amenities, arguing that the desire to feel a sense of ownership over one's underwear was "a backslide into darkest capitalism… [a] prejudice originating in a petit-bourgeois ideology".

1920s architects took on the task of designing new housing units for the new way of life. The Association of New Architects held design competitions: the result of one of these can be found on ulitsa Lesteva near Shabolovskaya metro station. The Shabolovka housing estate with its five- to seven-storey houses included communal facilities as well as balconies and courtyard gardens. Further examples of Moscow Constructivism can be seen on nearby ulitsa Ordzhonikidze, where one of the student hostels of the Friendship of the Peoples' University—formerly the Patrice Lumumba University for training students from the developing world—dates from the late 1920s and was built by Ivan Nikolayev as communal housing. The building bears strong traces of the influence of the visionary French modernist architect Le Corbusier, a much-feted figure in Moscow architectural circles at this time. Le Corbusier spent time in Moscow during the 1920s and 1930s, and the office block of the State Statistical Commission, the former Tsentrosoyuz Building on Myasnitskaya ulitsa near Chistye Prudy metro station, was built by him.

Another interesting approach to housing that was tried out during the 1920s can be seen in the streets near Sokol metro station, just off Leningradsky prospekt, north-west of the city centre. In the area around ulitsa Vrubelya, ulitsa Polenova and other streets named after famous artists one can wander through a little settlement of wooden houses, reminiscent of a traditional Russian village. Pioneered by the architect Nikolai Markovnikov and built in the 1920s, the Sokol development involved the construction of small individual wooden cottages in a traditional style with plenty of green space around them, all forming part of an attempt to create a Russian variant of the garden city movement. The experiment was eventually rejected as too costly but the houses remain to this day.

Social Engineering

Communal living in its purest forms never really took off and the government was forced to explore other avenues in pursuit of a solution to the housing question. Housing was a critical issue for the post-revolutionary city authorities: on the one hand, reinventing the entire system by which living space was allocated to people offered a golden opportunity both to punish the former ruling classes and to inculcate the habits of communal living into the new citizens of the first socialist society; yet on the other hand, the authorities faced the urgent need to provide homes for the huge influx of migrants from the countryside who flooded into Moscow in a series of waves starting in the late 1920s. As in so many areas of Soviet life, the regime began by giving a free rein to radical experimentation and ended up being forced to take desperate measures to cope with a crisis that was entirely of their own making.

One of the earliest measures taken after the Revolution was to deprive the former ruling classes of their luxurious living-quarters, a process carried out spontaneously by anarchist groups. The British diplomat Robert Bruce Lockhart went to visit some of these houses on ulitsa Povarskaya after the anarchists had been expelled in spring 1918 and described the scenes that met his eyes:

The filth was indescribable. Broken bottles littered the floors, the magnificent ceilings were perforated with bullet-holes. Wine stains and human excrement blotched the Aubussan carpets. Priceless pictures had been slashed to strips. The dead lay where they had fallen.

Workers were resettled in these apartments, with their previous owners either forcibly evicted or, in some cases, permitted to retain one room for their own use. In *Dr Zhivago*, the Gromyko house is divided up after the revolution as Tonya and her father invite the Agricultural

Academy to take over part of the house. On his return to Moscow, Yury approves of the new living arrangements, commenting that

> there really was something unhealthy in the way rich people used to live. Masses of superfluous things. Too much furniture, too much room, too much refinement, too much self-expression. I'm very glad we're using fewer rooms. We should give up still more.

Not everyone dispossessed by the Revolution shared this positive attitude: many propertied Muscovites fled the country, smuggling out whatever jewellery they could, and carved out new lives for themselves in the émigré communities of Berlin, Paris and New York.

Filip Filipovich Preobrazhensky, the professor in Bulgakov's comic novel *The Heart of a Dog*, in which an incautious scientist transplants the heart and pituitary glands of a man into the body of a dog, provides a good literary example of the kinds of difficulties that could beset members of the Moscow intelligentsia after the Revolution. He finds his life severely inconvenienced by the hordes of new tenants who are moved into the apartment building where he lives. Although the professor succeeds in claiming protection from a well-connected patron and is able to keep his unheard-of luxury of having seven rooms to himself against all the attempts of the new House Committee to requisition his living space, he finds that his new neighbours make his life unbearable:

> "I have been living in this house since 1903. And from then until March 1917 there was not one case—let me underline in red pencil **not one case**—of a single pair of galoshes disappearing from that rack even when the front door was open... One fine day in March 1917 all the galoshes disappeared, including two pairs of mine, three walking sticks, an overcoat and the porter's samovar. And since then the rack has ceased to exist. And I won't mention the boiler. The rule apparently is—once a social revolution takes place there's no need to stoke the boiler... I ask you... Why can't the proletarians leave their galoshes downstairs instead of dirtying the staircase?"
>
> "But the proletarians don't have any galoshes, Filip Filipovich," stammered the doctor.

... *"Nothing of the sort!... The proletarians do have galoshes now and those galoshes are—mine! The very ones that vanished in the spring of 1917."*

Following the Revolution, the municipal authorities created a new system whereby rent collection and the management of buildings was supervised by elected house committees. We witness one such committee meeting in *Doctor Zhivago* when Yury visits a patient living in "an old brick barrack of a house built round a courtyard and with covered wooden stairs running up the courtyard walls". A representative from the local Soviet attends the meeting where the caretaker complains about residents failing to carry out their cleaning duties in the communal areas. "Don't worry, Fatima, we'll show them," says the official. "What kind of a house committee is this anyway? They're hopeless. Criminal elements are given shelter, people of doubtful morals stay on unregistered. We'll get rid of them and elect another."

"By the way," Tonya informed Yury, "we don't say rooms any more, it's called living space nowadays." Joint occupation in the notorious communal apartments or *kommunalki* was to become the norm for many Muscovites in the Soviet era and under new housing regulations passed in the 1920s each citizen was entitled to nine square metres of living space. Many had far less and, in any case, the living space directive took no account of the fact that part of the space would inevitably be taken up with walls and corridors. House committees were elected in many apartment blocks to take decisions about communal affairs. From the authorities' point of view, of course, communal apartments provided a useful, as well as an ideologically acceptable, way of ameliorating the housing crisis. Cramming people together in this way brought another advantage: it meant that neighbours could spy on one another.

Communal apartments could be truly ghastly places, throwing together complete strangers often from entirely different generations and backgrounds who, rather than discovering the joys of collectivism through enforced sharing, came cordially to loathe one another. If anything, it fostered greater individualism as people became increasingly possessive about their own property when forced to share with others. Even the authorities recognized this: a report in a communist newspaper in 1920 noted with displeasure that "we have brought our petty bourgeois habits along with us into our communes. Everyone cooks in his own pot, hides in his own room, procures food and utensils for his own family, etc." The lack of available housing meant that divorced couples often had to continue living with one another long after relations had broken down, and feuds between neighbours were commonplace. The novelist Mikhail Bulgakov had his fair share of communal living and the appalling neighbours who often went with it. Confiding in his diary in October 1923 he wrote:

> *This first day of heating was marked by the fact that the notorious Annushka left the kitchen window wide open all night. I positively don't know what to do with the swine who inhabit this apartment.*

Vladimir Mayakovsky described the cramped conditions of one communal apartment room that he lived in during 1919:

> *Twelve*
>   *square yards of living space,*
> *Four of us*
>   *in the room—*
> *Lilya,*
>   *Osya,*
> *I,*
>   *And the dog*
> *Shchenik.*

Sir E. D. Simon, who headed a British commission visiting Moscow in 1936 to examine Soviet methods of town planning, was shocked by the overcrowding that he witnessed:

> *The overcrowding in Moscow is appalling… what life must be like, under such conditions, is difficult to imagine. How is it possible for people to keep their temper and health under the constant irritation of such close quarters, how brain workers can show anything approaching their full efficiency, is an insoluble riddle to the Englishman…the worst overcrowding in Moscow may not be much worse than the worst in London or Manchester, but in England this bad overcrowding is confined to one or two per cent of the*

*population; in Moscow it is nearly universal... it is safe to say that
90 per cent of the families in Moscow would improve their housing
conditions beyond recognition if they could have to themselves one
of these houses which are being pulled down in Manchester as unfit
for human habitation.*

Migration and Overcrowding

In this sense, housing conditions in Moscow actually got worse in the
1930s, as the overcrowding suffered by a minority of Muscovites in the
late nineteenth century became the norm for all but the most
privileged. The city's population had increased rapidly in the later
nineteenth century as Russian industrialization proceeded apace: from
around 600,000 inhabitants in 1871 to nearly two million on the eve
of the Revolution. Housing development failed to keep pace with the
increasing numbers. Pre-revolutionary housing betrayed the social
standing of its occupants: from the ornate classical facades of the
aristocratic mansions along ulitsa Prechistenka and the Art Nouveau
houses built by wealthy merchants in the late nineteenth century, to the
wooden shacks and factory barracks beyond the Garden Ring that
provided workers with a place to sleep at nights. The lack of an efficient
public transport network meant that factory workers tended to live
close to their workplaces. The poorest of the poor rented a corner
somewhere: sharing a basement room with other families or bedding
down in the hostels of the Khitrov market district.

The municipal government was responsible for making a number
of improvements to living conditions within the city in the later
nineteenth century, but it was starting from a very low base indeed. In
the 1870s the streets of Moscow had been described by a foreign visitor
in the following terms:

*in spring... owing to bad paving and draining, every street is either
a water-course or a morass...the stones sink and become displaced
and the black mud oozes between them. A horse that has sunk up
to the belly in mud is no uncommon sight in the streets of Moscow...
I have in my time seen bad roads of all descriptions, and on both
sides of the world, but I have never seen any roads in town or
country so atrociously bad as in the streets of Moscow.*

By the end of the century, the situation had certainly been improved as dynamic merchant-mayors such as Nikolai Alekseev launched ambitious street-paving programmes as well as building underground sewers and improving the water supply. By the turn of the century, most streets in the city centre had been cobbled or paved. Housing problems continued, however, with a 1915 study indicating that on average, there were 8.7 people living in each apartment in Moscow, compared with figures of around half that for western European capitals. Although the Revolution stopped the city centre from turning into an upper-class ghetto, it did nothing to stem the problem of overcrowding in the longer term.

Population increase was not a steady process: a graph for the post-revolutionary years would indicate sharp falls and equally sharp rises. The Civil War waged from 1918 to 1921 between the Bolsheviks and their "White" opponents turned Moscow into a ghost town. Hunger, disease and emigration slashed the city's population in half. Workers rediscovered their peasant roots and returned to the villages in search of food; members of the former ruling classes fled the country if they could. The upheaval of these years created thousands of homeless children, usually orphans, who became a serious social problem for the city authorities to deal with. These *bezprizorniki*, as they were known, often lived in and around railway stations or in the Khitrov market and begged or turned to crime or prostitution to save themselves from starvation. Moscow was regarded as an attractive destination for these children, in the belief that access to food and shelter might be easier in the capital city. The chief of the secret police, Felix Dzerzhinsky, wrote of how, during the Civil War:

> *It would be difficult to find in the entire republic a city or town from which there has not been a pilgrimage to Moscow of abandoned children...* [Moscow] *has become the national refuge to which bezprizornye stream from all ends of the country.*

According to an estimate dating from 1923, there were around 20,000 homeless children living on the streets of the city. They made shelters for themselves along the city walls, and when road repairs required boilers of asphalt to be set up on street corners, the children would flock to these places in search of warmth. One resident described the scene on the Arbat after the tram lines had been ripped out and the asphalting was in progress: "there were dozens and scores of them there, tattered, half-famished, dirty, all of them sneaking about these big warm boilers like little animals."

The U-turn in economic policy at the end of the 1920s and the advent of state planning brought a massive influx of new migrants into the city. The population is estimated to have increased by seventy per cent between 1928 and 1933 as 1.5 million people flooded in to work in the new factories and on construction sites such as the metro system. Overcrowding was probably worse in Moscow during the First Five Year Plan period than at any time before or since. Workers either lived in shanty towns on the outskirts of the city, in makeshift wooden buildings with no plumbing, electricity or paved roads and grew much of their own food; or they slept in barracks provided by the factories where they worked. These barracks sometimes entailed three people sharing a single bed on an eight-hour shift system. An account by an American visitor describing barracks housing in 1936 describes how in a room with around 500 beds

there were no screens or wall to give any privacy to the occupants of the barracks... I could not stay in the barracks very long. I could not stand the stench of kerosene and unwashed bodies. The only washing facility was a pump outside. The toilet was a rickety, unheated shanty, without seats.

Many such buildings lacked a water supply altogether: in 1928 only two-thirds of houses in Moscow had access to the city's water services.

For many of the newcomers from the villages life in the big city could be quite insulated. Peasants tended to move to districts where they already had acquaintances from back home who could help them find work in factories. Lack of transport connections in the early Soviet period meant that they were unlikely to see much of the city centre; descriptions of the lives of factory workers told of how they simply got up and went to work, then returned home to sleep. Moscow may have offered plenty of attractions for new migrants—shops, parks, cinemas and clubs—but many were in no position to take advantage of them.

A Room of One's Own

Living in barracks or communal flats obviously meant giving up any kind of personal privacy. This was far from a new phenomenon: the Marquis de Custine had commented on the "lack of private space" in Russia when he visited in the 1830s, and some would argue that Russia does not really share the western concept of privacy at all (the word itself is difficult to translate accurately). Mary Leder certainly thought so. An American Jew whose family migrated temporarily to the Jewish homeland of Birobidzhan, set up by Stalin in a mosquito-infested swamp in Siberia, she ended up staying in the USSR for more than thirty years. In the early 1930s she spent some months working at an electric motor factory in the Proletarskayay district of Moscow and sharing a room with three other girls plus a colony of bedbugs and cockroaches in a workers' commune belonging to the factory. The desire for that unattainable goal of privacy consumed her thoughts:

> *An empty room! A room of my own where I could close the door and shut out the world—I was obsessed by this dream. It was a fantasy I dreamed of nearly all the years I lived in the Soviet Union.*

Leder subsequently moved to live in a curtained-off corner of a room in a communal apartment together with a woman who moonlighted as a prostitute; when she moved out six months later, the woman changed the locks and she was unable to retrieve her suitcase of clothes. Her next home was a room in a communal apartment that she shared with an illiterate old woman who had been a servant in the house prior to the Revolution; later she moved to a shared room in a student hostel in Ostankino with no indoor plumbing. Her experiences were by no means untypical for Muscovites in the Stalin era.

Internal Passports

With the continuing stream of migrants into the city, even squashing people together in communal apartments could not completely solve the housing crisis. The serious famine of 1932 that hit southern Russia and Ukraine, causing somewhere in the region of four to five million deaths (some would argue that this figure should be considerably higher), brought floods of peasants into the cities seeking to escape starvation. It was in response to this sudden crisis that the authorities decided to clamp down on people's freedom of movement and internal passports were introduced. These passports included a residence permit or *propiska*, allowing the government to regulate how many people were allowed to live within the city. Periodic campaigns to remove unregistered residents were launched: in 1931 homeless children were rounded up and dispatched to orphanages and children's colonies, effectively reform schools for juvenile delinquents. Nikolai Ekk's famous 1931 film *Road to Life*, which enjoyed some success abroad, depicted the work of once such colony. Unregistered workers, including those who had been brought into the city in order to help build the metro, were also expelled.

The residence permit became like gold dust for many. Margaret Wettlin, an American woman who married a Muscovite theatre director in the 1930s recalled in her memoirs how "residence registration buttoned every Moscow citizen onto a square of living space." Her own husband had given up his registration when he divorced his first wife, and she commented that this was "not a dire state in those early days but a fatal one later on when a person could be expelled from the city in twenty-four hours if it was discovered he had no place to call his own."

Mikhail Bulgakov's novel *Master and Margarita* is full of satirical commentary on the housing question. After the literary editor, Berlioz, has his head cut off in an unfortunate accident involving a tram, his uncle comes up from Kiev, desperate to take over his late nephew's Moscow apartment.

> *An apartment in Moscow is a serious thing!... this was a moment it would be sinful to let slip... despite all obstacles, he had to succeed in inheriting his nephew's apartment on Sadovaya [the Garden Ring]. Yes, it was difficult, very difficult, but these difficulties had to be overcome at whatever cost. The experienced Maximilian Andreevich knew that the first and necessary step towards that had to be the following: he must get himself registered, at least temporarily, as the tenant of his late nephew's three rooms.*

Taking his papers to the management of the apartment block, Maximilian Andreevich is met by one of the devil's accomplices, the black cat Behemoth, who looks at his passport and comments "I know that office, they issue passports to anybody. Whereas I, for instance, wouldn't issue one to the likes of you!" Behemoth then flings the passport to the floor and orders the uncle to return to his place of residence at once.

As the devil and his associates explore Moscow further they notice all kinds of interesting phenomena related to the housing crisis. They cite how a Muscovite expanded his living space by partitioning a room to add an extra bedroom and then swapped what was now a four bedroom apartment for two separate apartments, one with three rooms and one with two, then swapping the three roomed apartment for two further ones, each with two rooms, making six rooms altogether. His next trick was thwarted "when his activity ceased for reasons independent of him," and we are left to suppose that his energetic house-moving had attracted the unwelcome attentions of the authorities and he had been arrested. Commenting on how Muscovites had changed over recent years, the devil, Woland, remarks that "they're people like any other people... In general reminiscent of the former ones... only the housing problem has corrupted them."

Stalin's Terror brought with it all sorts of opportunities for poorly housed Muscovites to better themselves as people began to disappear from their apartments at night. Margaret Wettlin, who was a strong supporter of the Soviet system at the time of moving from the US, gave an honest account of her feelings on hearing the news that apartments made vacant by the arrests were to be redistributed:

> Did the announcement cause me palpitations of the heart? It did. Did it raise my hopes? Oh, yes! Did I have no qualms about stepping into dead men's shoes? What qualms could there be when the shoes stood empty and my cramped feet were aching so cruelly? Besides, the shoes had belonged to people who had attempted to undermine all that I held most dear.

She and her husband with their two children eventually managed to wangle two rooms in an apartment that was only shared with two other people. Strange as it may seem in a supposedly socialist state, the Wettlin family was not unusual in having the services of a maid: figures dating from 1933 show that 53,000 Muscovites worked as domestic servants.

Elite Housing

As the pigs make clear at the end of George Orwell's *Animal Farm*, "All animals are equal, but some animals are more equal than others." Despite the existence of a supposedly classless society, some Soviet citizens were certainly very much more equal than others—and they had the accommodation to prove it. As we have already seen, members of the Politburo and government officials often had housing within the Kremlin; the Cavalry Guards Barracks and the Poteshnyi Palace were given over to apartments for somewhere in the region of five hundred people. Natasha Andreeva, the daughter of one of Stalin's magnates, recalled some of the down-sides of a childhood spent living in such exalted surroundings:

> *We didn't want to live in the Kremlin. We were constantly told by our parents not to be noisy. "You're not in the street now," they'd say. "You're in the Kremlin." It was like a jail and we had to show passes and get passes for our friends to visit us.*

Indeed, one Party worker turned down the opportunity to live there in the late 1920s because of the overbearing security presence: "your every step was noted and you could not even sneeze without the GPU [forerunner of the KGB] knowing it."

Other government workers were housed in the enormous grey apartment block that stands on ulitsa Serafimovicha opposite the Kremlin known as the House on the Embankment. Built in the late 1920s by Boris Iofan, it offered more than five hundred apartments arranged around three courtyards together with facilities including a supermarket, gymnasium, cafeteria, kindergarten, clinic and the Udarnik cinema. The luxury apartments were given to elite Party workers and VIPs; plaques run all along the sides of the building detailing some of the famous residents. The block became notorious in the 1930s for the midnight knocks on the door as the secret police came calling. Yury Trifonov's 1976 novella, *The House on the Embankment*, takes this building as its subject. Trifonov was the son of an old Bolshevik, a hero of the Revolution and Civil War, and he lived here as a child. His father was arrested in the building in June 1937 and never seen again; the novel describes how each morning the porters would tell other residents in the building about who had been arrested during the night.

The house is described by Trifonov as "a huge, grey house with a thousand windows that was like a whole city or even country... The grey colossus loomed over the narrow lane..." The main character in the story, Glebov, is invited to visit a school-mate who lives there and he marvels over the chandeliers, the wide hallway, "so long that you could ride a bike in it" and all the other luxuries enjoyed by privileged Muscovites. Today, there is a private museum in the building, run by a long-term resident, which tells the stories of some of those who were arrested here. Members of the Party elite are probably turning in their graves these days as their former home is now topped by large advertising signs for Adidas sportswear or Mercedes cars.

Party workers were not the only elite members of Soviet society entitled to better housing. Writers, scholars, scientists, composers and other professional or artistic groups also did better than their peers in the housing lottery. A law passed shortly after the Revolution entitled intellectuals to more living space than other people, recognizing the need for an extra room to work in at home. Construction cooperatives were formed to build special apartment blocks for groups of professionals, and these houses sprang up all over the city. Let us explore just two examples, both dating from the 1930s: the Composers' House and the House of Polar Explorers. The Dom Kompozitorov or Composers' House can be seen if you take a short walk down Briusov pereulok from Tverskaya towards the Moscow Conservatoire on Bolshaya Nikitskaya: it is a tall yellow building on the corner of a small courtyard, just past the theatre director Meyerhold's old flat, easily identifiable by its treble clef sign. Other blocks in this area provided accommodation for people employed by Moscow theatres. The Dom Polyarnikov, the House of Polar Explorers, is located on the Boulevard Ring between Nikitskie vorota and the Arbat. It has a series of columns separating out the balconied apartments and a key hole shaped window above the main entrance. Originally built for members of the Navy, it was later allocated to Arctic explorers, and a small exhibition of their exploits can be found in the main entrance hall.

Private housing was very rare in the Soviet period, but one example in central Moscow is the Constructivist house built for his own family by Konstantin Melnikov on Krivoarbatsky pereulok just off the Arbat. Melnikov was a hugely successful avant-garde architect during the first decade of Soviet rule and he had close links with the authorities at this time: he won the competition to design the sarcophagus for Lenin's Mausoleum and designed the Soviet pavilion at the Paris Exposition of Decorative Arts in 1925. His own house was designed as two intersecting cylinders with massive glass windows on the side that faces the street and a pattern of hexagonal shaped windows on the cylindrical wall at the rear, it was built in the late 1920s; Melnikov's family has lived there ever since. The house is not open to visitors.

The post-war years witnessed an explosion in the construction of elite housing. Several of the seven great wedding cake skyscraper buildings were given over to nomenklatura apartments: the building on ploshchad Vosstaniya and the apartment building on the Kotelnicheskaya embankment to the east of the Kremlin, built by labour camp prisoners. The skyscrapers were the ultimate in Stalinist monumentalism; architects, ordered to create "outstanding works of socialist architecture which reflect the glory and the greatness of the Stalinist epoch" produced massive, striking structures that dominated the skyline of the capital. Gothic-style towers gave the skyscrapers their unique and extraordinary style. One official response to the appearance of these new buildings on Moscow's skyline extolled the way in which "these grandiose works carry us high into the light and the winds to meet the sun and the sky. Their splendid monumental shapes are triumphant symbols of the liberated work of men in our fortunate country."

Luxury apartments for members of the Party elite were put up on Kutuzovsky prospekt, west of Kievskaya metro and along ulitsa Gorkogo, as Tverskaya ulitsa was named in the Soviet period, from the late 1930s through to the 1950s. Distinguished by their immense size and their façades decorated with classical features—balconies, arches, decorative carvings and columns—these buildings offer an illustration of the "monumental" turn taken by Soviet architecture from the 1930s onwards. Henceforth, buildings in Moscow had to be of a scale and grandiosity commensurate with the prestige of the world capital of socialism. Other areas where elite housing was clustered included the area south of the Arbat, the Khamovniki area to the east of Park Kultury metro station and the Lenin Hills to the south-west, an area that has now returned to its old name of the Sparrow Hills. Brezhnev himself had an apartment on Kutuzovsky prospekt as well as a dacha in the Kuntsevo region, built in the 1970s, where he enjoyed luxuries such as

a heated swimming pool and a game park complete with a herd of reindeer.

Members of the Soviet elite not only had better housing; their living standards in general were of a higher order than that of the ordinary man in the street. With their chauffeurs and servants, luxury dachas, access to special shops and permission to travel abroad, they enjoyed a very privileged lifestyle in sharp contrast with the conditions that the majority of people experienced. Most Muscovites were familiar with a life of daily shortages and long queues for food and basic consumer goods. Food rationing was very much the norm, rather than the exception, in the first half of the Soviet period. It was not phased out until 1924, and rationing was then reintroduced from 1929 to 1935 and again from 1941 to 1947 during and after the Second World War.

"Khrushchev-slums" and "Micro-Regions"

It was only in the Khrushchev years that moves started to be made towards housing people in separate, rather than communal, apartments. Five-storey blocks to a standardized design went up in areas such as Novye Cheryomushki in the south-west and Izmailovo in the east. These *khrushchoby* or "Khrushchev-slums" as they came to be known were poor-quality, prefabricated constructions designed to provide mass housing for a population that by the mid-1960s had increased to 6.5 million people. The buildings lacked the extravagant exterior decoration of their Stalin-era counterparts: Khrushchev had made a public criticism of the wasteful expense of earlier building projects such as the skyscrapers.

Ulitsa Novyi Arbat, the "New Arbat", was created during the 1960s, a wide avenue stretching out from the Boulevard Ring as a continuation of ulitsa Vozdvizhenka flanked by multi-storey apartment blocks with shops and restaurants on the ground floors. The street does not make for user-friendly shopping, though, as the vast scale of the buildings and distance between them mean that it is something of a trek for potential customers wanting to visit more than one outlet. Formerly named Prospekt Kalinina after the Soviet President Mikhail Kalinin (it was not until the Brezhnev era that the Secretary-General of the Party combined his position with that of the Head of State), the avenue's construction brought about the demolition of many old houses and streets in the area. These included Sobachaya ploshchad, Dog Square, described by Alexander Pasternak as

> *a retired, pleasant little square whose insignificant and irregular shapes gave it a domestic quality unlike the civic pomp of the larger squares… There were many such squares in Moscow then; they have all gradually disappeared, taking with them a characteristic aspect of the vanishing city. Everything here was scaled for the individual, not the crowd as in our bustling central squares today.*

In Trifonov's 1966 short story, *Vera and Zoika*, a character discusses the demolition and rebuilding of parts of the capital with her taxi driver:

> *"I feel sorry for these little houses. After all, this is the Moscow of old, our history. Krasnaia Presnia… And here they are being mercilessly burnt down…."*
>
> *"And a good thing, too! You shouldn't feel sorry for them, they're only good for breeding bedbugs!" said the driver with unexpected spite. "People used to live on top of each other there, ten people for every seven metres! They don't need your history! Now at least they'll have somewhere to live that is fit for humans."*

Moscow's housing problems did not end with the renewed investment of the Khrushchev years, however. Living space was still restricted, waiting lists for housing were long and many people found themselves unable to move out of their communal flats. Even those lucky enough to move into one of the new apartments found cheap, shabby interiors and cockroach problems. The creation of new housing stock put considerable powers of patronage in the hands of local officials, and the composer Dmitry Shostakovich wrote an operetta about a corruption scandal in one of these new Khrushchev-era housing estates. *Moscow-Cheryomushki* (1959) tells the story of a group of prospective tenants of an estate who eventually succeed in overcoming the wicked plans of the local bureaucrats.

The later 1950s witnessed the beginnings of the creation of "micro-regions", *mikroraiony*, dominated by high-rise tower blocks encircling the outskirts of the city intended to provide all essential services for residents such as schools, food stores and child care facilities on a local basis. This model of housing development was continued into the 1970s and 1980s, with some outlying districts housing up to a quarter of a million inhabitants.

Housing cooperatives became an increasingly common feature of the Brezhnev era when groups of people from the same workplace or professional union could club together to buy an apartment block. This kind of housing was mainly available to professional people who were able to put down the necessary deposit. It was in intellectual homes that the "kitchen culture" emerged: groups of like-minded friends gathered round the kitchen table for food, drink and conversation. Dissidents in the 1960s met in friends' kitchens to swap carbon copies of underground literature, *samizdat*, works that could not make it past the censors.

The 1981 Oscar-winning film, *Moscow Does Not Believe in Tears*, plays out its rags-to-riches story against the backdrop of late Soviet housing problems. We first meet the heroine, Katya, when she is sharing a room in a workers' hostel with two friends from the countryside. When Katya is asked to house-sit for a professor, she and her friends organize a party in his apartment and invite eligible young men. Katya falls in love with one of these men, a young sports star, and ends up becoming pregnant but he abandons her when he discovers that she is not in fact a professor's daughter and does not have permanent residence in Moscow. The film then jumps on fifteen years and we see that Katya has now become a factory director and is living in a spacious apartment with her daughter. She falls in love with a factory worker, Gosha, and although she feels she has to hide her superior social status from him to begin with, the film concludes with a happy ending as they marry and he moves in to become the head of the household. Appropriately, for this Soviet version of the Cinderella story, the prince turns out to be a manual worker and the palace a three-bedroom apartment.

Residence permits, as Katya's errant lover recognized, were a serious business. It was felt by many within the city authorities that without restrictions on in-migration Moscow could become vastly overpopulated, with shanty towns spreading all around the outskirts. The *propiska* system was therefore strictly policed. For new migrants to acquire a *propiska* they could either marry Muscovites, bribe a corrupt official or find an enterprise that was willing to sponsor them. Unsurprisingly, fictitious marriages between city residents and out-of-towners were not uncommon. The most common means of gaining residency by legal means was to become one of the *limitchiki*, migrants who were given temporary permits for three to five years to work in unpopular jobs. Following this period, when they were generally housed in hostel accommodation, these people could usually find a way to get themselves onto the housing list and gain permanent residency. Well over half a million people worked in Moscow as *limitchiki* during the Brezhnev years before the system was formally suspended in 1986.

Even with the necessary paperwork, housing remained a real problem for Muscovites. The wait for housing on the city housing queue took years, years in which people might be forced to live with their in-laws, with their estranged spouse or to remain in student hostel accommodation or communal apartments. Popular discontent became more vocal in the *glasnost* era as people were encouraged to air their grievances in the press and in letters to the authorities. One complainant put the issue starkly in a letter to an architectural journal:

> *I would like to ask our city planners: in what other civilized capital would a woman take her husband for the night into a room where her mother is sleeping? No one finds that surprising here.*

According to statistics compiled in the late 1980s, four million people had less than the official nine square metres of living space that had been set as a "sanitary norm" back in the 1920s.

Post-communism
Since 1991 Muscovites living in municipal housing blocks have been able to apply to privatize their apartments and for a nominal fee they can gain the right to buy or sell their homes. The rules have been more complicated for tenants in communal apartments, where either all of the inhabitants would have to agree to go down the privatization route or those wishing to privatize would have to pay off their neighbours, buying up their rooms individually, or finding them alternative accommodation. Although the housing privatization scheme was popular in its early years, the poor state of many apartment buildings

deterred many city tenants who did not wish to take on the financial responsibility for maintenance of their homes.

The booming Moscow property market in recent years has led to a spate of reports about the activities of unscrupulous property developers. Tenants in prestigious neighbourhoods have found their houses bought up by developers who then try to force the long-term residents out in order either to let their apartments to wealthy clients or to demolish the old buildings and rebuild them from scratch. Scare tactics have been employed, with tenants finding their heating turned off in winter or gas taps turned on deliberately; other reports tell of frauds perpetrated on vulnerable, often elderly people to turn them out of their apartments. Violence is not unknown: in one case that reached the courts a group of former police officers were convicted of having murdered two Muscovites in order to seize their apartments.

Homelessness was a criminal offence in the Soviet period. Not to have a *propiska* meant that you were "without fixed abode" and could be punished by imprisonment; so too could long-term unemployment, described by the state as "parasitism". The two conditions went together, of course, because without a residence permit it was impossible to gain regular employment. Since 1991 the attitude to homeless people seems to have barely changed among officialdom. Police still routinely arrest homeless people, deporting those who are not Muscovites. Although some efforts have been made to provide shelters, these are usually unavailable to non-Muscovites, require medical checks prior to admission and are often run along the lines of a prison. There is a massive social stigma attached to homelessness, with widespread assumptions that these people are vagrants and criminals.

Even today, more than a decade after the end of communism, Moscow's housing situation remains a serious problem that has not yet been resolved. Ordinary Muscovites continue to put up with things that residents of western cities would refuse to endure: the ritual turning off of the hot water for a few weeks every summer while the municipal pipes are repaired; the disgusting state of common spaces in apartment buildings. Entrance hallways, lifts and stairwells are left with no one taking responsibility for their upkeep, with the result that if a resident returns home one night, blind drunk, and vomits in a common area, it is unlikely to get cleaned up for weeks afterwards. Even after seventy years living under communism, Muscovites have not yet mastered—

one might say, they have deliberately and strategically refused to master—many of the practicalities of communal, or even merely neighbourly, living.

Chapter Nine
CITY OF PALACES AND MONASTERIES

As befits a city of "forty times forty" churches, Moscow contains a great many monasteries and convents, some in the very centre of the city— the old Zaikonospassky monastery on Nikolskaya ulitsa where the Slavic-Greek-Latin Academy was set up; the Upper Monastery of St. Peter on Petrovka; the Convent of the Nativity on ulitsa Rozhdestvenka and the Ivanovsky Convent on ulitsa Zabelina, all within the White City—and others ringed around the southern edge of the medieval city. Several monasteries were destroyed, in whole or in part, during the Soviet period and all were turned over to secular purposes: it is only in recent years that monks and nuns have moved back in and church services have begun to be held again.

Moscow remained a popular haunt with members of the nobility after the capital was moved to St. Petersburg, and many aristocrats particularly enjoyed coming to the city for the winter months. The eighteenth century marked a significant period of palace-building in Moscow, and grand mansions, built both for the Tsars and for members of the Russian aristocracy, are dotted around the city, many on the outskirts in what were once grand country estates and are now city parks.

Lefortovo
An interesting architectural walking tour of late seventeenth- and eighteenth-century palaces can be made by exploring the Lefortovo district, clustered around the Yauza river to the north-east of the city centre. The nearest metro station is Baumanskaya on the dark blue line. This was the old Nemetskaya sloboda, the quarter where foreigners were required to live from the days of Tsar Alexei Mikhailovich in the mid-seventeenth century. The nearby Vvedenskoe cemetery was where many of these people, who were not Orthodox believers, were buried. Inhabited by people from a mix of different nationalities and professions, including soldiers, merchants and diplomats, the district

became a favourite spot with the young Peter the Great and he spent many evenings here playing drinking games in the company of his friends. At the very end of the seventeenth century a palace was built in this area for Peter's Swiss friend Franz Lefort: the shabby but still attractive yellow classical-style building with crumbling plasterwork and birch trees growing in the courtyard stands on 3 2-ya Baumanskaya ulitsa. Parties held in this palace in Peter the Great's day were said to be accompanied by "debauchery and drunkenness so great that it is impossible to describe it." After Lefort's death the palace was given to Prince Alexander Menshikov, one of Peter's closest associates, and it was in this building that Peter's grandson, the young Tsar Peter II, died of smallpox on his wedding day in 1730. The building fell into disrepair and was badly damaged by fire on more than one occasion. It is now the home of the state archives of military history and of sound recordings

Further down the same street stands another former palace building, now a higher educational establishment for training engineers. This suburban palace was built in the mid-eighteenth century and later became the property of Tsar Paul, the mentally unbalanced son of Catherine the Great. It was badly damaged in the 1812 fire, subsequently rebuilt and became the Imperial Moscow Technical Academy, a hotbed of revolutionary activism in the early twentieth century.

In the 1730s two palaces were put up on the opposite side of the Yauza from the Lefortovo Palace, built by the Italian architect Count Bartolomeo Francesco Rastrelli, who went on to construct many of the best known eighteenth-century buildings in St. Petersburg, including the Winter Palace. Originally erected in the grounds of the Kremlin, the Winter Annenhof, as one of these palaces was known, was moved here to stand alongside the Summer Annenhof, named after the Tsarina Anna for whom they were built. The Annenhof burnt to the ground in the mid-eighteenth century and the Catherine Palace was built on the site to a design by another Italian architect Giacomo Quarenghi. This palace, noted for its lengthy colonnade, was soon converted into a military barracks and continued to be used by the army into the Soviet period. Today it houses a tank academy. There is a park, and plans have been mooted to restore this space to its former glory by restoring the Annenhof Canal, with its bridges and embankment, as well as rebuilding the Winter Annenhof Palace and the earlier Golovin Palace on the site. Whether the funding for such a scheme can ever be raised remains to be seen.

The Lefortovo district contains many other examples of classical architecture, and it became a fashionable residential area in the late eighteenth century. Pushkin was born in a house here, on Baumanskaya ulitsa, in 1799, and Count Musin-Pushkin had a house on Spartakovskaya ulitsa. His famous library, including the priceless manuscript of the medieval epic poem *The Lay of Igor's Host*, went up in flames in 1812. Two museums can be visited in the area, the museum of the Ministry of the Interior on 9a Krasnokazarmennaya ulitsa, with displays covering various aspects of crime and punishment, and the Lefortovo Museum on 23 Kryukovskaya ulitsa, which tells the history of the area. Recent controversy over road-building plans had a successful outcome when the decision was taken to reroute an eight-lane highway that had been planned to cut through Lefortovo.

Izmailovo

Heading east from Lefortovo by trolleybus or taking the dark blue metro line for a few more stops will take you to Izmailovsky Park. Although most tourists come here to buy *matrioshka* dolls, wooden bears and Soviet kitsch from the large souvenir market, one can also visit Izmailovo to see the old royal estate, situated on an island in the park. Originally owned by the Izmailov family, the land later came into the hands of the Romanovs, who built an estate that they used as a summer residence. Most of the older buildings, including the Pokrovsky Cathedral, date from the late seventeenth century. A menagerie was kept here and game was reared for hunting. Peter the Great spent a lot of time at Izmailovo during his childhood; he learned to sail on the ponds and his "toy regiments"—troops whom he organized to play military games and who later became elite army regiments—held their manoeuvres in the park. The two "toy regiments" were named after the nearby villages that they came from, Preobrazhenskoe and Semenovskoe, both now subsumed within the city.

The Petrovsky Palace and Khodynskoe Field

After the capital of Russia had moved to St. Petersburg in Peter the Great's reign, tsars still had to visit the old city from time to time, not least in order to be crowned. In the 1770s Catherine the Great decided that she needed a new palace that she could use as a stopping point on the way into Moscow. Thus was the Petrovsky Palace built, on the road that leads to St Petersburg, Leningradsky prospekt, a short distance from Dinamo metro station on the green line. Vasily Bazhenov was first commissioned to undertake the design, but the task was later transferred to Matvei Kazakov. The resulting building is in the classical style but with some neo-Gothic touches, medieval decorative elements prefiguring the development of the Russian Style in the late nineteenth century.

The palace appears briefly in Pushkin's *Eugene Onegin* as Tatyana passes it on her way into Moscow:

Here stands, with shady park surrounded
Petrovsky's castle; and the fame
In which so lately it abounded
Rings proudly in that sombre name.

The fame in which so lately it abounded refers to Napoleon's brief stay in September 1812 when he escaped to the Petrovsky Palace from the burning city. One of his generals recalled the journey they were forced to make: "It was impossible to proceed thither by the direct road on account of the fire and the wind; one had to cross the western part of the town as best one could through ruins, cinders, flames even, if one wanted to reach the outskirts. Night had already fallen when we got there."

The park surrounding the palace was landscaped during the 1820s and became a popular spot for afternoon strolls. The literary critic Vissarion Belinsky described it as "a charming park. There is not one better in all of Moscow or the surrounding area. There is everything here: nature, country and city." The Yar restaurant moved nearby in the middle of the nineteenth century, and a restaurant with the same name is to be found within the nearby 1950s Stalin-style Sovietsky Hotel. After the Revolution the palace became an institute for air force engineers; Yury Gagarin was one of its better-known graduates. Most of the park has been swallowed up by surrounding roads and buildings, but part of it remains and plans are underway to convert the palace into a museum.

Just opposite the park is Moscow's central airfield, Khodynskoe Field. It was the site of a great public celebration in 1774 to mark the victorious conclusion of the Russo-Turkish war. Troops paraded triumphantly through the streets of the capital up to the Kremlin to be greeted by the Tsarina, Catherine the Great, and at Khodynskoe to the north a series of pavilions were built in the neo-Gothic style to represent the different Turkish, Tartar and Ukrainian towns where the battles had been fought. Free food including roast oxen was provided for all-comers, the fountains ran with wine and the evening ended with a fireworks display.

The name of Khodynskoe Field is principally remembered, however, for the tragic events of May 1896 when crowds gathered here for another mass festival, this time to celebrate the coronation of Nicholas II. The Tsar had come to Moscow, as was traditional, to be crowned in the Cathedral of the Ascension in the Kremlin, and a public celebration was laid on for the masses on Khodynskoe Field with free food, beer, souvenir coronation mugs and entertainment. Many thousands of people came from miles around, taking the train to Moscow in order to enjoy the festivities. A terrible accident took place that night: as a rumour spread that the free gifts had run out, the crowd surged forwards towards the stalls. Some people were crushed, others stumbled into trenches in the field that had not been properly covered over. Insufficient police were on hand to help control the crowd and more than 1,300 people died. One foreigner who witnessed the scene described how she saw "poor crushed peasants still in their gaudy festival clothes being driven through the city to the cemetery, followed by weeping friends." Other witnesses reported seeing rows of bodies lying at one end of the field while the festivities continued further away and photographs of the scene, as well as examples of the souvenir mugs, can be seen at the Museum of Modern History on Tverskaya. The Tsar did not emerge with credit from this incident. He let the celebrations continue, and appeared callous and unfeeling by attending the French Ambassador's ball on the evening after the tragedy had occurred.

Kolomenskoe

Kolomenskoe is a former royal estate that lies to the south of the city; it has its own metro station on the green line. During Tsar Alexei Mikhailovich's reign in the mid-seventeenth century a great wooden palace was built, a rambling collection of buildings covered with towers and domes and all linked together with interconnecting passageways. The palace was designed to be used both for official functions and for private life, and play rooms were included for the children of the royal household. The exterior of the building had elaborate wooden carvings and thousands of windows gave light to the many rooms hung with grand portraits and maps. The Tsar's throne in the throne room was flanked on either side by copper lions which contained a complex mechanism enabling them to roll their eyes and roar. In the words of the erudite monk Simeon Polotsky:

> In one word this palace is perfection,
> A great construction worthy of the Tsar;
> Magnificent, like the Tsar's own honour,
> There is nothing better, except in heaven.
> The ancient world had but seven wonders;
> Our own age has an eighth—this splendid house!

Sadly, the palace was pulled down on the instructions of Catherine the Great a century after it had been built because the buildings were thought to be in danger of collapsing. A model of the palace can be seen in the Kolomenskoe museum. It was also in the reign of Tsar Alexei Mikhailovich that the Church of Our Lady of Kazan was constructed; like the Kazan Cathedral on Red Square it was built to honour the

victory against the Poles in 1612. Alexei was also responsible for extending the gardens on the estate.

Kolomenskoe had been a spot favoured by the Russian royal family before Alexei Mikhailovich ever built his palace. The Church of the Ascension, the white tent-roofed church that overlooks the bend in the river, was built in the 1530s during the reign of Grand Prince Vasily III to mark the birth of his son, who would grow up to be called Ivan the Terrible. The church was particularly distinctive in that it took traditional wooden design and reproduced it in stone. The French composer Hector Berlioz, who visited it three hundred years after it had been built, was captivated by its beauty:

> *Here before my gaze stood the beauty of perfection and I gasped in awe. Here in the mysterious silence, amid the harmonious beauty of the finished form, I beheld an architecture of a new kind. I beheld man soaring on high. And I stood amazed.*

Various noteworthy incidents of Russian history have connections with Kolomenskoe: Dmitry Donskoi is said to have assembled his troops here after the Battle of Kulikovo Field in the late fourteenth century; it was here, too, that Ivan Bolotnikov, the leader of a peasant rebel army during the Time of Troubles, set up camp in October 1606 and laid siege to Moscow before going out to fight (unsuccessfully) against Tsar Vasily Shuisky. The Patriarch of Moscow, Germogen, wrote that

> *The rebels stay in Kolomenskoe near Moscow and write their cursed leaflets, ordering the boyars' slaves to kill their masters, promising them their wives and estates, urging them to massacre all the merchants and to seize their goods and summoning them to the rebel camp.*

Bolotnikov's army was defeated although he himself escaped on this occasion; after a further defeat in the south he was captured, had his eyes put out and was drowned.

It was also at Kolomenskoe that the copper riots of the early 1660s took place, a popular protest against the debasing of the silver coinage and the inflation that had resulted. An angry crowd of demonstrators marched on Kolomenskoe to remonstrate with Tsar Alexei Mikhailovich: he summoned his troops and a massacre took place. Reports claimed that seven thousand people were killed and twice that number had terrible punishments inflicted upon them, including branding and amputation of limbs. Some have argued that Peter the Great was himself born at Kolomenskoe: a poem dating from more than a hundred years after Peter's birth describes Kolomenskoe as the "Russian Bethlehem" which "delivered Peter to the light."

Peter may or may not have been born here, but he certainly spent time at the estate: his "toy regiments" conducted operations in the park at Kolomenskoe and his daughter Elizabeth was born here. Some of the oak trees in the park date from his time. Of the other buildings around the park, some are originals and have been here since they were first built, such as the seventeenth-century Water Tower near the Church of the Ascension; it used to pump up water from the river for use in the palace. Others were brought here during the early Soviet period when the park was made into a museum of wooden architecture under the direction of the conservationist Pyotr Baranovsky. A wooden watch tower from Siberia and a gate tower from a Karelian monastery are two of the structures that were moved here in the twentieth century, as was Peter the Great's log cabin brought to Moscow from Arkhangelsk (Archangel) on the White Sea.

Tsaritsyno

The suburban estate of Tsaritsyno is a little way south of Kolomenskoe, a few stops further on the green line. The land, which used to go by the charming name of *Chernaya Gryaz* or Black Mud, passed from the Godunov family to that of Prince Kantemir (sometimes Cantemir) and was bought from that family in 1775 by Catherine the Great, who renamed the estate and decided to build a palace here. Vasily Bazhenov was commissioned to design the buildings and he spent nearly ten years working on the project, which was completed in 1785. The Governor General of Moscow wrote to Catherine with his impressions of the design: "the building has been marvelously done... the first view of Tsaritsyno is so fine, so pleasant, so splendid... truly I have seen nothing to compare with it."

Bazhenov's estate included two separate palaces, for Catherine and for her son Paul as well as servants' quarters, a smaller palace suitable for private receptions, an opera house and a number of follies dotted around the park. The distinctive buildings were constructed in the neo-Gothic style from red and white brick. Catherine came to see her new palace in 1785, shortly after its completion, and took a violent dislike to the place. She ordered that the buildings be torn down and commissioned Matvei Kazakov to rebuild the palace anew. The reasons for her extreme reaction have long been debated: she was perhaps horrified by the thought of sharing the estate with her much-unloved son Paul or perhaps it was all connected with her fears of a conspiracy against her on the part of the Freemasons. Bazhenov himself was a Mason and he included Masonic symbols in his designs: a pair of compasses appear to be hanging down from the centre of the archway of the Grape Gates, a little way beyond the Opera House.

Not all of Bazhenov's original buildings were destroyed although his two palaces did go, to be replaced by a single Great Palace building designed by Kazakov. An Oxford don who looked around the newly-rebuilt estate in the 1790s thought it hideous:

> [it was] *built in a taste meant to be gothic but fantastical and quaint beyond any thing of that kind that I ever saw… These buildings are also crowded together in such a manner that one could fancy it the object of the Architect to shut out as much as possible the beauties of the situation…*[this] *imperial bauble… will not hand down to posterity, if it is as they say her own plan, any very favourable idea of her Majesty's taste… I grudged the labour and particularly the fine stone which has been thrown away in this motley and tasteless undertaking.*

Catherine herself lost interest in the whole scheme and no one ever lived here. In the nineteenth century a local factory removed some of the bricks, leaving the estate in ruins—which is how it remains today. The park is a popular spot with the *Tolkinisty*, Russian fans of the novels of J. R. R. Tolkien, who come here dressed in costume as elves, dwarves and hobbits to take part in role-playing games, usually involving sword fighting. The *Tolkinisty* began as a student society in the 1980s but its popularity has greatly increased since the films of *The Lord of the Rings* came out in Russia. Families come here in the winter months to go sledging on the slopes of the park.

Moscow's Monasteries

Novodevichy Convent, the New Maiden's Convent, was founded in 1524 by Grand Prince Vasily III to mark the recapture of Smolensk from the Polish-Lithuanian occupation. It stands in the western quarter of the city alongside the river and can be reached either by taking a trolleybus out along Prechistenka and all the way down Bolshaya Pirogovskaya ulitsa; alternatively, it is a short walk from Sportivnaya metro station on the red line. The Smolensk Cathedral, the largest church building in the complex which was built at the time of the convent's foundation, was inspired by the design of the Cathedral of the Assumption in the Kremlin. Novodevichy had royal associations from an early stage. The widow of Tsar Fyodor Ivanovich, Ivan the Terrible's feeble-minded son, entered the convent after her husband's death; her brother Boris Godunov is said to have been staying here in 1598 when crowds arrived demanding that he accept the throne, an episode depicted in the opening scene of Musorgsky's opera *Boris Godunov.*

Another royal woman with close connections to the convent was Sophia, the sister of Peter the Great, who was the beneficiary of the first *streltsy* rebellion in 1682. She made generous endowments to the convent during the 1680s, and it was at this time that the churches over the northern and southern gates of the complex were built: the Church of the Transfiguration and the Church of the Intercession. According to the contemporary writer and poet Karion Istomin, during Sophia's regency:

> *The walls surrounding the convent were heightened with bricks, and the towers were given various fine embellishments. Holy churches were also built with magnificence and splendour within the Convent and over the gates on the walls, and were decorated inside with all manner of finery.*

The tall octagonal bell tower, rising to a height of two hundred feet also dates from this period, as does the iconostasis in the Smolensk Cathedral. After the failure of the second *streltsy* rebellion in 1689, Sophia was sent to live in Novodevichy under effective house arrest. After the third and final attempt by the *streltsy* to oust Peter in favour of his sister had been crushed in 1698, the Tsar took his revenge. The errant musketeers were interrogated, tortured and many of them were

executed. In a gruesome description left by an Austrian diplomat, in front of the convent

> *there were thirty gibbets erected in a quadrangular shape, from which there hung two hundred and thirty streltsy. The principal ringleaders, who presented a petition to Sophia… were hanged close to the windows of that princess, presenting, as it were, the petitions that were placed in their hands, so near that Sophia might with ease touch them.*

Sophia took the veil and lived out the rest of her life in the convent under the name of Susanna. She died here in 1704. Peter the Great's first wife, Yevdokia Lopukhina, lived in the convent from the late 1720s after being rejected by the Tsar: she gave her name to the Lopukhin Chambers to the right of the main entrance. During the French occupation of Moscow in 1812 the convent was used for storing food by the French. They attempted to blow the place up when they left, but were thwarted, it is said, by vigilant nuns who cut the fuses and thus avoided disaster. After the Revolution, the convent was used for workers' housing and it later became a museum. It was returned to the Church after the Second World War and is still a working convent to this day.

The extensive cemetery is adjacent to the main convent complex, accessible through the gate on Bolshaya Pirogovskaya ulitsa. It is famous as the resting place of many of the great artistic figures of the nineteenth and twentieth centuries: Gogol, Chekhov, Mayakovsky, Bulgakov, Stanislavsky, Eisenstein, Prokofiev and Shostakovich were all buried here. It was also the place where those politicians and military officers who did not win for themselves a coveted burial spot by the Kremlin wall ended up. Stalin's wife Nadezhda Alliluyeva, who shot herself in 1932, was buried here, as was Stalin's foreign minister Vyacheslav Molotov, the man after whom the incendiary Cocktail was named. (Finnish partisans made the homemade bombs in order to throw them at Russian soldiers during the Winter War of 1940-1.) Nikita Khrushchev's grave can also be found here. Some of the military graves are worth exploring, as several are adorned with sculptures of tanks, rocket launchers or detailed maps of their most famous military victories.

Several of the graves at Novodevichy were moved here from other cemeteries. In some cases, like Gogol, this happened because the graveyards where they were originally buried were being destroyed or severely reduced in size; in others they were transferred back here from abroad. Chaliapin's grave is one such example; the singer's remains were moved to Moscow from their original Parisian resting place in 1984. An attempt was made in 2001 to transfer the ashes of the ballerina Anna Pavlova, the star whose tutu provided the inspiration for a meringue, back from Golders Green in London to Moscow for reburial at Novodevichy; this failed after objections by relatives.

Novodevichy is only one of the six walled monasteries that once formed a defensive ring around Moscow's southern flank. Going from west to east and starting from Novodevichy, the next monastery you would reach is the Donskoi Monastery, hidden behind thick red brick walls a short walk from Shabolovskaya metro station. Built in the 1590s during the reign of Boris Godunov, it was supposed to have been founded on the spot where Dmitry Donskoi mustered his troops before setting off to do battle with the Mongols. It was expanded considerably a century later during the reign of Sophia when the huge New Cathedral was built. This was the place where the Archbishop Amvrosy was beaten to death by an enraged crowd during the Plague Riots of 1771. After the Revolution, the monastery became home to a museum of atheism and later to an architecture museum. A crematorium was opened in the new cemetery next door to the monastery complex, and the bodies of many Terror victims were incinerated here. Memorial stones mark the spot of the mass graves where those who were shot during the Stalin period lie buried.

From the Donskoi Monastery it is a short trolleybus ride to the Danilov Monastery. Although it is said to be the oldest of the six monasteries, the visitor might not think so because many of the buildings within the monastery complex are modern and because of the presence of cars parked within the monastery walls. Even the paving stones have a modern feel to them and the gardens are tidily laid out and well maintained. It nevertheless remains the case that the Danilov Monastery was founded in the late thirteenth century by Prince Daniil of Moscow, the son of Alexander Nevsky and father of Ivan I. Further buildings were added to the complex over the years that followed, with the Cathedral of the Trinity built in the 1830s by Bove. It became a children's institution, largely inhabited by orphans, after the Revolution but was returned to the Church in the 1980s. It now serves as the administrative centre of the patriarchate, and some of the more modern buildings serve as offices for the Department of External Church Relations and as one of the official residences of the Patriarch. The Millennium Chapel with its gold dome was built to celebrate the millennium of Russian Orthodoxy in 1988.

The Simonov Monastery is best reached by metro to Avtozavodskaya station on the green line and then walking up Vostochnaya ulitsa and on to Simonovsky val. Only a small part of the original monastery complex remains, although you can see part of the massive brick walls and defence towers as you walk along Simonovsky val. Founded in the late fourteenth century, it had an unfortunate history. Although the monastery survived an attempt by the French army to blow it up in 1812, it did not survive the Soviet assault. Most of the main buildings including the bell tower were destroyed in the early 1930s in order to create space to allow for the expansion of the car factory and the building of the Palace of Culture, a Constructivist-style workers' club built in the 1930s by the Vesnin brothers.

Taking the trolleybus north along Simonovsky val will take you past the Krutitskoe podvore, the site of an old monastery that was used by the Metropolitan of Moscow after the creation of the Patriarchate in the sixteenth century. After the fall of Constantinople in 1453 many of the institutions of the Byzantine Church were recreated in Russia to help secure its claim as the new centre of Eastern Christianity. The dilapidated brick buildings, including a Cathedral of the Assumption and an arched *teremok*—a covered walkway lined with painted tiles— mainly date from the late seventeenth century. In the nineteenth century it was used as a military prison (Alexander Herzen was held here for a short period in the 1830s). A plaque commemorates the work of the Soviet-era conservationist Pyotr Baranovsky.

The Novospassky Monastery (the New Monastery of the Saviour) is just across the road from the Krutitskoe podvore. It dates from the late fifteenth century although most of the main buildings are later constructions. The Cathedral of the Saviour in the centre of the complex contains the burial vault of the Romanov family; the Grand Duke Sergei Alexandrovich, who was assassinated in 1905, was reburied at Novospassky in the 1990s. The monastery became the home of the first Soviet forced labour camp, set up not long after the Revolution, and it was also used as a burial ground for Terror victims. Dress code rules are strict here: women need to wear long skirts and to cover their heads and shoulders. A recent visit in the summer provided a vivid illustration of Orthodox sexism: having forgotten to take a headscarf with me, I was given a piece of cloth to use for this purpose at the entrance gate; I then entered the monastery, only to find the whole place swarming with topless (male) builders.

Finally, the Andronikov Monastery stands on the banks of the Yauza river, not far from Taganka. It was established in the mid-fourteenth century, and the famous white Saviour Cathedral was built a century later. It became a forced labour camp and later a workers' hostel during the Soviet period, before finally being turned into a museum of early Russian art. The monastery is forever associated with the name of Andrei Rublev, the monk and icon painter who died here around 1430. Some of his greatest works can be seen in the Tretyakov Gallery, including the icons he painted for the Trinity Monastery at Sergeev Posad and for the Cathedral at Zvenigorod, both a short distance outside Moscow. Rublev owes his international reputation in part to the film made about his life, *Andrei Rublev*, by Andrei Tarkovsky. Initially banned by the authorities, who were always touchy about any artistic treatment of a religious theme, the film was only released in the early 1970s after an hour's worth of cuts had been made to the original material. Rublev was canonized by the Orthodox

Church in 1989 and there is a statue of him just outside the monastery gates

The Sheremetyev Estates: Kuskovo and Ostankino

Two noble estates in the north and the south of the city both belonged to the same family, the Sheremetyevs. In the eighteenth century, the Sheremetyev family was the biggest landowner in Russia apart from the Tsar. They owned hundreds of thousands of serfs, many of whom were given an artistic training so that they could work for the serf theatre troupe either as actors, singers or dancers or as backstage mechanics and craftsmen. Serf architects were responsible for building the palaces at Kuskovo and at Ostankino, the two country estates near Moscow that have now been swallowed by the ever-expanding city. The Kuskovo Palace in south-east Moscow, a bus ride away from Ryazansky prospekt metro station on the purple line, was built in the 1770s and set within lavish formal gardens that included cottages built in different styles, a hermitage and a grotto; the estate was described by one visitor as Moscow's answer to Versailles and by another as a "scaled down transfer of Eden". Two theatres were constructed, an indoor stage and an outdoor amphitheatre, and it was here that Count Nikolai Sheremetyev first set eyes on the serf girl, Praskovya Zhemchugova whom he would later and scandalously marry. Concerts are held at Kuskovo in the ornate ball room

In the 1790s the Count had a new palace built for himself at Ostankino (near VDNKh metro station), an estate that the family had acquired through an auspicious marriage into the Cherkassky family. The pink and white palace is entirely constructed from wood with plaster mouldings and papier-mâché used in the interior to resemble marble, bronze and malachite. The theatre was even bigger and more elaborate than the one at Kuskovo. Following the Revolution, the two estates were preserved as museums: the fact that serfs had been so involved in their creation may well have worked in their favour. A ceramics museum was set up at Kuskovo, and Ostankino became known as the Museum of Serf Art.

FURTHER READING

Alexander, John T., *Bubonic Plague in Early Modern Russia: Public Health and Urban Disaster*. Baltimore: Johns Hopkins University Press, 1980.

Ball, Alan M., *And Now My Soul is Hardened: Abandoned Children in Soviet Russia, 1918-1930*. Berkeley: University of California Press, 1994.

Barber, John, "The Moscow Crisis of October 1941", in Julian Cooper, Maureen Perrie, E. A. Rees, eds, *Soviet History, 1917-1953*. Basingstoke: Macmillan, 1995.

Bartlett, Rosamund and Benn, Anna, *Literary Russia: A Guide*. London: Picador, 1997.

Bartlett, Rosamund, *Chekhov: Scenes from a Life*. London: Free Press: 2004.

Benedetti, Jean, ed, *The Moscow Art Theatre Letters*. London: Methuen, 1991.

Benjamin, Walter, *Moscow Diary*. Cambridge MA: Harvard University Press, 1986.

Berton, Kathleen, *Moscow: An Architectural History*. London: Tauris, 1990.

Bertensson, Sergei, & Leyda, Jay, *Sergei Rachmaninov: A Lifetime in Music*. Bloomington: Indiana University Press, 2001.

Binyon, T. J., *Pushkin: A Biography*. London: Harper Collins, 2002.

Boym, Svetlana, *Common Places: Mythologies of Everyday Life in Russia*. Cambridge MA: Harvard University Press, 1994.

Bradley, Joseph, *Muzhik and Muscovite: Urbanization in Late Imperial Russia*. Berkeley: University of California Press, 1985.

Braun, Edward, *Meyerhold: A Revolution in Theatre*. London: Methuen, 1995.

The British Church of St Andrew, Moscow: Handbook for the Members of the Congregation. Printed by C. Grossmann, Moscow: 1912.

Brumfield, William Craft, Ananich, Boris V., and Petrov, Yury A., eds, *Commerce in Russian Urban Culture, 1861-1914*. Washington DC: Woodrow Wilson Center Press, 2001.

Bulgakov, Mikhail, *Manuscripts Don't Burn: A Life in Diaries and Letters*. Compiled by J. A. E. Curtis, London: Bloomsbury, 1991.

Bulgakov, Mikhail, *The Master and Margarita*. Translated by Michael Glenny, London: Vintage, 2003.

Bulgakov, Mikhail, *The Heart of a Dog*. Translated by Michael Glenny, London: Collins and Harvill, 1968.

Bullard, Reader W., *Inside Stalin's Russia: The Diaries of Reader Bullard, 1930-1934*. Edited by Julian and Margaret Bullard. Charlbury: Day, 2000.

Bushkovitch, Paul, *The Merchants of Moscow, 1580-1650*. Cambridge: Cambridge University Press, 1980.

Bushnell, John, *Moscow Graffiti: Language & Subculture*. Boston: Unwin Hyman, 1990.

Carroll, Lewis, *The Russian Journal and other Selections from the Works of Lewis Carroll*. Edited by John Francis McDermott. New York: Dover, 1977.

Chekhov, Anton, *Plays*. Translated by Michael Frayn, London: Methuen, 1988.

Chekhov, Anton, *The Lady with the Little Dog and Other Stories, 1896-1904*. Translated by Ronald Wilks. London: Penguin, 2002.

Anton Chekhov, *A Life in Letters*. Translated by Rosamund Bartlett and Anthony Phillips. London: Penguin, 2004.

Colton, Timothy, *Moscow: Governing the Socialist Metropolis*. Cambridge MA: Belknap Press of Harvard University Press, 1995.

Engelstein, Laura, *Moscow, 1905: Working Class Organization and Political Conflict*. Stanford: Stanford University Press, 1982.

Feinstein, Elaine, *Marina Tsvetaeva*. Harmondsworth: Penguin, 1989.

Figes, Orlando, *Natasha's Dance: A Cultural History of Russia*. London: Penguin, 2002.

Figes, Orlando, *A People's Tragedy: The Russian Revolution, 1891-1924*. London: Jonathan Cape, 1996.

Forest, Benjamin and Johnson, Juliet, "Unraveling the Threads of History: Soviet-Era Monuments and Post-Soviet National Identity in Moscow", *The Annals of the Association of American Geographers*, 92:3, September 2002, 524-547.

Frankland, C. Colville, *Narrative of a Visit to the Courts of Russia and Sweden, in the Years 1830 and 1831*. London: 1832.

Garros, Veronique, Korenevskaya, Natalia and Lahusen, Thomas, eds, *Intimacy and Terror: Soviet Diaries of the 1930s*. New York: New Press, 1995.

Gattini, Andrea, "Restitution by Russia of Works of Art Removed from German Territory at the End of the Second World War", *European Journal of International Law* 1996, 1-88.

von Geldern, James, "Putting the Masses in Mass Culture: Bolshevik Festivals 1918-20", *Journal of Popular Culture*, 31:4, Spring 1998, 123-144.

Gillespie, David, Iurii Trifonov: *Unity Through Time*. Cambridge: Cambridge University Press, 1992.

Hoffmann, David L., *Peasant Metropolis: Social Identities in Moscow, 1929-41*. Ithaca: Cornell University Press, 1994.

Hughes, Lindsay, *Russia in the Age of Peter the Great, 1682-1725*. New Haven: Yale University Press, 1998.

Kelly, Laurence, ed., *Moscow: A Traveller's Companion*. London: Robinson, 2004.

Kennan, George F., *Memoirs, 1925-50*. London: Hutchinson, 1968.

Kiernan, Maria, *Moscow: A Guide to Soviet and post-Soviet Architecture*. London: Ellipsis, 1998.

Kirichenko, Evgeniia, *Russian Design and the Fine Arts, 1750-1917*. New York: Abrams, 1991.

Kivelson, Valerie A., *Autocracy in the Provinces*. Stanford: Stanford University Press, 1996.

Koenker, Diane, *Moscow Workers and the 1917 Revolution*. Princeton: Princeton University Press, 1981.

Leach R. and Borovsky, V., eds, *A History of Russian Theatre*. Cambridge: Cambridge University Press, 1999

Leder, Mary, *My Life in Stalinist Russia: An American Woman Looks Back*. Bloomington: Indiana University Press, 2001.

Lilley, Ian K., ed, *Moscow and Peterburg: The City in Russian Culture*. Nottingham: Astra Press, 2002.

Lilly, Ian K., "Conviviality in the Pre-Revolutionary 'Moscow Text' of Russian Culture", *Russian Review* 63, July 2004, 427-48.

Bruce Lockhart, R. H., *Memoirs of a British Agent*. London: Putnam, 1932.

Londonderry, the Marchioness of, *Russian Journal of Lady Londonderry, 1836-7*. Edited by W A L Seaman and J R Sewell. London: John Murray, 1973.

McVay, Gordon, *Esenin: A Life*. London: Hodder and Stoughton, 1976.

Maes, Francis, *A History of Russian Music: From Kamarinskaya to Babi Yar*. Berkeley: University of California Press, 2002.

Magarshack, David, *Gogol: A Life*. London: Faber and Faber, 1957.

Mandelstam, Nadezhda, *Hope against Hope*. Translated by Max Hayward. London: Harvill, 1999.

Mawdsley, Evan, *Moscow and Leningrad*. New York: W. W. Norton and Co (Blue Guide), 1991.

Merridale, Catherine, "Redesigning History in Contemporary Russia", *Journal of Contemporary History*, vol. 38 no. 1, 2003, 1-28.

Merridale, Catherine, *Night of Stone: Death and Memory in Russia.* London: Granta, 2000.

de Mertens, Charles, *An Account of the Plague which Raged at Moscow, 1771.* Newtonville MA: Oriental Research Partners, 1977.

Nivat, Anne, *The View from the Vysotka: A Portrait of Russia Today, Through One of Moscow's Most Famous Addresses.* New York: St Martin's Press, 2004.

Olearius, Adam, *The Travels of Olearius in Seventeenth Century Russia.* Edited by Samuel H Baron. Stanford: Stanford University Press, 1967.

O'Mahony, Mike, "Archaeological Fantasies: Constructing History on the Moscow Metro", in *Modern Language Review*, vol. 98, no. 1, January 2003.

Owen, Thomas C., *Capitalism and Politics in Russia: A Social History of the Moscow Merchants, 1855-1905.* Cambridge: Cambridge University Press, 1981.

Pankhurst, Sylvia, *Soviet Russia as I Saw it.* London: Dreadnought Publishers, 1921.

Parkinson, John, *A Tour of Russia, Siberia and the Crimea, 1792-4.* Edited by William Collier. London: Frank Cass, 1971.

Pasternak, Alexander, *A Vanished Present: the Memoirs of Alexander Pasternak.* Edited by Anna Pasternak Slater. Oxford: Oxford University Press, 1984.

Pasternak, Boris, *An Essay in Autobiography.* Translated by Manya Harari. London: Collins Harvill, 1990.

Pitcher, Harvey J., *Muir and Mirrielees: The Scottish Partnership that Became a Household Name in Russia.* Cromer: Swallow House, 1994.

Pitcher, Harvey J., *When Miss Emmie was in Russia: English Governesses Before, During and After the October Revolution.* London: Century, 1994.

Porter, Cathy and Jones, Mark, *Moscow in World War II.* London: Chatto & Windus, 1987.

Poznansky, Alexander, *Tchaikovsky Through Others' Eyes.* Bloomington: Indiana University Press, 1999.

Alexander Poznansky, *Tchaikovsky: The Quest for the Inner Man.* London: Lime Tree, 1993.

Rachmaninoff, Sergei, *Rachmaninoff's Recollections, told to Oskar von Riesemann.* London: George Allen & Unwin, 1934.

Rayfield, Donald, *Anton Chekhov: A Life.* London: Harper Collins, 1997.

Ruble, Blair A., *Second Metropolis: Pragmatic Pluralism in Gilded Age Chicago, Silver Age Moscow and Meiji Osaka*. Cambridge: Cambridge University Press, 2001.

Saul, Norman E., *Distant Friends: The United States and Russia, 1763-1867*. Lawrence KA: University Press of Kansas, 1991.

Saul, Norman E., *Concord and Conflict: The United States and Russia, 1867-1914*. Lawrence KA: University Press of Kansas, 1996.

Simon, Sir E. D. *et al, Moscow in the Making*. London: Longmans, Green & Co, 1937.

Smith, G. S., *Songs to Seven Strings: Russian Guitar Poetry and Soviet "Mass Song"*. Bloomington: Indiana University Press, 1984.

Richard Stites, *Revolutionary Dreams: Utopian Vision and Experimental Life in the Russian Revolution*. Oxford: Oxford University Press, 1989.

Thurston, Robert W., *Liberal City, Conservative State: Moscow and Russia's Urban Crisis 1906-14*. Oxford: Oxford University Press, 1987.

Tolstoy, Leo, *War and Peace*. Translated by Rosemary Edmonds, Harmondsworth: Penguin, 1982.

Tolstoy, Leo, *Anna Karenina*. Translated by Rosemary Edmonds, Harmondsworth, Penguin, 1978.

Ward, Charles A., *Moscow and Leningrad: A Topographical Guide to Russian Cultural History*. Munich: K G Saur, 1992.

Wettlin, Margaret, *Fifty Russian Winters: An American Woman's Life in the Soviet Union*. New York: Pharos Books, 1992.

INDEX OF LITERARY & HISTORICAL NAMES

INDEX OF PLACES & LANDMARKS